Paper Valley

GREAT LAKES BOOKS

A complete listing of the books in this series can be found online at wsupress.wayne.edu

Editor

Thomas Klug
Sterling Heights, Michigan

PAPER VALLEY

THE FIGHT FOR THE FOX RIVER CLEANUP

P. DAVID ALLEN II AND SUSAN CAMPBELL

WAYNE STATE UNIVERSITY PRESS

Detroit

ISBN 978-0-8143-4958-8 (paperback)
ISBN 978-0-8143-4959-5 (e-book)

Library of Congress Control Number: 2022946520

Cover image © Anton Balazh / Shutterstock.com
Cover design by Brad Norr Design

Wayne State University Press rests on Waawiyaataanong, also referred to as Detroit, the ancestral and contemporary homeland of the Three Fires Confederacy. These sovereign lands were granted by the Ojibwe, Odawa, Potawatomi, and Wyandot Nations, in 1807, through the Treaty of Detroit. Wayne State University Press affirms Indigenous sovereignty and honors all tribes with a connection to Detroit. With our Native neighbors, the press works to advance educational equity and promote a better future for the earth and all people.

Wayne State University Press
Leonard N. Simons Building
4809 Woodward Avenue
Detroit, Michigan 48201-1309

Visit us online at wsupress.wayne.edu

To Dale Patterson and all the other civil servants in the Wisconsin Department of Natural Resources—and in local, tribal, state, and federal agencies throughout the United States—who quietly strive to do what's right while their bosses play politics.

CONTENTS

CAST OF CHARACTERS

U.S. Fish and Wildlife Service ("Fish and Wildlife" or "FWS," part of the Department of the Interior or "Interior"): The federal agency that forced the Superfund law into the Fox River cleanup. Led by **David Allen** in Green Bay, Wisconsin with his key partner **Frank Horvath** in Fort Snelling, Minnesota and their regional leader **Bill Hartwig** in Fort Snelling.

Green Bay Press-Gazette: The local paper in Green Bay, Wisconsin that made the Fox River cleanup a major story for the state and region, led by environmental reporter **Susan Campbell**, with support from the paper's top editor and editorial staff.

U.S. Department of Justice ("Justice" or "DOJ"): The center of the legal team that took Allen's case seriously from the very beginning, starting with **Matt Richmond** in Milwaukee, then **Susan Schneider** in Washington, DC.

U.S. Environmental Protection Agency ("EPA"): The federal agency that reluctantly invoked its Superfund cleanup authorities on the Fox River, but eventually charged ahead with the largest PCB cleanup in history, led by **Jim Hahnenberg**, **Roger Grimes**, and their acting regional administrator **Dave Ullrich**, all three located in Chicago.

Wisconsin Department of Natural Resources ("DNR"): The state agency whose leaders followed Governor **Tommy Thompson** to partner with the paper companies in open opposition to the federal government and the Superfund law, led by DNR secretary **George Meyer** and powerful manager **Bruce Baker**, all in Madison, Wisconsin.

The paper companies: Led by the makers of carbonless copy paper,

NCR and **Appleton Papers**, and the recyclers of it, **P. H. Glatfelter** and **Fort Howard**.

The Fox River and Green Bay: The forty river miles and fifteen hundred square miles of open water polluted with hundreds of thousands of pounds of the toxins known as **polychlorinated biphenyls** ("PCBs") (Swackhamer and Armstrong 1987).

TIMELINE

1991   Water Resources to lead Fox River NRDA for DNR

DOI NRDA training for DNR

FWS R3 NRDA hires

1992   DNR says no FWS NRDA in Wisconsin

Fox River Coalition begins

FWS NRDA Nemadji River

1993   FWS NRDA Lake Geneva

FWS invites DNR to Green Bay NRDA

1994   FWS Green Bay NRDA starts; DNR declines

FWS identifies paper companies as potentially responsible parties

DNR asks Congress for $30 million for Fox River cleanup

Paper companies form the Fox River Group

1995   Governor Thompson asks Secretary Babbitt to stop Green Bay NRDA

FWS Regional Director Bill Hartwig says new direction for Green Bay NRDA

DNR settles Nemadji River unilaterally

1996   Last Fox River Coalition meeting

FWS Assessment Plan for Green Bay NRDA

Green Bay NRDA ranked first for DOI funding

Governor Thompson to Secretary Babbitt: concept paper

1997   DNR signs $10 million unilateral deal with Fox River Group of paper companies

1998   DNR forces then cancels Theo Colburn meeting

DNR heckles FWS at governmental meeting in Boulder

FWS NRDA: fish consumption advisories

1999   FWS NRDA: bird injuries

FWS NRDA: PCB pathways

FWS NRDA: water and fish injuries, recreational fishing damages

2000   DNR: SMU 56/57 demonstration project disaster

FWS calls for unilateral orders at SMU 56/57

DNR pretends to join Green Bay NRDA while making secret deal with Fort Howard

DNR attacks FWS Green Bay NRDA during meetings

EPA order at SMU 56/57; DNR unilateral deal at Sheboygan NRDA

$40 million Green Bay NRDA/cleanup deal with Appleton Papers

FWS Green Bay NRDA: final determination: RCDP

DNR attacks FWS Green Bay NRDA publicly

"Fox River Sellout?" story runs

2001   Governor Thompson leaves Wisconsin

Deal canceled between DNR and Fort Howard

EPA/DNR Fox River cleanup plan

INTRODUCTION

It's a hot August afternoon in Green Bay, Wisconsin. People stroll down the Fox River waterfront along the popular downtown CityDeck, a broad promenade that extends a quarter mile beside the river's east bank. Others rest on benches or sip drinks at one of several riverfront cafes as bicyclists thread their way along the boardwalk. Children shout as they're pelted by water spouting from a nearby splash pad. Upriver, thousands more enjoy boating and sport fishing in the river or are connected to its waters via the twenty-five-mile Fox River Trail.

The Fox River cuts a broad course straight through the middle of the city, its waves catching glints of sunlight and tossing ashore a breeze that refreshes riverfront regulars and tourists alike. When the CityDeck celebrated its tenth anniversary in 2019, city leaders said the original $13 million investment had attracted nearly $150 million more in direct investment for nearby projects (Gamble and Heyda 2016). That, in turn, had led to nearly $80 million in additional tax base for the city, including luxury apartments and condos overlooking the river.*

The Fox River's current appeal is a recent phenomenon, however.

Thirty years ago, the cleanup of the grossly contaminated Fox River was held hostage by a popular and powerful politician willing to ignore facts, laws, experts, the press, and even the institutions he had

---

* *CityDeck Great Places Award 2018*, *YouTube*, October 8, 2018, https://m.youtube.com/watch?fbclid=IwAR334N-s75Lga_PzfpDyt5PL7HdfIgqV01ZFqR1f4bjsW0pShNTyXb-pGk4&v=su0GfA14RK8&feature=youtu.be.

sworn to lead. He aimed a hair-triggered belligerence at anyone not in lockstep with his ideology. His anti-environmental, anti-regulation, anti-federal rhetoric made Governor Tommy Thompson the perfect ally for the powerful Fox River paper companies seeking to avoid paying for the costly cleanup of their mess, especially under the federal Superfund law.

What follows is the true story behind the turbulent battles throughout the 1990s that led to one of the largest, most divisive, most politically charged environmental river cleanups in the history of Superfund: the $1 billion fix for widespread chemical contamination of the Fox River to save the imperiled bay downstream. It is a complex story of how science, facts, community support, and individual perseverance overcame the persistent advantages of corporate polluters and their political allies. It's a story that resonates not only in Wisconsin but in communities around the country struggling to reclaim damaged waterways and protect the wider bays and lakes that suffer from decades of careless industrial practices.

It took another twenty years after Tommy Thompson left the governorship before massive dredges finally removed the contaminated muck and launched the restoration of the Fox River and bay of Green Bay. Today, most of the toxic chemicals that once lined the Fox River are gone. Contaminants no longer pour from the Fox into the bay of Green Bay, one of the most prominent ecological and recreational jewels of the entire Great Lakes, which themselves form the largest surface freshwater system on earth. The restoration of the Fox River and Green Bay is a clear win for the environment that can be replicated in any of the eight Great Lakes states and beyond. More than that, it's a win that can be replicated wherever and whenever political ideologues try to ignore facts, the law, and the people they are elected to serve.

We are David Allen and Susan Campbell, a former government scientist and a former reporter, respectively, who were at the center of the Green Bay drama that unfolded in the 1990s. We will take turns telling you about that drama, labeling our narrative voices accordingly as we share our two perspectives, and we encourage you to visit *www.papervalley.org* for the extensive documentary evidence we assembled for this book.*

We will tell of how one of us dreamed of managing nature sanctuaries, only to find a new professional "oasis" dominated by hulking paper mills, overwhelming industrial odors, and widespread ecological damage. We will tell of how a small, unlikely team fought to overcome a decade of hostile opposition, from multi-billion-dollar corporate polluters to the state regulators that Governor Tommy Thompson chose to direct the cleanup.

We will tell how the battle for the water and for the health of the community's people and wildlife played out on the front pages of the local *Green Bay Press-Gazette*, jockeying for space with articles about Titletown's fabled Green Bay Packers and quarterback Brett Favre. We will describe how a determined editor of that newspaper published hundreds of stories about a divided public, injured wildlife, and a relentless march to bring justice to a community that had nearly lost hope of ever healing the scarred river and saving the magnificent bay. As the case builds, we will take you ringside to the highly contentious emerging national debate among scientists and environmentalists that holds implications for human health the world over: what risks do PCBs, the same chemicals that lined the Fox River, pose to human health throughout the industrialized world?

In 2020, nearly three decades after the launch of the Fox River and Green Bay project, its completion was celebrated. Hailed as the largest PCB cleanup in history and the largest river cleanup completed anywhere in the world, the project saw a staggering 6.5 million cubic yards of contaminated sediment removed from the riverbed—enough to fill Green Bay's storied Lambeau Field Stadium six times over. Another thousand acres of chemical pollution lie entombed in the river beneath sand and specially engineered caps. And thousands of acres of critical habitat continue to be restored all around the bay to this day.

---

* In a few cases, multiple events or conversations have been combined, and some quoted conversations are approximations based on memory. In all instances, we have attempted to convey both the spirit and substantive details accurately.

All of the restoration work was funded not by taxpayers but by the polluters, which were first identified back in the mid-1990s. What we didn't know at the time was that our actions and reporting would unleash power plays, intrigue, and an epic public battle to bring about one of the world's biggest environmental comebacks.

PART I

MAKING A FEDERAL CASE, BY ACCIDENT

For every ailment under the sun
There is a remedy, or there is none;
If there be one, try to find it;
If there be none, never mind it.
                    —W. W. Bartley

Aerial photo of P. H. Glatfelter (Bergstrom Paper) in 1973, with discharges visible in Little Lake Butte des Morts at the upstream portion of the Lower Fox River, later known as Operable Unit 1. (Wisconsin DNR, circa 1990s)

I

GREEN BAY CONVERGENCE

FEDERAL TRANSFER

David Allen

Making paper can be a messy business. Turning trees into magazines and tissues requires a lot of energy, water, and chemicals.* A big river makes the job easier. Flowing water powers large machines, fills giant paper vats, and carries away tons of inconvenient waste. Paper companies discovered in the late 1800s how to harness the Fox River in northeast Wisconsin to make enough money to drive most of the local economy, as it does to this day. Fox River paper mills have made more paper—and more money—than most people can imagine.

Making all that paper meant that huge volumes of contaminated waste were pumped directly into the Fox River—though the nature of the pollution changed over the decades. How much waste? From the 1920s to the 1950s, the mills discharged so much sulfite liquor into the river that most of the many fish that had historically thrived in the river were killed. This early waste used up nearly all of the river's life-giving oxygen.

---

* Throughout this book, a primary source is David Allen's notes taken while working at the federal government from 1991 through 2001. Transcribed notes are available at Allen 2018a. Handwritten notes are available at Allen 1991, 1992a, 1993, 1994a, 1995a, 1996a, 1997, 1998a, 1999, 2000a, 2001.

Aerial photo of Fort Howard in the 1970s, with discharges visible below the De Pere Dam in the Lower Fox River, later known as Sediment Management Unit 56–57 and Operable Unit 4. (Wisconsin DNR, circa 1990s)

The State of Wisconsin basically invented the legal tools that would later become the guts of federal water pollution law: governmental requirements for wastewater treatment. The state began legal investigations and enforcement against Fox River paper companies in the 1920s with the legislature's State Committee on Water Pollution. It took decades of enforcement and court cases, but Wisconsin, eventually with help from the Feds, forced the paper companies to stop discharging most of the worst oxygen-depleting sulfite liquors into the Fox River.

Fish began returning to the river, only to face a more insidious problem—polychlorinated biphenyls, or PCBs. Paper mills began spewing these dangerous chemicals in the 1950s. PCBs were much harder to notice than the earlier forms of pollution since the fish didn't quickly suffocate and float, belly up, to the water's surface. PCBs were harder for wastewater plants to treat, too. The PCBs spread much further and lasted much longer than sulfite liquors. So even after the Department of Natural Resources (DNR) and the Environmental Protection Agency

(EPA) forced the paper mills to stop discharging PCBs from their pipes under the federal Clean Water Act in the late 1970s and early 1980s, Fox River sediments full of PCBs kept flowing from the river bottom to the entire bay.

Aerial view of the Lower Fox River. (Photo courtesy of the Wisconsin Department of Transportation)

Paper bales outside the Green Bay mill of Fort Howard Corporation in June 1973. (U.S. National Archives and Records Administration, photograph by Ted Rozumalski for the Environmental Protection Agency)

In 1980, the federal Superfund law hit the books.* This law taxes the chemical and petroleum industries to create the Superfund, which EPA and state cleanup agencies like Wisconsin DNR can use to clean up abandoned or uncontrolled hazardous waste sites even when no polluter can be found to pay. The agencies can also sue for all of the cleanup costs when polluters are still in business. The law also confers police powers on EPA and state agencies to order polluters to clean up a pollution emergency, and gives EPA huge advantages in court—most polluters do not want to face these kinds of legal proceedings.

Most people have heard of a Superfund site. It's usually a forgotten landfill where EPA forces some company to clean up leaking barrels of toxic waste that were dumped back in the day when nobody was watching. However, the Superfund law is broader and more powerful than most people realize. It can be used almost anywhere hazardous substances are present, even giant rivers and bays where chemicals have spread for decades. And the law has a special superpower that allows for something more than cleanup: a Natural Resource Damage Assessment, or NRDA, conducted by specific tribal, state, or federal agencies other than EPA. These agencies figure out how much the public has lost that cannot be replaced by cleaning up a polluted site, no matter how vigorously. These agencies can't use the money in the Superfund, and they can't use police powers like EPA, but they can still sue polluters for enough money to restore the natural resources lost to the public because of the pollution—such as water, fish, wildlife, and habitat.

At most sites, such as common landfill sites, the restoration costs from damage assessments are small compared with cleanup costs. Digging up leaking barrels and disposing of them safely is expensive, but most landfills have a pretty small footprint. Plus, unlike EPA, the agencies conducting damage assessments can't use many of the legal advantages Superfund gives EPA for cleanup.**

---

* Comprehensive Environmental Response, Compensation, and Liability Act ("Superfund"): 42 U.S.C. §§9601–75.

** EPA's cleanup lawsuits are based on their administrative record and they win as long as that record does not show EPA to be "arbitrary and capricious." Trustee agencies build

EPA ramped up its Superfund program in 1981, right after the Superfund law was passed by Congress. The same urgency that motivated Congress to pass Superfund for sites like the notoriously polluted Love Canal neighborhood in New York motivated EPA to act quickly. Superfund soon became one of EPA's largest programs. Even so, there were so many contaminated sites that EPA could barely keep up. States joined in soon after with their own large cleanup programs under Superfund. Wisconsin DNR was among them.

It took longer for most agencies to create viable damage assessment programs. Wisconsin DNR and the U.S. Fish and Wildlife Service both started theirs in the late 1980s. Even then, most didn't fully grasp the potential of this new superpower, but everybody did realize that preparing intricate court cases from scratch for damage assessments would be harder to accomplish than EPA's more direct power to compel cleanup.

Throughout all of these decades of changing pollution from Fox River paper mills and waves of enforcement by state and federal governments, the people of so-called Paper Valley and Green Bay argued about whether turning trees into money made all the pollution worth it. Fox River paper companies and the many thousands who worked for or otherwise benefited economically from them tended to see the tradeoff as a pretty good deal, but Green Bay anglers usually disagreed. Environmentalists and conservationists fought with industrialists and entrepreneurs over what to do about the pollution. In 1992, when I arrived in Green Bay, environmentalists argued, "The companies made most of the money and most of the mess. Shouldn't these same companies fix the lingering PCB problems now?"

My new job was to help build a Natural Resource Damage Assessment for the Fox River and bay of Green Bay. My agency, Fish and Wildlife, figured it might be a big case requiring its normal expertise in fish and wildlife toxicology and habitat restoration. However, my agency probably didn't expect Wisconsin DNR to suddenly abandon its role as the lead on the damage assessment—just as I was hired. My new bosses

---

their NRDA cases from scratch (de novo), which is harder, more time consuming, and more difficult to win.

certainly didn't expect Wisconsin DNR to also abandon the Superfund law altogether, both the cleanup side with EPA and the NRDA side with Fish and Wildlife. Nobody expected Wisconsin DNR to publicly oppose, for the first time in seven decades, all legal enforcement against the paper companies by *any* agency.

At most sites, an NRDA is a formality, an afterthought that gets settled at the same time that the bigger cleanup is resolved by EPA. But the Fox River and bay of Green Bay PCB problem was exponentially bigger than most Superfund sites, and it had no cleanup agency willing to use Superfund, at least back in 1992 when I moved to Green Bay. So when I proposed to use an NRDA by the U.S. Fish and Wildlife Service to force the Superfund law at the Fox River site, most people thought I was nuts. Fish and Wildlife had never launched a Superfund case completely on its own. And no trustee agency had ever tried to force EPA's hand over the objection of a state. Plus, nobody had ever used the NRDA provisions under the Superfund law to accomplish everything the cleanup agencies normally tackle with their stronger authorities under the same law. I didn't agree with the skeptics. It might have been a long shot, but moving my agency forward without EPA and DNR was the only chance the river, the bay, and the public had.

When I arrived in Green Bay, I knew that the local rhetoric about voluntary cleanup by the paper companies was a pipe dream. Most people thought a complete cleanup of the Fox River would cost far more than it would cost the paper companies to fund their defense in court. I realized that the bank interest alone on those cleanup costs would exceed the expense of their defense. No company officer or stockholder would forego that much money without a fight. I was sure from the start that I was right about those officers and shareholders. And I never lost sight of this fundamental truth as I developed my strategies for Green Bay.

I often worry that I fit a bit *too* well into the relatively rare INTJ category of Myers-Briggs personality tests, sometimes labeled "strategist." The classic INTJ character traits include a penchant for questioning authority, fiercely independent thinking, and single-minded determination to follow one's own vision regardless of what others think. It probably explains some of my successes—but also my struggles.

As a youngster, I joined teams and organizations mostly to please friends or mentors, but abandoned them whenever coaches, teachers, or leaders failed to explain the big-picture goal and why it was worthwhile. For instance, I joined middle school basketball for my tall and lanky childhood friend Bill Conlon. But no coach ever took the time to explain the game to me, so I sat on the bench bored out of my mind and mostly daydreamed about my next trombone lesson. Music was the only part of my life that didn't seem to need any strategic thinking. Its meaning somehow arrived without need for explanation.

After high school, I had to learn the value of difficult and sometimes tedious work the hard way. I explored a sense of uninhibited freedom as an undergraduate at The Ohio State University. My classes had to compete with an array of other interests, and uninteresting classes didn't stand a chance. Three of my six college roommates flunked out of school, and Bill Conlon came close to it. I nearly flunked out as well, but managed to pull up just in time.

Graduating with a bachelor's in science and mediocre grades in zoology, I knew I faced a tough employment road ahead, and trombone gigs were never going to pay the bills. I proposed marriage to my girlfriend, Darlene, but she wanted to know I was serious about our future. So I took a shot at flying jets with the U.S. Air Force. It took just two days for me to fly out of Officer Training School when I realized I'd have to memorize volumes of materials as an exercise to prove my willingness to process complex information for no reason other than it was mandatory. Another strike.

I took my GRE tests soon after marrying Darlene and tried one-on-one persuasion with OSU professors to attend the School of Natural Resources. A wildlife biology professor told me he liked my test scores but wasn't about to award me one of his rare grad posts unless I proved myself. He signed me up for two quarters of classes as a test. At the same time I was shouldering the ridiculously difficult course load to satisfy my professor, I took on a paper route to satisfy Darlene. The combination nearly did me in. During the first two weeks I finally learned to study, but I also learned the larger life lesson that hard work pays dividends. A woman on my paper route—younger than me—who answered the door and announced, "Honey! Paperboy is here to collect" gave me all the motivation I needed.

By the time I was officially in graduate school, two quarters later, I had a whole new set of work habits that I would draw on for the rest of my academic life and career. Hard work, even if it was tedious, was strategic if it ultimately got me what I wanted. Plus, I soon learned how to conduct field research in the woods, live-capturing and tracking white-tailed deer with radio transmitters.

After grad school, Darlene and I moved to Chicago, where I became EPA's technical expert on regional water quality standards, and I interacted with each of the region's Great Lakes states: Illinois, Indiana, Michigan, Minnesota, Ohio, and Wisconsin. I soon learned about EPA's Great Lakes priorities, which included PCB contamination in the bay of Green Bay. Darlene arranged a transfer within her company from Ohio to a building a few blocks from my federal building in downtown Chicago. We took the train together to work. We were both in our twenties, and big-city life was a great adventure for us both.

At EPA, I began working on water quality issues in Ken Fenner's group of about one hundred federal employees. I was only twenty-seven, but I was eager to learn, so he mentored me. I dived into the technical and legal intricacies of the Clean Water Act with enthusiasm. However, he taught me much more than how to read a federal statute. He showed me how to use facts and the law to limit the authority of powerful bureaucrats—even elected officials. He taught me how to spar with state agencies completely outside my line of command and, critically, helped me develop stamina in the face of extended expert opposition. Most important of all, he taught me how to "read the room," whether literally during meetings with representatives of companies seeking discharge permits, or figuratively while finessing just the right paper trail to influence targeted factions within EPA.

Once Fenner took me under his wing, I learned to operate the bureaucratic tools within my reach. I learned that my own EPA group looked to Wisconsin as a powerful innovative trendsetter, but also that

Wisconsin DNR's Bruce Baker was a regular visitor to our Chicago office and a skilled adversary when he disagreed with EPA priorities. My EPA office had many divisions, with about eighteen hundred people on multiple floors of a Chicago skyscraper; I made it my business to find like-minded, capable people no matter which floor they occupied. I discovered people who were engines for regulatory action, even when it required litigation, but many others who preferred giving grants, conducting research, and avoiding controversy.

While learning the ropes from Fenner at EPA, I met Ken Stromborg from the U.S. Fish and Wildlife Service. We started collaborating on water quality standards to protect fish and wildlife throughout the Great Lakes. Ken was already famous in my agency because he had literally crashed into Green Bay in a small airplane. His plane had run out of fuel as he was following cormorants, big black seabirds, to see how far they flew from their nests to feed (Custer and Bunck 1992). He had somehow emerged without a scratch. Once I got to know him, it made sense that no crash could bring him down—in body or in spirit. In 1991, Ken told me he was about to advertise a position in his Green Bay office. Classified as a "Fish and Wildlife biologist" post, the actual title was "Natural Resource Damage Assessment specialist." My heart skipped a beat. Here was an opportunity to learn a whole new federal statute, the Superfund law, which had been on the books eleven years and already had some impressive successes under its belt.

The Fish and Wildlife position Ken dangled in '91 hinted at a new and different life, but one that had its own allure. Beyond tackling a potentially big case like Green Bay, it was a chance to join the same agency that housed the National Wildlife Refuge System, which included the Seney National Wildlife Refuge. The refuge was located near my family camp in Michigan's Upper Peninsula and my dream job, since boyhood, was to someday manage it. My formative years and memories had been shaped by annual trips to the camp, which was located in northern Michigan's Hiawatha National Forest. My friend Bill Conlon had been a regular fixture there, too, as he would be for many years. My father and grandfather had stepped in as unofficial surrogates when Bill's father died, back when he and I were in third grade. As kids in the 1960s, we

David Allen at his camp in the Hiawatha National Forest in
the Upper Peninsula of Michigan, circa 1973. (Ann Allen)

had explored the woods and learned to fish on Michigan's Big Bay de
Noc at the very north end of the bay of Green Bay.

In 1992, when Ken Stromborg offered me the U.S. Fish and Wildlife
Service position in Green Bay, it meant I could combine my lifelong
predilection for strategic thinking, sharpened by Ken Fenner for the
regulatory world of EPA, with my passion for the woods and the water,
sharpened by my graduate degree and field research at OSU.

Darlene was quickly accepted into the University of Wisconsin at
Madison, and Ken Stromborg agreed to let me live in that city while she
finished her graduate degree. I steeled myself for the daily two-and-a-
half-hour commutes between Madison and Green Bay.

REPORTING TO GREEN BAY

Susan Campbell

"Are you sure you'd want to live there?" asked the voice at the other end of the line.

I was taken aback. "Why not?"

"Well, most people around here don't want to live near the water," the voice said.

I was embarrassed by my obvious outsider's ignorance. And frustrated. On the map, the city of Green Bay, Wisconsin looked ideally situated at the junction of a broad river and the bay of Green Bay. The opportunity to live near a large body of water, affordably, was one of the major draws to moving back to the Midwest to work at a local newspaper. The closest body of water to my apartment in suburban Philadelphia was the Atlantic Ocean, and you had to cross New Jersey to get there. I turned to my husband after getting off the phone. "Tom, there's only one apartment complex near the bay and apparently most people wouldn't want to live near it."

"Why? What's wrong with the water?" he asked.

"Polluted," I said. "I asked the apartment manager if the water was really dirty or smelled bad, and he said no. So how bad can it really be?"

I had been calling papers around the Midwest looking for reporting jobs during the recession of the early '90s, a time when newspaper layoffs were commonplace. The search was made more complicated by the need for two reporting jobs, one for me and one for Tom, and the fact that more and more cities had become single-newspaper towns.

Through our first years at small newspapers, Tom and I had watched a number of friends and colleagues leave journalism for more lucrative jobs and predictable 9–5 schedules. But journalism was our calling, our chance to serve the public interest, and we were committed to making it a long-term career.

Now, here we were, circling above Green Bay from the air before touching down for our respective job interviews at the *Green Bay Press-Gazette*. I felt immediately at home with the rolling countryside, the small, manageable city, and all that glorious blue-green Lake

Michigan water. It was freshwater, not saltwater—part of the same lake system that included Lake Superior, the Great Lakes' crown jewel, where as a child I'd vacationed every year with my family.

Growing up in Minnesota had meant having room to breathe and dream. Even the urban landscape of Minneapolis was home to several of the state's renowned ten thousand lakes, many connected by miles of winding bike trails, parks, and wooded walking paths. As is often the case, it wasn't until I'd moved away that I truly appreciated what this part of the country had to offer. Now twenty-seven and having lived more than a decade on the East Coast, I was angling to return, to be closer to my family in Minneapolis and closer to the Great Lakes.

The *Press-Gazette*'s executive editor took us to lunch at a local supper club overlooking the Fox River, but not before circling nearby Lambeau Field, home of the famed Green Bay Packers, two, maybe even three times. It was clearly a major selling point for working at the paper. Driving around Green Bay, I couldn't help noticing that even the fire hydrants here were painted Packers' green and gold. At lunch, the conversation included talk of the "emerging" Brett Favre who, in just his second year as the Packers' quarterback, already carried the hopes and dreams of the entire community. We also learned about the Monfils murder, an apparent inside job by union brothers working at one of the prominent paper mills along the Fox River.

I recalled my phone call with the apartment manager and made a point of asking the executive editor about the polluted river and bay of Green Bay. I got a brief answer about paper mills and PCBs. Whatever PCBs were, I thought to myself, they weren't enough to thwart my enthusiasm for moving back to the Midwest.

Our hosts told us that no visit to Green Bay would be complete without visiting neighboring Door County, the "thumb" of Wisconsin jutting out into Lake Michigan that separates the lake from the bay. Door County had a reputation as "the Cape Cod of the Midwest," and Tom and I had spent many a weekend driving up Massachusetts's Cape Cod peninsula during our college years in Boston.

Now, in the waning summer light of early September, the breathtaking drive up the Door Peninsula did not disappoint. Flanked by the sparkling bay of Green Bay on one side and the wilder Lake Michigan on the other, Door County had its own allure. I pulled into a marina in the first town we reached and we raced each other to the water's edge. Here was beauty in every direction. The village of Egg Harbor was a safe haven of cottages, with shops behind them to the east. Wooded limestone cliffs encircled the harbor's southern and western shores before giving way to the open waters of Green Bay to the west. The bay broadened northward to mix, some thirty-five miles away, with Lake Michigan's deeper, darker blue waters.

A strong wind was blowing, whipping up whitecaps on the water and driving tall waves into the harbor where we stood, faces to the wind. We knew, in that instant, this was where we wanted to be.

The call from the *Press-Gazette* came not long after the interviews. Just three weeks later, we were packed and ready to leave our old newspaper jobs in suburban Philly, the stifling late-summer heat, and the East Coast. We said good-bye to friends and colleagues, enduring the Wisconsin jokes about recreational "cow-tipping" and the loyal Cheeseheads who worshiped the Green Bay Packers. Then we crammed our belongings into already overstuffed hatchbacks and rolled out into the night, heading west on the Pennsylvania Turnpike for a new beginning.

There's a saying in journalism that reporters are listed right at the top of crazy people's phone books. And there's a corollary, which some reporters subscribe to more than others: listen to those people. For amid the random calls about the neighbor's rabid dog, the rumored philandering city councilor, and the occasional hoax would come a gem. You just never knew when. Everyone had a story to tell, and a good reporter had to listen to them all to find it.

I took this as gospel and had practiced it informally long before becoming a reporter. I genuinely liked talking with people and was by nature a good listener. I also had a knack for getting information, even unintentionally. "I don't know why I'm telling you this" was something I often heard in conversation. Depending on the situation, the words either made me perk up my ears or find a quick exit. I'd learned the hard way my relatability could be a great asset, except when it wasn't—for instance, when I'd call in an order and spend twenty minutes hearing the life story of the salesperson at the other end of the line. Tom would often catch me mid-call and ask afterward whom I was talking with. "I thought it was your mom," he'd say with a smirk.

It turned out that being a good listener was a major asset indeed for a reporter. My first editor, a crusty former *Boston Globe* editor in semi-retirement, had nicknamed me the "baby-faced assassin" and "smiling barracuda" not long after my start in the business. Just twenty-one at the time and fresh out of college, I didn't like how coldhearted the sobriquets sounded. I never betrayed a source's confidence and was a strict observer of "off the record." I often winced inwardly when a story made a source look bad, even if the source was the one who had held up the mirror. But I did get information, and my first editor's labels had stuck.

In Green Bay, the Fox River saga would bring together all the elements I valued in a good story: intrigue, science, politics, nature, and more than its share of interesting, peculiar people. I told myself I would make it my business to get out of the newsroom office to meet them and listen to their stories as often as I could. The core of my reporting, however, would be undertaken in the newsroom and on the phone—and would eventually center on David Allen at the U.S. Fish and Wildlife Service.

At the same time that Tom and I were trying to find reporting jobs near the Great Lakes, a little-known scientist in Washington, DC, was gearing up to publish a book that soon would send shock waves throughout the scientific community and the chemical industry.

The book would be hailed by many as the next *Silent Spring*, and its coauthor, Theo Colborn, as the next Rachel Carson—whose seminal work had helped spark the modern environmental movement some thirty years earlier. Carson was among the first to write about the harmful effects of synthetic chemicals on people and wildlife. Her writings were based on research on DDT done by the Fish and Wildlife lab in Patuxent, Maryland, which would later discover PCBs in Green Bay gulls and was coincidentally the same lab that years later would hire

Ken Stromborg at the start of his federal career at the U.S. Fish and Wildlife Service.

Colborn was about to take it to the next level, taking special aim at PCBs and other synthetic chemicals accumulating in the environment and its inhabitants. She theorized that these chemicals, known to cause reproductive problems, deformities, and even death in some wildlife, might also have harmful effects on people. There was already some evidence they did, and Colborn was about to publicize it to the world.

In 1991, she was one of twenty-one scientists who signed a solemn two-thousand-word consensus statement warning, in part, that the reproductive problems reported in wildlife should be of concern to people dependent upon the same resources—in this case contaminated fish. "The impacts on wildlife and laboratory animals as a result of exposure to these contaminants are of such a profound and insidious nature that a major research initiative on humans must be undertaken," the scientists wrote (Colborn, Dumanoski, and Myers 1996, 256).

The consensus statement was signed after a several-day multidisciplinary workshop at a sprawling thirty-six-acre campus in Racine, Wisconsin on Lake Michigan's western shore. The ringside seat to Lake Michigan was no accident: the Great Lakes were a living laboratory for studying the problem. The mostly self-contained and slow-moving system served as a natural holding pen for PCBs and other toxic contaminants, and many of the world's leading researchers in the field were training their lenses on the Great Lakes.

Colborn's own research was rooted there. Having earned her PhD in zoology from the University of Wisconsin–Madison in 1985 as a fifty-eight-year-old grandmother, she had soon been hired to assess the environmental health of the Great Lakes for a nonprofit DC think tank.

She found study after study showing problems in Great Lakes wildlife. Although the Great Lakes had been cleared of most of the visible pollution that plagued them in the 1960s and '70s, biologists in the field were reporting that things were still seriously amiss: a crash in the mink population; crossed bills, missing eyes, and clubbed feet in double-crested cormorants; female herring gulls nesting with other females; and Forster's terns with little interest in guarding or incubating their eggs. Biologists were also reporting large numbers of eggs that never hatched, and seemingly healthy chicks that mysteriously wasted away.

Everywhere Colborn looked around the Great Lakes, she saw signs that something was seriously wrong. How they all fit together was a puzzle, however. Her fresh perspective would assemble the pieces in a new and controversial way, and would attract a particularly attentive audience from Green Bay to Paper Valley.

It took decades, but Green Bay was already becoming the epicenter of the Great Lakes PCB story even before Theo Colburn began sharpening the focus. In the early 1960s, researchers were surprised to discover that Green Bay herring gull eggs were full of chemicals known as organochlorines (Keith 1966). Labs hadn't yet figured out how to separate the hundreds of man-made chemical compounds that comprise organochlorines, among them PCBs, dioxins, furans, and pesticides like DDT. All of these compounds were notorious for their high toxicity, slow breakdown, and tendency to accumulate in the bodies of fish and wildlife. And each of them behaved differently in the environment and in the bodies of their hosts. Decades of groundbreaking local research ensued.

Over time, labs determined that PCBs comprised most of the organochlorine chemicals in the eggs. The findings also determined that PCBs were in many other local species, and that the chemicals sometimes caused adverse health effects in those species. Hundreds of people worked on dozens of studies, many of which were now well known in the scientific literature (Allen 2018b).

A number of the scientists from the University of Wisconsin–Green Bay wanted to study the contaminant problem in their backyard. The university was located near the shores of Green Bay in the shadow of the Niagara Escarpment, a rocky ridge that runs east to New York before dropping off precipitously to form Niagara Falls. The campus was founded on a mission of sustainability in the run-up to the first Earth Day in 1970. Soon called Eco U, it was one of just three colleges at the time to pioneer environmental programs, and it attracted talented, idealistic professors and students—some of whom played key roles in the unfolding Fox River drama.

A part of the university, the Richter Museum of Natural History, became an archive of one of the most historically important collections of birds and mammals in the western Great Lakes states. The museum's metal filing cabinets in UW–Green Bay's Cofrin Hall catalogued more than fifty thousand animal, fossil, mineral, and anthropological specimens, including one of the ten largest bird egg collections in the world.

The museum's collections were essential fodder for decades of studies by Great Lakes scientists, UW–Green Bay researchers, and graduate students. As far back as 1968, scientists used measurements from the archive's herring gull egg sets to analyze for historical levels of the chemical DDT in avian food webs, leading Wisconsin to become the first state to ban the use of DDT pesticides.* The extensive collections of gulls, herons, terns, egrets, and pelicans were directly involved in many of the critical studies that first discovered organochlorines in Green Bay birds, as well as subsequent exploration of PCBs and their effects on wildlife.

The corridor just outside the museum was lined with large displays accessible to the public whenever the university building was open. But the heart of the museum—a large, windowless space—was viewable by appointment only. Tucked away here in wide metal drawers were the museum's carefully catalogued bird specimens, many scarred with twisted bills and other gross deformities. Others were packed and pickled in jars, and still others, preserved and mounted, stared out from shelves and glass cases.

This was also where the museum curator held court. He was a researcher in his own right. Passionate, intense, and a bit wild-eyed at times, he'd been studying birds on the bay of Green Bay since the 1960s. During that time, he had seen and coauthored a number of scientific studies on cormorants, terns, and other bay birds born with twisted legs, beaks, and wings. He'd recorded many birds born with deformed

---

* "Richter Museum of Natural History," https://www.uwgb.edu/biodiversity/richter/; and "Cofrin Center for Biodiversity," https://www.uwgb.edu/biodiversity/about/mission.asp.

and partial feet, and birds that didn't sit on their nests long enough to hatch their young (Kubiak et al. 1989). He'd seen the decline or disappearance of the bay's populations of terns—fast-flying, elegant birds that resemble agile gulls.

Although bird-banding records on the bay dated back to 1926, he often pointed out that no bird deformities had been recorded there until the 1970s, soon after various chemicals, classified together as organochlorines and including PCBs and DDT, began showing up in bird samples. The source of the problem was no mystery to him. He told anyone who asked that the museum's macabre mix of mutant birds clearly derived from the bay's potent cocktail of PCBs and other organochlorines (Campbell 1998i, 2000d).

"The problem is much greater than people thought," the museum curator had warned CNN reporter Robert Vito in a 1980s news broadcast about the high prevalence of PCBs and bird deformities in the bay. "I think we should start monitoring the fish, and I think we ought to start monitoring the people who eat [the] fish."

By 1987, Canada and the United States had jointly identified forty-three critically impaired areas around the Great Lakes, including Green Bay because of its widespread chemical contamination (International Joint Commission 1990; Great Lakes Water Quality Board 1987). EPA and DNR went on to fund a landmark study of how PCBs move in the Fox River and Green Bay that involved a whopping $16 million* for data collections from riverbed muck, water, fish, and other biota, and development of computer models to track and try to predict PCB movement (Velleux and Endicott 1994). The rich data sets allowed researchers to model how the river's waters ebbed and flowed, how the water moved PCBs along the river bottom and lakebed, and how PCBs accumulated in fish and wildlife. Many of the country's top experts in this field of modeling assembled to sift through and build models from the data (see

---

* The often-cited figure of $11 million (1990s dollars) from EPA's Great Lakes National Program Office does not include the $5 million (also 1990s dollars) from the Wisconsin DNR.

Connolly et al. 1992; DePinto et al. 1994; Eadie, Bell, and Hawley 1991; Gailani, Ziegler, and Lick 1991; Manchester-Neesvig, Andren, and Edgington 1996; Pearson et al. 1996; Sweet et al. 1993; Velleux et al. 1995).

Soon after I arrived at the *Green Bay Press-Gazette*, I discovered that Green Bay was being called the most studied PCB site in the world.

BLINDSIDED

David Allen

On Sunday, March 22, 1992, I left my Chicago apartment for the last time and drove to my temporary quarters at the Residence Inn on Webster Avenue in Green Bay. I was leaving my wife, Darlene, behind for a couple of weeks, and my job at the U.S. Environmental Protection Agency forever. I was excited to begin exploring northeast Wisconsin, especially the Door Peninsula, Chicago's playground. As I drove north on Webster, though, I caught glimpses of Fort Howard's towering smokestacks just across the Fox River. Fort Howard was the best-known paper company in Green Bay and likely to be my biggest adversary in an enormous environmental case. Door County fun might have to wait.

When I exited my car at the hotel parking lot, an odd pungent odor jolted me into the present. I'd been warned by an EPA colleague who had worked near Green Bay that the whole region smelled like rotting eggs or decaying cabbage at times because of some of the paper mills. My new office mates at the U.S. Fish and Wildlife Service in Green Bay would tell me, "It's the smell of money."

To say that papermaking ruled the economy and quality of life here, in a community better known nationally as football's "Titletown," was an understatement. Situated along part of the forty-mile Lower Fox River that runs from Lake Winnebago northeast to Green Bay, "Paper Valley" had for more than a century been home to dozens of paper mills, at one time boasting the largest concentration in the world (Dobkin 2010). The monolithic plants rose up from the banks along the river, their towering smokestacks and blinking lights cutting into an otherwise pastoral landscape.

These companies produced publishing-grade paper, their goods lined grocery shelves around the world, and they dominated the commercial paper market. The reach and economic might of Paper Valley became expansive: millions of tons of paper products each year traced their beginnings to this region. The paper mills themselves shaped the local community as surely as they shaped the landscape. Together, they helped power the economy of the Fox River Valley and Green Bay, directly employing tens of thousands of workers, indirectly employing many more, and reaping over a century of economic success in the process.*

Despite the very real economic benefits to the region, it was hard for outsiders to understand how locals accepted the recurring—but legal—stench of sulfur compounds from papermaking as a cost of living downriver from Paper Valley.

It turns out sulfur was the least of what the mills were spewing into the local environment. From the late 1950s through the '70s, some mills were discharging hundreds of thousands of pounds of an odorless, invisible group of far more worrisome compounds. These toxic chemicals—known as polychlorinated biphenyls, or PCBs—were discharged to the Fox River by the manufacture or recycling of carbonless copy paper.

The National Cash Register company had invented carbonless copy paper in 1953 so that people could make multiple copies all at once when using a pen, as when filling out forms in triplicate or making receipts. They called it "no carbon required" or NCR paper. They made a lot of it—and a lot of money—at the Appleton Papers mill in Paper Valley. The company used PCBs to encapsulate and transfer ink between the multiple layers of paper. Unfortunately, the manufacturing process spilled PCBs into the Fox River. Plus, other mills, such as Fort Howard, recycled NCR paper. Their recycling processes sent mostly clean fibers into the new paper and most of the waste products, including PCBs, directly into the river.

Congress banned production of PCBs in the 1970s, citing concerns about their cancer-causing properties. Unfortunately, by then hundreds

---

* Wisconsin Paper Council, https://www.wipaper.org/economic-impact.

of thousands of pounds of PCBs had already been dumped into the Fox River by paper companies. Worse, the PCBs were flowing every year from the river sediments into the bay of Green Bay. By the 1990s, more of the paper mills' PCBs had spread throughout fifteen hundred square miles of the bay than remained in the river, though the river still had far higher concentrations than the bay. By this time, three decades of scientific research had accumulated showing health problems for fish and wildlife throughout the bay, and new research was beginning to prove how PCBs moved from the river into the bay. State advisories warned anglers that most of the fish and waterfowl in the Fox River and bay were unsafe to eat because PCBs, a known carcinogen, were found in fish throughout the system and, in turn, in the birds that fed on them. Some bay wildlife showed aberrant behavior like failing to protect nests, and male-female ratios that were sufficiently out of balance to affect reproductive success. Some birds were born with deformities like backward wings and twisted bills. For nearly three decades, scientists had been assembling a jigsaw puzzle that was beginning to link fish and wildlife exposure to PCBs with many of these unusual problems in the bay.

All of this might add up to evidence of a major disturbance throughout the local ecosystem caused by the paper mills' PCBs, but nobody had ever tried to turn the three decades of research into a court case. None of the researchers had ever thought about how to collect data for the Superfund law or under judicial rules of evidence.

The stakes were high, and the smell of money might prove a powerful lure to government officials, bureaucrats, lobbyists, lawyers, scientists, consultants, and politicians from the highest levels in Washington, DC (Allen 2019b). Leaning against my car in the hotel parking lot, I looked over toward the river and Fort Howard. For just a second I felt a pang of panic. What had I gotten myself into?

My first couple of months with the U.S. Fish and Wildlife Service were interesting ones. After two weeks of temporary quarters at the hotel in Green Bay, Darlene and I moved into an apartment in Madison. Right away, I began dividing my time among introductions at Wisconsin

DNR's main offices in Madison, fieldwork on the Door Peninsula northeast of Green Bay, and the regular two-and-a-half-hour commute from Madison to my new office in Green Bay. My DNR introductions started with a staffer named Dale Patterson. He was an exceedingly helpful scientist and manager who knew all about the Fox River.

However, as I wandered between offices in DNR's Madison headquarters, I often felt too many eyes watching me, as if people had been warned to be careful around me. I'd worked with DNR staff while I was at EPA, and this was not the usual stiffness that occasionally strained interactions between states and the Feds. It was soon clear that Wisconsin had become nervous about the very idea of damage assessments. As Dale became more comfortable with me, he began relaying stories, then documents, about DNR's early damage assessment efforts, and the ax that fell on them soon after seeking clearance from Governor Tommy Thompson. The governor had a growing disdain for environmental regulation, even by his own Department of Natural Resources. This was particularly true in Paper Valley, one of his key political strongholds.

Back in Green Bay, local environmentalists and academics began whispering in my ear. Most of them were convinced that the important decisions about the Fox River had already been made. They assumed Governor Thompson and paper company executives had struck a quiet deal to prevent legal mechanisms with real leverage from being used against the paper companies. Whatever details remained to be worked out for a wholly voluntary river cleanup would be handled by DNR— perhaps with minor input from EPA, Fish and Wildlife, and environmentalists. Nobody thought I would be able to influence the Fox River cleanup much.

I soon discovered that the paper companies had an army of polished PR men, lawyers, lobbyists, technical reps, and local allies who relied on their favor. They sent them to every gathering that might involve a whisper about Fox River PCBs or what to do about them. These paper company "ambassadors" angled to look reasonable and in line with the state officials controlled by Governor Thompson while discouraging any mention of their own responsibility for their mess and the laws that could hold them accountable. And they fed endless discussions of technical and procedural minutiae, populating each new subcommittee with men who were ever watchful, ever whispering in friendly ears, ever warning anyone who stepped out of line.

In those early days, I considered the paper companies' arguments. Perhaps little could be done about Fox River PCBs. Maybe the problems caused by PCBs would never justify the expense of a cleanup that could make a real difference, such as dredging most of the river PCBs to make sure the wide-open PCB spigot to the bay was finally closed.

On the other hand, many constituents, activists, experts, and officials were demanding that something be done. Many in the community wanted to remove enough PCBs from the river, *now*, so that fish and waterfowl throughout the bay would become healthier and safe to eat in a few years rather than many decades or longer. Patience was wearing thin.

Unfortunately, any talk of using Superfund or other laws to require the paper companies to clean up their mess was met with hostility, not only from the paper companies—which everyone expected—but from DNR, an agency with decades of successful environmental protection and stewardship. Instead, meetings were carefully steered toward more study, open-ended discussion, and proposals for taxpayer funding. In 1992, hundreds of people began spending thousands of hours talking and analyzing, but legal leverage was a topic strictly forbidden by the DNR leaders and paper company reps running the meetings. By the time I arrived in Green Bay, many seemed disgusted that these tactics were starting to work, but few wanted to risk derailing the voluntary talks to consider leverage that seemed so unlikely to ever materialize.

Most of the arguments during meetings ping-ponged between two factions. One faction, led by the paper companies, wanted to delay cleanup action altogether. The other, led by Wisconsin, wanted a quicker cleanup, but paid for with whatever public monies could be used and maybe some ancillary contributions by the paper companies. Both factions refused to look at the broader, more vibrant, more valuable bay of Green Bay as additional justification for a cleanup that focused, for practical engineering reasons, on the river only. And neither faction tolerated talk of legal tools aimed at the paper companies. Against this backdrop, most estimated that funding for the Fox River cleanup would top out at a few million dollars, perhaps even a few tens of millions.

In surveying the situation, two facts emerged of which I was absolutely certain: first, that preventing legally enforceable actions under the Superfund law was a mistake for everybody—except the paper companies—and second, that focusing exclusively on the Fox River instead of the bay was a mistake for everybody—except the paper companies.

And I'd started suspecting an even larger truth almost immediately after arriving in Green Bay. The decades of PCB consumption advisories on waterfowl and nearly every species of sport fish throughout the entire river and bay, as well as mounting evidence of PCB-caused health effects in fish and wildlife throughout the bay and parts of Lake Michigan, all seemed to point to one inescapable conclusion: local cleanup cost estimates were too low by several orders of magnitude.

On my very first day at the U.S. Fish and Wildlife Service in March 1992, I began helping my new supervisor, Ken Stromborg, sort through the stakes we used to mark cormorant nests on tiny Spider Island in Lake Michigan. We were collecting data on bird injuries in eggs, embryos, and hatchlings caused by PCBs, which we hoped could be used in the Green Bay Natural Resource Damage Assessment. Ken had been investigating potential links between bird injuries and various chemicals for fifteen years, before the damage assessment came along, and our agency had been studying Green Bay PCBs and bird injuries for decades, long before the Superfund law was conceived.

After the regular workday, we loaded equipment and attached the boat to a four-wheel drive pickup. Then, we drove north to Rowley's Bay on the northeast corner of Wisconsin's Door Peninsula. We ate at the Wagon Trail restaurant, then dressed for the trip to Spider Island, one of two uninhabited islands in Lake Michigan with restricted access that made up the Gravel Island National Wildlife Refuge.

The spring water temperature ranged from the 30s to low-40s degrees Fahrenheit, and the air temperature was often colder still, particularly after sunset. Our first layer of clothing was polypropylene from neck to feet. Next, standard-issue Fish and Wildlife uniforms. Then, a warm coat and insulated chest waders. Finally, a full-body orange floatation survival suit—Ken called them "monkey suits" or "slow-death suits." They looked like an ultra-bulky jumpsuit and weighed about twenty pounds. Putting one on after chest waders while prone required a Herculean effort. Standing was a considerable challenge, as was controlling feelings of claustrophobia. Ken also warned against falling in shallow water, having once nearly drowned—facedown in water just deep enough to prevent his arms and legs from finding purchase on the bottom and just shallow enough to prevent coordinated swimming maneuvers.

On the island, Ken showed me how to mark the nests so we could track the success of each egg and compare success rates between colonies with different levels of PCBs. He showed me how to quickly grab cormorant nestlings by the neck before being accosted by their sharp, serrated bills; to flip them upside down and hold them by a leg, then place a band with just enough room and the right oval shape to allow for growth without pinching or rubbing. The bands would enable us to track the birds after they left to winter in the Gulf of Mexico. He showed me how to keep accurate field notes in the middle of the night while herring gulls dive-bombed our heads to drive us away from their nests, and double-crested cormorants expelled rank-smelling liquids— half-digested fish regurgitated from one end, completely digested fish defecated from the other. We did not start banding until after dark, and did not quit until nearly sunrise—a way to prevent vigilant gulls from spotting and eating cormorant eggs after their parents had fled from the men in strange suits disturbing their nests.

I learned to love the evenings spent sitting on the rocks of the shoreline of Spider Island waiting for night to fall. The sky often darkened from turquoise to deep indigo while the black and white silhouettes of cormorants and gulls circled overhead. Eventually, stars appeared, then the Milky Way, and then the dust clouds of the Milky Way. Some nights, curtains of Northern Lights would glimmer in greens, reds, or whites along the northern horizon above Lake Michigan's waters. I was mesmerized, and happier with my Fish and Wildlife workspace than any

Double-crested cormorant with a crossed bill. (Ken Stromborg)

cubicle I'd occupied during my former job in Chicago at the U.S. Environmental Protection Agency.

I had heard about the unusual occurrence of "crossed-billed cormorants" in the bay for years before coming to Green Bay. An EPA colleague had even thought "crossed-billed cormorant" was the name of a species there. During my first season of studying the effects of PCBs on these birds, I saw dozens of crossed bills on the bay and in lake colonies. A cormorant's bill is normally long and straight with serrations to help it catch fish. However, some of these birds had grossly deformed bills curved to the left or right, often wildly, and sometimes with the upper and lower mandibles curving in opposite directions. These unfortunate birds, often as many as one in a hundred in Green Bay (orders of magnitude more than in healthy ecosystems), could not catch fish and starved to death soon after the adults stopped feeding them.

Still, nothing could have prepared Ken or me for what we witnessed one spring morning working on Green Bay's Hat Island, located off the Door Peninsula. While collecting cormorant data, we noticed an astonishing number of deformed bills around this colony. One in twenty was afflicted. We had never seen such high prevalence, nor had Ken heard of a colony having deformity rates this high anywhere.

Later, we returned to collect all the doomed birds with deformed bills. A colleague examined their tissues to try to determine more about the nature and causes of the deformities. We held a meeting in Madison, including follow-up calls involving half a dozen top bird experts from the University of Wisconsin and various research labs. Together, we talked for hours about whether the deformities were caused by genetics, environmental influences, or both, and discussed experimental questions and hypotheses that might help us find answers. We explored the avian wildlife literature and wondered whether laboratory experiments, field studies, or both might be needed to sort out why so many Hat Island birds were deformed.

I was intrigued to have witnessed such an obvious problem in the field with such a visible effect. I was thrilled to be discussing such interesting scientific questions with top-notch researchers, all focused on what Ken and I had witnessed.

I had yet to decide where cormorant research fit in with the damage assessment my office was planning in Green Bay. But this was clearly a fascinating, if haunting, finding that deserved scientific study.

While Ken and I were collecting cormorant data in Green Bay and Lake Michigan, another story was unfolding along the Fox River. Every morning at the river's edge, a solitary man dropped a line in the water and waited. He was soon joined by another. And another. They stood there, alone together, still profiles against a slowly brightening sky. Suddenly, a pull and a tug on one man's line. He pulled back with a small cry, then reeled in a fish.

Up to this point, there was nothing remarkable about the scene, which played out daily along the banks of the Fox River. It was what came next that mattered. The man unhooked the struggling white bass and dropped it into his bucket, where within hours the fish was joined by twenty more of its kind.

At day's end, he brought them all home to his wife and children to eat.

The man was a member of Green Bay's Hmong community, one of many who brought their subsistence fishing culture from Laos to

Wisconsin and regularly fished the Fox as a way to help feed their families. He was aware of state fish consumption advisories warning anglers against eating many—in some cases any—of their catches because of the river's PCB contamination. But, like many other local Hmong, he ignored them. "Catch and release" was a senseless concept, and there was no word for this sort of invisible pollution in his native tongue.

"The water is not dirty," he said in broken English. "It's clean enough."

On May 14, 1992, during my third month at Fish and Wildlife, I attended a meeting in Madison that was a harsh slap in the face. I found myself looking on in amazement as Carroll "Buzz" Besadny, the head of the Wisconsin Department of Natural Resources, unloaded on one of the top five guys in my Fish and Wildlife region of eight states and about a thousand federal employees. My regional office in Fort Snelling, Minnesota had arranged the meeting in Madison to talk about the proposed Green Bay Natural Resource Damage Assessment. My federal agency wanted to partner with Wisconsin because its DNR had extensive expertise and a long history of exemplary environmental protection. Unfortunately, Governor Thompson wanted no part of environmental enforcement, especially by the Feds. Besadny was about to prove his loyalty to his governor, at my regional leader's expense.

My regional office sent one of its leaders to impress upon DNR's highest officials that Fish and Wildlife was serious about fixing the bay of Green Bay. It was one of the biggest pollution problems in the whole country, especially for the creatures inhabiting the fifteen hundred square miles of what was otherwise an ecologically vibrant bay. My agency had been studying PCB problems in the bay's fish and wildlife for three decades. It was time to act.

Our host, DNR secretary Besadny, was an imposing man with considerable political skill, forty years of experience in state government, and roots in northeast Wisconsin, home of the Fox River. He easily commanded everyone's attention. After quick introductions, Besadny took the floor.

Something was up. He was making too much eye contact with his senior staff—like they were about to launch a well-rehearsed plan. Then, he let us have it with both barrels, angrily describing how Fish and Wildlife was fumbling every one of its programs in Wisconsin. One by one, Besadny listed the programs and recounted the numerous bitter complaints from his staff in offices throughout the state. He lambasted the refuge system, the private lands program, federal law enforcement, fisheries programs, endangered species work, permit reviews, research, the contaminants program and, of course, Natural Resource Damage Assessments. It didn't seem to matter to Besadny that we were only there to talk about the Green Bay damage assessment, or that we had nothing to do with most of the programs Besadny was listing. In fact, it was obvious to me that the ambush was the point. Besadny wanted to scare my leaders right out of the state. Besadny's voice was artificially harsh and his delivery quick, as if to keep us silent and off balance. He paused just long enough at times to glance at his staff, who smiled knowingly and chuckled, right on cue. It was a bizarre performance, shattering the norms that usually guide high-level interactions between agencies, particularly agencies that share environmental purposes and mandates.

Before my guy could transform his wide-eyed look of astonishment into a complete sentence, Besadny delivered a punch line that would seal the fate of the Fox River cleanup for years to come—though, ironically, not as he'd intended. He asserted that Fish and Wildlife had no legal authority to conduct damage assessments within the constitutional boundaries of Wisconsin without DNR permission. No such permission would be granted on the Fox River, he said, until Wisconsin exhausted all opportunities to convince the paper companies to voluntarily clean up the Fox. "Period," Besadny declared imperiously. He placed his palm firmly on the table and looked away, apparently signifying that the matter was now closed.

I wondered if Besadny had ever read the U.S. Constitution, the U.S. Code for the Superfund law, or the federal regulations that spelled out federal, state, and tribal jurisdiction for Superfund under the National Contingency Plan. I wondered if he really believed that his governor's rhetoric about states' rights mattered more than the constitutional, statutory, and regulatory underpinnings of my agency's authority, even within the great state of Wisconsin. I wondered if he really believed that senior federal officials scared so easily.

Besadny's senior staff then played good cop. One of them actually seemed enthusiastic about how DNR had the Fox River situation under control. But the other, Bruce Baker, could only manage a bored monotone. He probably didn't remember me, but I knew him from my time at EPA in Chicago. Most of my circle believed he had even more power than his relatively high rank within DNR gave him—though nobody could explain how. Besadny closed the meeting by inviting us to continue participating in the various plodding committees that advised DNR about the Fox River.

I had just been thrust into the most hostile intergovernmental relationship I would ever experience in my entire thirty-year career working for dozens of local, state, and federal governmental agencies in twenty-five states. I'd been warned that Governor Thompson had begun sowing discord between his DNR and federal agencies, but was taken aback by Besadny's unexpected and unrelenting attacks on a senior federal official in the room that day. The state DNR and federal Fish and Wildlife Service were already very much in each other's way on the Fox River by the time I'd arrived at the Green Bay office. Now, Besadny had just blindsided my regional leaders. It had probably been a while since they had been treated with such condescension. I made a mental note to use the incident to keep them motivated in the coming months, should it be necessary. I had already learned, from my past few years of working for EPA, that Wisconsin DNR—especially Bruce Baker—had a knack for wearing down senior federal officials in order to prevail. Wisconsin was a national leader in environmental regulation, but DNR could be a hostile adversary when the Feds tried to intrude on state preferences.

Yet I figured DNR would soon revert to its role as natural, if prickly, ally of the U.S. Fish and Wildlife Service and U.S. Environmental Protection Agency, particularly as DNR had mobilized its own Natural Resource Damage Assessment program back in 1989 in addition to its active Superfund cleanup program.

After sending dozens of staff for training about new damage assessment regulations, the department had hired an attorney experienced with damage assessments in Montana to organize a new NRDA program for Wisconsin. He was one of the few attorneys in the country with real experience in this field, so hiring him indicated that DNR was initially serious about moving forward with damage assessments in Wisconsin. A team of forty staff across several divisions, with relevant legal, economic, and scientific expertise, was identified to work on any damage assessments pursued by DNR in Wisconsin, including at the Fox River. DNR managers also began meeting with Fish and Wildlife to figure out how the two agencies could work together. I was then hired specifically to help Fish and Wildlife support the DNR on a damage assessment of the Fox River and bay of Green Bay.

Despite this promising start, by the time I arrived in Green Bay, discussions had stalled between DNR and Fish and Wildlife about working together. Rumors had been swirling for months that DNR was reconsidering the wisdom of pursuing damage assessments anywhere, particularly on the PCB-laden Fox. Besadny had just added an exclamation point by throwing down the gauntlet.

Over several weeks following the meeting with Besadny, I did some sleuthing and found that the rumors were true. DNR was serious about stopping any Fox River damage assessment dead in its tracks. Besadny had prepared for his attack on Fish and Wildlife by sending requests to DNR's offices throughout Wisconsin for any complaints about my agency before the meeting. Plus, just as Besadny appeared to be volunteering to be Governor Thompson's right-hand man, Bruce Baker seemed to be volunteering to be Besadny's. Baker, the titular chief of just one of the agency's water bureaus, was in practice one of the most powerful bureaucrats within the entire DNR. Baker had used his personal internal connections to assert control over any DNR program that might touch the Fox River—even the state Superfund division. Thus, DNR's new attorney with damage assessment experience from Montana had been recently reassigned within DNR before any state damage assessment had begun. He was now prohibited from working on any of DNR's damage assessments, assuming one was ever launched. DNR's damage assessment team had been dissolved at the same time.

In June came another blow to my hope for eventual intergovernmental cooperation: DNR announced formation of its voluntary "Fox River Coalition," which would operate under the thumb of Baker and a newly appointed operative, Maryann Sumi. Sumi had her own access to the governor, despite working within the DNR bureaucracy. The coalition appeared to be designed by the paper companies and Governor Thompson to prevent any mention of litigation, particularly federal litigation. Instead, the paper companies would bask in the positive PR of purportedly working hand in hand with state and local stakeholders without any risk of enforcement leverage that might lead to sufficient cleanup of their PCB mess. The new coalition was a cynical but brilliant ploy to effectively prevent a costly PCB cleanup—one large enough to make a practical difference for the bay and the public. It would be championed for the next several years by Governor Tommy Thompson, DNR secretary Besadny, his successor George Meyer, and DNR's senior Fox River staff, Maryann Sumi and Bruce Baker. Baker, in particular, would sit at the center of state power, highly attuned to the political winds blowing from the governor's office but also manipulating the levers of DNR's bureaucracy. He was a man of small physical stature but his reach had snaked for decades throughout the halls of DNR. He would outlast a string of governors and DNR leaders and never lose his seat at the Fox River table.

I would soon discover skepticism within DNR to Besadny's proposition to rely on paper company volunteerism. Many staff didn't buy that paper companies were a safe bet for determining what a Fox River cleanup should look like, how it should proceed, and how the public's rights should be protected.

Dale Patterson worked in Bruce Baker's group, but he was one of those staff. He didn't look or act anything like a troublemaker, seemingly too mild mannered and wary to risk Baker's disapproval or Governor Thompson's wrath. So I was skeptical when my boss Ken Stromborg suggested Dale would be helpful. Dale was soft spoken and seemed to have an innate ability to evade attention—characteristics that no doubt helped him fly under the radar within Baker's group. His shoulders slightly hunched over his computer, Dale could seem a little distracted, as though he had work waiting for him. I even worried at our first meeting that he was suspicious of me, but in time I would learn he was simply cautious by nature. Dale was at ease with his data, though. A shared understanding of particularly consequential data would add a gleam to his eye, and sometimes even a smile to his face.

Dale was a gold mine of information. He knew the entire history of the Fox River, its paper mills, its pollution, its PCB data, and the paper companies' modus operandi of outmaneuvering governmental agencies. More than that, I quickly discovered Dale knew where all the best files were kept, where the most helpful DNR staff sat, and where hostile ears might be listening.

Within days of our first meeting, Dale and I were candidly discussing how PCBs moved in the river and bay. Within weeks, he was introducing me to DNR staff in Madison and Green Bay who also doubted that the paper companies would follow DNR's mandates and data with the same rigor as agency officials. Within months, he was showing me key documents and data that were central to determining the scale and details of PCB cleanup that could be justified under the law, as well as DNR's responsibilities under its own regulations and previous management decisions. That was before Governor Thompson intervened in DNR's early plans for using the law to force Fox River cleanup, and before Besadny and Baker aligned themselves more with their governor's political ambitions than with their duty to protect Wisconsin's natural resources.

I started assembling an arsenal of information. The results of decades of research on PCB exposure and adverse effects in fish and wildlife throughout Green Bay were suddenly being scientifically linked with historical PCB contamination of the Fox River from the paper mills along the river, rather than to hundreds of other PCB sources all around Lake Michigan and elsewhere. It was a ridiculously large amount of information, which had to be sifted and organized.

Local discussions had often assumed the paper mills were the main source of PCBs in the bay, but the scientific research was finally providing a means to potentially prove it. These dots were much harder to connect than most people realized. At least, they were hard to connect well enough for a federal court in front of skeptical defense attorneys.

This is the story of how my team connected them.

After that fateful meeting with DNR secretary Besadny, I devoted myself to competing tasks: fieldwork to investigate PCB-caused injuries to birds in support of a case that DNR might eventually lead, and creating an infrastructure in my agency capable of conducting the entire damage assessment on its own. I returned to my graduate school roots and conducted field investigations of wild animals with Ken Stromborg and his colleagues, measuring how PCBs move in water, sediments, and organisms, and the injuries to fish and wildlife that result. We hoped the information might eventually serve as evidence in a Green Bay damage assessment under the Superfund law, whoever conducted it.

At the same time, I began following the flow of power that emanated from Governor Thompson through the Wisconsin DNR to protect the paper companies from Superfund and any other legal enforcement tool. The governor was already relying on Besadny at the top of the DNR, which had been clear from our meeting with him in May 1992. The governor and Besadny assigned Maryann Sumi to lead the Fox River Coalition, which kept open-ended discussions far from the legal tools I'd need to build a credible damage assessment against the paper companies. Bruce Baker volunteered his masterful control of the powerful DNR bureaucracy to outmaneuver EPA and my agency. Paper companies locked arms with Governor Thompson, and DNR's Fox River leaders aimed to satisfy him. So I quietly started building administrative momentum within the U.S. Fish and Wildlife Service. I was hedging my bets in case my agency found itself forced to lead every element of the entire assessment under Superfund, rather than merely assisting DNR.

I resolved in 1992 to systematically build a damage assessment against the paper companies even if it required confronting DNR's unnatural public hostility toward my agency, even if it required overcoming Paper Valley's natural affinity for its industrial patrons, and even if it required neglecting the scientific fieldwork I loved. Paying careful attention to the facts and legal authorities involved in the case, I worked to prepare the U.S. Fish and Wildlife Service for action—and controversy.

Step 1 was to ready my office for upstream progress under its own power, likely in the face of increasing hostility. I steered into opportunities aggressively and began engaging opponents head-on. I relished countering disingenuous arguments. The more insincere and contrary to clear public rights and mandates these were, the less I could resist enthusiastic engagement.

In this way, Wisconsin DNR leaders were about to keep me highly motivated for most of a decade. The electricity of these disputes would eventually attract attention from experts, lawyers, managers, the press, the public, and politicians from Wisconsin to Washington.

2

THE FEDS DON'T TAKE WISCONSIN'S HINT

BUILDING THE TEAM

David Allen

The Fish and Wildlife Service was much different than the Environmental Protection Agency. Fish and Wildlife was smaller, less centralized, and less of a regulatory powerhouse. But it had advantages: its considerable expertise was closer to the field and the public, and decentralized authority might just work to the advantage of an obsessive strategist.

My new program, NRDA, as it was known, was a sleeping giant: asleep because it was so new, a giant because the environmental stakes involved could be just as big—or bigger—than those targeted in an EPA cleanup.

In Green Bay I saw a huge opportunity to awaken the sleeping giant and unleash its superpower. Even more important than fixing a large contaminated site like the Fox River was the fact that governmental success at a few big, difficult sites could convince industrial polluters, real estate and insurance agencies, banks, and lawyers throughout the country to finally police themselves in order to avoid liability for damaging the public's shared environment and resources. This was the real power and beauty of the Superfund law. Agency success at a few big sites could change the pollution landscape of the whole country. Looked at the other way around, of course, it meant that agencies had to prove themselves with their first significant cases. That's where I figured I fit in.

But I needed allies. I found four quickly: Ken Stromborg in my field office in Green Bay; Frank Horvath in my regional office in Fort Snelling, Minnesota; Matt Richmond in the U.S. Department of Justice (DOJ) in Milwaukee; and Susan Schneider, also at DOJ, in Washington, DC.

In the field office, Ken Stromborg and I were a good match. Ken was a sturdy Swede with curly brown hair and a quirky sense of humor. He was originally from the south side of Chicago but earned his PhD in wildlife toxicology from Michigan State before joining Fish and Wildlife's research division at Patuxent, Maryland. We complemented each other's strengths. Ken focused on the science and I concentrated on how to use the results as evidence in a damage assessment we both fully expected the DNR to lead. We also enjoyed each other's company. We talked for hours about topics both lighthearted and serious.

Our office gave me considerable culture shock, though. On my first day of work I dreaded traveling Green Bay's outer belt during rush hour, having assiduously avoided peak driving times to my EPA job in downtown Chicago. Instead of working in the heart of a megalopolis, I was now working on the rural edge of the small city of Green Bay. I laughed out loud when I first encountered Green Bay's light "rush hour" traffic at 8 a.m. And I laughed louder at the utter lack of fanfare with which my new building proclaimed its identity as a federal office serving the public. I had traded a skyscraper for a nondescript building with about fifteen staff on the rural edge of the city of Green Bay, which boasted a population of just under one hundred thousand.

Inside, the office continued to underwhelm and entertain. It was a relatively new building, apparently designed from the ground up by and for local staff, but it already looked decades old. The layout was haphazard, and the decor drab, cheap, and worn. Within, staff mostly wore brown polyester, government-issued uniforms, rather than the fashionable suits and ties worn in the Chicago office.

Staff eccentricity also seemed more prevalent in my new office, which offered still more visual cues that I'd moved far from the bustle of

The Green Bay Field Office sign, U.S. Fish and Wildlife Service, 1992. (Kay Thomson)

EPA and Chicago. Ken occupied an office and lab near the front door. Shelves and glassware lined the walls, but the entire lab space was little more than an overflow receptacle for his tiny office. The actual office had a door, but the room was smaller, darker, and more uncomfortable than any office cubicle I had ever seen. Mounds of paper and field notebooks, complemented by coolers, field equipment, and computer accessories strewn throughout the lab, completed the look.

I also had to adjust to my new office's field equipment. My assigned vehicle was a rusting, puke-brown Suburban from the 1970s with two-wheel drive. It leaked and burned enough oil that I had to keep several quarts with me in the truck at all times. My colleagues were delighted and took pictures whenever I buried the Suburban in mud at tree swallow study sites. The office's main boat was a 1970s Aquasport with a six-foot crack in the hull and a motor several sizes too big. The office

The Green Bay Field Office building, U.S. Fish and Wildlife Service, 1992. (Kay Thomson)

The Green Bay Field Office's Aquasport boat at Spider Island in Lake Michigan, with David Allen and Ken Stromborg, 1992. (Ken Stromborg)

David Allen's 1974 International Harvester Scout II, 1983. (Darlene Allen)

employed an even older Boston Whaler that routinely took on enough water over the stern to make the level inside the boat even with the lake water outside.

Substantively, however, the Green Bay staff had considerable local expertise and ability. Fish and Wildlife was a great place to work for people more interested in critters and dirt than pretty offices, fine clothes, and litigation. Truly, I was in heaven. It wasn't that different from my camp in the North Woods where I'd always found ways to make aging equipment serve in the field. And I found my new colleagues were largely compatible. Everyone participated enthusiastically in Tuesday morning discussions about the latest TV episode of *Northern Exposure*, and we all seemed to recognize our own foibles in the show's quirky characters, places, and pursuits—which seemed at times to hit a little too close to home.

=

A six-hour drive to the west, in Fort Snelling, Minnesota, Frank Horvath held court as damage assessment coordinator for our entire Great Lakes region. Like me and unlike most of our Fish and Wildlife colleagues, he was a recent arrival to Fish and Wildlife and had a regulatory background. We were outsiders, but we were just the right kind of outsiders to be highly useful to our new associates and supervisors.

Frank often wore a tense look that easily shifted between worry and determination. His otherwise even temper and steady hand were girded by a quiet but fierce resolve that had been sharpened by years of service in the U.S. Army. He was about fifteen years older than me, had a fisheries background, and had most recently worked at the Michigan Department of Natural Resources.

Our shared regulatory experience made us highly compatible, as did the fact that we had both grown up in Ohio and attended OSU, both adored the Great Lakes, and each owned our own boat. We were also both natural introverts, eschewing social gatherings after long meetings

David Allen's boat at South River Bay on Garden Peninsula, later known as the natural resource trustees' Garden Bluffs Restoration Project and the Nature Conservancy's Haunted Forest Preserve, 1997. (Ann Allen)

and heading straight to our respective hotel rooms. And we both were habitually circumspect, particularly when preparing for potential litigation. Most important, we shared a keen desire to use legal leverage expertly within our new agency and its new damage assessment program to further the public interest.

Frank, Ken, and I naturally assumed Wisconsin DNR would provide the administrative momentum—as well as the legal, economic, and PCB-pathway modeling expertise—for a damage assessment. We planned to work with Wisconsin to establish the extent of PCB exposure and injuries, with Fish and Wildlife studying birds and fish, and Wisconsin focusing on fish and mammals.

Unfortunately, our meeting with Secretary Besadny had made it clear DNR would neither take the lead on the case nor invoke other statutory authority available to Wisconsin, despite its earlier efforts that had seemed so promising. The Green Bay field office and the Fort Snelling regional office would have to join forces, then go it alone (Allen 1992b).

Meanwhile, DNR continued to escalate its opposition to damage assessments in general, and to Fish and Wildlife in particular. Ironically, Wisconsin's increasingly hard line both freed and empowered me. I decided to test my agency's rhetoric about the critical need for action in Green Bay by catalyzing progress everywhere at once. I wasn't about to wait for explicit permission and risk losing valuable time and momentum for the case. I would push Frank and Ken as far as they could tolerate, and maybe just a bit more when really necessary.

I had a game plan: Frank and I would build our team upward through management, and begin assembling the details of our administrative leverage. Ken and I would build our team outward to technical experts, and amplify our discussions with local constituents involved in the publicly contentious Fox River PCB issue—including learning how to engage the press.

My colleagues relied on me to secure help beyond the normal reach of our offices, and they also counted on me to ignore the predictable bureaucratic resistance to opening these atypical lines of communication. We needed economists, so I began discussions with UW–Madison's Dr. Rich Bishop, one of the most respected and famous natural resource economists in the country. We needed expertise in PCB discharges and movement, so I began talking with experts in Dale Patterson's section of DNR, who cared more about the river's health than their managers' disputes with Fish and Wildlife. We needed damage assessment know-how, so I began talking with other agencies with NRDA programs. We needed leverage for cleanup, so I began talking to colleagues from my previous employer, EPA in Chicago.

We also needed a legal team to prepare for litigation. It wouldn't be easy. The U.S. Department of the Interior, of which my agency was a small part, kept all its attorneys in one division. They had to provide legal advice to all of Interior's many bureaus. Indeed, it was hard for Frank, Ken, and me to appreciate just how much competition we were up against. Sometimes called "the Department of Everything Else" because of its wide range of responsibilities, Interior also included the Bureau of Land Management, the National Park Service, the U.S. Geological Survey, the Minerals Management Service, the Bureau of Indian Affairs, and many other more obscure offices.

My entire region of Fish and Wildlife, with about one thousand federal employees scattered throughout eight states, relied on one tiny office in Fort Snelling with four Interior attorneys to handle whatever legal issues might arise, damage assessments among them. Unfortunately, the small office had little experience with Superfund or environmental litigation, little time to spare, and even less tolerance for advice from outsiders—including the Fish and Wildlife staff it was tasked to represent.

We worked hard to forge a relationship with the Fort Snelling attorneys, but we worked harder still to create momentum for Green Bay. To avoid jeopardizing the Green Bay case, we started with small cases in the Wisconsin communities of Lake Geneva and Superior. These were essential to laying the groundwork for Green Bay, serving as a proving ground for our fledgling administrative procedures, relationships with Wisconsin and EPA, and attempts to build a viable legal team. Surprisingly, our assigned Interior attorneys gave us zero support to assemble a Green Bay legal team. Worse, they tried to thwart our efforts to bring in legal expertise from elsewhere, including Interior's Washington, DC, lawyers—and any lawyers from other federal agencies. Strangely,

I found our attorneys' resistance almost equal to Wisconsin's—and equally unfounded.

Soon, I decided to focus my efforts on more capable and willing attorneys. Assistant U.S. Attorney Matt Richmond, who worked for the U.S. Department of Justice in Milwaukee, was tall, fit, blond, well dressed, and drove a Mitsubishi 3000GT sports car. He was confident but also well aware of the sources and limits of his power. He was comfortable in his own skin and had an easygoing manner that masked, when he wished, a sharp wit and the aggressive instincts of a good trial attorney. He looked and acted every bit the part of a successful big-city lawyer.

Matt was enthusiastic about nearly any natural resource case, which seemed pretty unusual for a federal prosecutor. Six months after we started working together on the small initial case in Lake Geneva, though, it was obvious that Matt was as passionate about hunting and fishing as he was about the law. Our small case sparked something bigger, too. EPA was learning it could not avoid Superfund cases launched by Fish and Wildlife in Wisconsin. Just as important, I solidified my relationship with Matt. The alliance had started simply as a means to bypass resistance. But he soon was comfortable enough around me to admit he was bored with his routine cases, which seldom involved fish and wildlife, or much factual or legal complexity, for that matter. The admission set off a light bulb in my head. Matt was going to love the case I had in mind for Green Bay.

Soon after DNR launched its Fox River Coalition of paper mills working toward a voluntary cleanup, I convinced Matt to quietly attend an upcoming coalition meeting. Fish and Wildlife was on deck to explain the need to move forward with its Green Bay Natural Resource Damage Assessment.

The presentation was hardly well received by Maryann Sumi or the paper companies. One mill executive even threatened to abandon the coalition. His theatrics worked, alarming DNR and eliciting objections from most of the others in the room. He had expertly escalated the public blackballing of the federal damage assessment. Sumi glared at the Fish and Wildlife reps and said she looked forward to writing the state's response if the Feds dared send a formal invitation.

Matt saw all he needed to see. Immediately after the meeting, he grabbed me and whisked me away in his sports car. He was clearly excited about the case. "The paper companies will never take voluntary action unless we build real leverage," he told me.

Matt and I were on the same page. The lawyer, whose heart was at home in Wisconsin's woods and waters, was already hooked.

Soon, we had made enough waves at Lake Geneva that Interior assigned a more experienced lawyer from Washington, DC, but Matt and I knew we needed more horsepower than that. So we headed to Main Justice, DOJ's headquarters in DC, and found senior attorney Susan Schneider.

She was a seasoned mid-career lawyer who had been involved in some of the big precedent-setting cases pursued by EPA-Chicago in prior decades. She had extensive experience with big environmental cases in the Great Lakes. Equally important, I would learn, Susan did not suffer fools. She was hard driving, with a quick wit and sharp tongue. She commanded respect, even from defendants, and could aim her considerable personal forces quickly and accurately. I admired Susan's no-nonsense, direct speech, her deep understanding of the practicalities of litigation, and her close attention to and understanding of factual detail.

She also brought us a bonus: DOJ quickly assigned half a dozen attorneys to our case.

Our Interior attorney was instantly outnumbered, and already distracted by other cases from all around the country. My agency, together with Justice, soon overwhelmed her with an avalanche of work from the Green Bay case. At the same time, she bitterly resented direct communications between the Justice attorneys and me, mirroring long-standing turf wars between the two agencies. The attorneys from Justice matched my own willingness to break down traditional communication barriers to move the case along. But it was always a delicate balancing act. Working too closely with Justice triggered outright territorialism from Interior that threatened, at times, to cost me my growing autonomy on the case.

Early evidence of this erupted during a trip to Washington, DC, when I was invited to stop by Justice for a chat with Susan Schneider.

Arriving at the appointed hour, I found she had packed the conference room with fellow DOJ attorneys, including Matt, who "just happened" to be in from Milwaukee. All were eager to talk about the details and next steps of the Green Bay case. My "chat with Susan" would last most of the day.

In the early afternoon, a worried receptionist interrupted to pull Susan away. A few minutes later, Susan returned with an equally worried look on her face. "David, I think you're in trouble," she said. "Interior is on the phone for you."

My Interior attorney had been trying to reach me all day, as well as Susan, Matt, and the rest of the Justice attorneys. Our meeting without Interior's attorney was an obvious breach of etiquette, and I was keenly aware she was in a position to inflict considerably more pain on me than on the Justice attorneys in the room. They looked sheepish now—and a little amused.

I strode to the phone at the front desk to take my medicine. My Interior attorney was livid and she read me the riot act. She mandated a series of directives about how the case would operate in the future, then issued an ultimatum: no more communication with *any* Justice attorney on *anything* without her being present.

Feeling my own adrenaline surge at this threat to my much-needed autonomy on the case, I fought back. "Are you telling me I have to refuse calls asking for the time of the next meeting if they happen to come from DOJ?" I asked.

"Uh . . . well . . . no."

"Withhold consequential information necessary for DOJ deliberation?"

"Uh . . . no."

For the next five minutes I spoke more than I listened, and we ultimately reached an uneasy détente.

After the call, Susan Schneider looked relieved. We both knew consequences still lay ahead, but we also knew we could handle them. Back in the conference room, I felt a new level of acceptance from the attorneys assembled there; their glances told me they had not expected me to return.

It wasn't easy. I had to be vigilant to avoid getting edged out of my own case. The more the case advanced, the more I found myself racing along what seemed an ever-lengthening tightrope that required my total concentration and commitment. There was no veering off course. No pausing to rest. Any misstep risked others running downfield without me, and likely without the public's best interest in tow.

The case demanded more than vigilance, however. It required being confrontational, a mode I was certainly capable of, but didn't seek out. I was happiest in the woods or on a lake—alone or with Darlene, Bill Conlon, or other close friends. The truth was I was more interested in contemplating the mystery of existence than winning some damned case. Professionally, my aim was still to manage a wildlife sanctuary. I was a wildlife biologist, and the forest was my church.

Yet I found it impossible to stand down when others threatened to subvert the law to suit their own goals or ambitions, especially when it shortchanged the public. In all my life endeavors, I strove to be the consummate team player, whether as a trombone player in an orchestra or an agency coordinator on a major damage assessment case.

Whatever role was available to me in Green Bay, I was determined to play it to the best of my ability.

CAREER-ENDING INJURY?

Susan Campbell

My *Press-Gazette* duties quickly took a downturn. Tom's and my hiring meant that one of us had to become the paper's designated weekend reporter. It unfortunately fell to me, which meant that after covering city hall during the week, I worked Friday and Saturday nights reporting police news and local events. Accustomed to reporting on politics and the courts back in suburban Philly, I did everything I could to convince the editors to take me off the weekend beat. At the end of nearly every weekend shift, I spent another couple of hours writing in-depth stories about my regular city hall beat. With music blaring in my headphones and chain-drinking coffee, I typed until my fingers and arms burned and ached, then typed more. The practice eventually caught up with me, crippling both my hands to the point I couldn't move my fingers without excruciating pain. Diagnosed with multiple tendonitis and fit with immobilizing braces on both hands, I was relegated to scheduling focus groups for readers to come to the office and brainstorm story ideas for other reporters.

It was easier on my hands but numbing to my mind and crushing to my ego. I was finally off the weekend beat but further from my reporting ambitions than ever before. Still, I embraced my newfound home of Green Bay—especially the water. Tom and I had found a favorite park perched on an overlook to the north of the city. There the bay was a little wider, the trees and wildlife a little wilder. The woods and water held restorative powers for my fettered hands and spirit, and so I retreated there often.

On my way home on an especially frigid January night, I slowed while crossing the Tower Drive Bridge, a dramatic two-hundred-foot-high span that arched over the Fox's east and west banks and marked the river's entry to the bay of Green Bay. The bay was as black as the night. But the view along the river was unforgettable. Towering white steam plumes rose from the paper mills and from the blinking coal-fired power plant at the river's mouth, then hung in the icy air for miles to the south before curling and snaking along the river.

The sheer magnitude of industry in this small city was arresting, and I had a hunch it had left an invisible mark that was equally so. The bay needed help, I thought, though what form that might take and what role I might play eluded me.

MAKING SENSE OF A BAY FULL OF INFORMATION

David Allen

During a break, Frank Horvath reminded me to talk to Lisa Williams. "She's a bona fide expert on PCBs. Got her PhD in John Giesy's lab at Michigan State." We were at a regional Fish and Wildlife meeting about pollution, held at the gorgeous Minnesota Valley National Wildlife

Refuge. The fourteen-thousand-acre refuge stretched for miles along the Minnesota River in the Twin Cities' suburbs. Lisa had been hired for damage assessments in Michigan at around the same time I was hired in Green Bay.

I remembered seeing a recent publication of her work at Michigan State, probably in my growing database of scientific papers for the Green Bay damage assessment. I looked it up on my laptop as I waited for the current work session to end. "Jesus, I'll say she's an expert!" I thought.

The citation showed she was lead author with Giesy on a 1992 paper (Williams and Giesy 1992). The paper was about the relationships between early mortality in salmon from Lake Michigan, chemical PCBs, and dioxin—specifically 2,3,7,8-TCDD, the most potent form of dioxin and a contaminant in Agent Orange, the notorious herbicide used in the Vietnam War. Lisa's only coauthor, Giesy, was one of the most famous environmental toxicology professors in the Great Lakes; he had taught a long list of grad students who had gone on to their own fame.

I had talked with Lisa several times about our new assignments. She was instantly a tremendous ally: smart, enthusiastic, dedicated, and already well connected with Michigan's university system and its civil servants working on a damage assessment in Saginaw. I envied her easy relationship with state counterparts. Now I began to envy the depth of her expertise.

At the end of the session, I cornered Lisa at the back of the room. She had a gift for distilling complex science into layman's terms, and I wanted to know more about what made PCBs so especially damaging. She explained:

So, the backbone of biphenyl is just two rings of carbon stuck together at one place. You can think of them as two hexagons with a carbon at each of the six corners, and the rings connected to each other at one corner. That leaves ten corners where hydrogen atoms are attached. A chlorine atom can replace any of the hydrogen atoms. There are exactly 209 ways to attach one to ten chlorine atoms on the biphenyl hexagons, which is why there are 209 different PCB congeners— or compounds.

So far, so good. I already knew this much. And I knew that the six carbons shared electrons and bonds all around the ring, sort of like glue. It made the rings, and PCBs, very strong, which also made them particularly durable and resistant to breaking down in the environment. But now Lisa turned to the reason some PCBs were so toxic:

Dioxin, really a particular dioxin with four chlorine atoms in just the right places, is toxic at incredibly low concentrations because it's shaped like a key that fits the lock of important enzyme systems in living cells. It screws up how those systems normally work, which can really wreak havoc. Dioxins look like PCBs, except the two hexagons are attached by two corners each, instead of just one. That means they're locked together in a single plane—they can't spin. Well, the really toxic PCBs tend to stay in a single plane, just like dioxin, because they don't have chlorines near the bridge between the two rings.

Lisa held up her hands, pointed her index fingers together, and showed how much easier it was to spin her hands around where her index fingers touched if she kept her other fingers—representing the chlorines that would repel each other because of their negative charge—out of the way. "Like that!" she said with a smile.

Then she explained that the whole list of individual PCB congeners was numbered, as easier shorthand. "So, you can just say 'PCB 126' to identify one of the highly toxic co-planer congeners, rather than trying to remember the chemists' name for it."

Lisa's explanations rang true, as I had been reading about the manufacturing of PCBs for months. The PCBs used in NCR paper started with a very particular recipe over at the Monsanto plants in Sauget, Illinois and Anniston, Alabama (Versar 1976). There, vats of biphenyl were cooked with chlorine gas until the whole mixture was 42 percent chlorine, by weight. This particular recipe was signified by the number 12, and the amount of chlorine was signified by the chlorine percentage, 42. Thus Monsanto sold this particular commercial mixture under the name Aroclor 1242. It usually included about 130 of the different

PCB congeners. It was a liquid at temperatures ranging from minus 2 to about 650 degrees Fahrenheit. It was extremely stable and could last decades or more, even under harsh conditions. It dissolved much more easily in oil than in water (DeVoogt and Brinkman 1989).

The National Cash Register company purchased Aroclor 1242 from Monsanto because it was good at dissolving, holding, and transferring ink between the layers of paper used in carbonless copy paper. The finished paper product was about 3 percent PCBs, by weight. The industrial processes for making carbonless copy paper resulted in the leaking of some PCBs into drains and collection systems, some of which made it into the Fox River. The papermaking also led to rejected sheets and edge trimmings, which were sold as "broke" to paper recyclers, especially mills situated on the Fox River that invented processes to remove the coloration from NCR paper (FWS 1999d).

Fort Howard and P. H. Glatfelter recycled a lot of NCR paper. The paper had high-quality fiber, and the companies knew how to clean it up. Unfortunately, the recycling operations sent the waste directly into the Fox River.

Once in the river, PCBs stuck to paper fibers and other organic particles suspended in the water. Wherever the water currents slowed, the organic particles settled into the riverbed sediments, along with their attached PCBs. Whenever water currents sped up, during storms, for example, the particles were picked back up until currents slowed again. Over time, the slow parts of the river and bay accumulated most of the particles contaminated with PCBs. Dozens of so-called PCB "hot spots" developed in the slower parts of the thirty-two miles upriver from the De Pere Dam.

The last seven miles of the river, from the De Pere Dam to the bay of Green Bay, were all slow. This section became one giant hot spot with ten times more PCBs than the entire thirty-two miles above the dam. The bay of Green Bay was also slow moving. So every spring snowmelt and every rainstorm picked up Fox River sediments and the clinging PCBs and dropped them into the bay. The bay ended up with even more PCBs than the river. Over the decades, the PCBs had also spread into Lake Michigan and beyond.

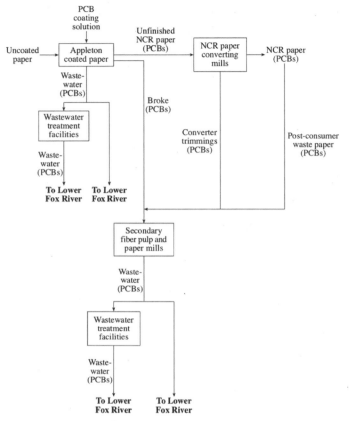

Schematic of how Fox River paper companies released PCBs into the Fox River. (U.S. Fish and Wildlife Service Restoration and Compensation Determination Plan, October 25, 2000)

The sediments of the river and bay were home to multitudes of insects, worms, and other invertebrates. They made their living by eating organic particles. If they happened to live in a PCB hot spot, they also consumed the PCBs that had glommed onto the organic particles. The PCBs accumulated in the fatty tissues of these creatures for the same reasons they stuck to organic particles. Some of the PCBs also activated or disrupted enzyme and genetic systems in cells by acting like microscopic keys in microscopic keyholes.

Bigger critters ate smaller ones, including the ones that lived in or emerged from the sediments. If the bigger ones fed at PCB hot spots, they ended up with even more PCBs in their bodies than the smaller ones. Every step up the food chain increased the body burden of PCBs. Eagles that ate cormorants that ate large fish that ate small fish that ate tiny fish that ate insects that ate sediment—all ingested a lot of PCBs.

The same was true of people who ate large fish.

Vanishingly small amounts of PCBs alter liver enzyme systems and can also affect genetic systems. Playing with such delicate cellular machinery easily leads to all sorts of havoc, including reproductive failure, behavioral problems, and cancer.

I would sometimes imagine a PCB molecule that was created in a Monsanto vat in 1954. It helped dissolve ink on a sheet of NCR paper in 1955, but the PCB was situated near a trimmed edge of the sheet. So it went to Fort Howard to be recycled to make new paper. Mostly clean fibers went into new paper, and mostly dirty ones went into the Fox River, including the one with the PCB molecule. The molecule stayed many years in what would one day be called Sediment Management Unit (SMU) 56–57, below the De Pere Dam. It was buried deeper for a while, then mixed during storms into shallower sediments, a sequence that repeated over and over again. Finally, in 1993, a large storm moved the particle with the PCB molecule into Green Bay. It moved up and down in those sediments as well, until two years later when a mayfly larva ate it. The larva emerged from the sediment in the spring, only to be eaten by a minnow. The minnow was eaten by a perch, the perch by a walleye that made it onto the dinner table of a local fisherman.

Now the PCB lives in a human fat cell. Will it eventually find its way to genetic machinery? Will it unlock the wrong door?

There was only so much I could learn from reading a book about PCBs or talking to Lisa Williams for a couple of hours at a meeting. I realized any case threatening to force well-financed and sophisticated defendants to pay hundreds of millions of dollars or more also needed great technical experts.

The bay of Green Bay, as a large, complicated system, required data and expertise in all kinds of subjects. I needed expertise in the engineering of papermaking and recycling at paper mills that had released PCBs into the Fox River. I needed expertise in environmental chemistry and the movement of PCBs through the sediments, water, and biota of the Fox River and Green Bay. I needed expertise in fish and wildlife toxicology and ecology, habitat preservation and restoration, and natural resource economics. And I needed expertise in engaging the public and the press.

I was well aware that the best technical experts were already committed to following their own prescribed research agendas. They had funding sources to address long-standing research questions, which is how they'd become leading experts in the first place. "Hired guns"—scientists routinely available for hire on legal cases—were less valuable than independent researchers, as the latter's goals were rooted more in pure science than in helping clients build cases for a living.

I knew this would be critically important to judges or juries weighing the credibility of our technical experts if the Green Bay case ever made it to court. The trick was to first size up the pool of experts most likely to develop data I could use as evidence, then convince them to adjust their research priorities to answer questions more central to our case.

Once I'd found our technical experts, it was hard work to keep them legitimate and independent, yet still on track. It also required a measure of self-control from me. Ken Stromborg and his colleagues in the research arms of several agencies and universities offered me opportunities to join cutting-edge studies already in progress. I was tempted but stayed on mission. The ramifications of the Green Bay case were bigger than any of us.

Fish and Wildlife had tremendous in-house expertise in the areas of fish and wildlife toxicology, ecology, and habitat restoration. But I needed still more horsepower for the damage assessment. There was also a complicating factor: controversy lurked at the heart of my agency's internal expertise. That controversy took the shape of crossed bills and other deformities appearing in droves of double-crested cormorants living on the bay of Green Bay. I myself was still haunted by the memory of my field research on the bay's Hat Island, where Ken Stromborg and I had seen as many as one in twenty cormorants crippled by wildly deformed bills.

Ken was personally involved in millions of dollars' worth of research by Fish and Wildlife to investigate whether, to what extent, and how PCBs might have caused the birds' crossed and twisted bills. He was adamant that environmentalists were too eager to accept a PCB connection before the scientific foundations were laid. But Tim Kubiak, a Fish and Wildlife colleague who had been Ken's predecessor in Green Bay before moving to Michigan, was a strong supporter of the PCB link.

Ken and Tim were entrenched in opposite camps of an internal debate that Ken sardonically dubbed "the Cormorant Wars." Both were colorful characters, but the similarities ended there. Tim was meticulous and organized; Ken was scattered. Tim was a voracious reader and advocate of the scientific literature implicating PCBs in crossed bills and other wildlife deformities; Ken was a traditional researcher who tried to disprove critical hypotheses. Both worked on field and lab studies published in the scientific literature, but each typically reached opposite conclusions about whether and how their studies answered the simple question of whether PCBs caused crossed bills. The two had overlapped only briefly in Green Bay, but long enough to ignite a personal and mutual dislike that would seal their reputations as mortal enemies.

In a rare point of agreement, Ken and Tim had put it to me that the Green Bay damage assessment should answer two central questions: Were the paper mills' PCBs injuring the cormorants? And, if so, what should the agency do about it?

The first question was especially important because the birds' deformities were visible, tangible, and grotesque. They attracted the interest of the press and public in ways that other examples of potential PCB damage often didn't. Images of Green Bay's starving birds with crossed bills appeared on page 1 of the local newspapers and on the evening news. Experts, including local experts at UW–Green Bay, discussed the birds at conferences. Fish and Wildlife itself fueled the concern while investigating the freakish phenomenon, regularly toting Henrietta—a disfigured stuffed cormorant—to Congress, state legislatures, public meetings, and museums. Last but not least: the cormorant conundrum was what had lured my agency into the Green Bay damage assessment in the first place.

Strategically, I knew that even if the crossed bills could be linked to the paper company PCBs, it might have limited bearing on our overarching arguments about PCBs' health effects on fish and wildlife. The cormorants comprised a subset of just one species amid hundreds on the bay.

Yet the cormorant question demanded an answer; without one, critical progress on the damage assessment threatened to bottleneck. I would have to determine just how much more effort we should invest in finding the answer.

HEALING HANDS

Susan Campbell

My hands were healing, but my fingers were still too weak to pound out news stories on the computer. The paper had loaned me a pedal-operated Dictaphone to record interviews over the phone, and I was dictating short news stories to an assistant. After months of this came a breakthrough. There was a new product out: voice-activated software that would enable me to dictate stories directly to the computer. A professional trainer was flown in from New York. Every day for a week we sat side by side in the newsroom as he taught me how to enunciate words and speak them one at . . . a . . . time, while simultaneously employing an extensive list of verbal commands to move the cursor, and to cut, paste, and move text. It was like learning a whole new language, and it was grueling.

But my new "voice machine" meant freedom—freedom to report and write again, to return to what I loved and felt I was meant to do. When the paper's executive editor announced that the *Press-Gazette* was resurrecting its environmental post and offered me first crack at it, I didn't hesitate.

BUILDING MOMENTUM

David Allen

Bringing U.S. EPA into the case to leverage its substantial cleanup powers under Superfund was the key to ultimate success in Green Bay, or at least would make success more likely. Without EPA on our side, Susan Schneider, Matt Richmond, Frank Horvath, Ken Stromborg, and I worried we would also fail to bring Wisconsin into the fold—a bleak scenario in which the paper companies would continue to influence the governor and his DNR, and perhaps prevail.

I realized I would need to muster all the finesse I'd learned from Ken Fenner at EPA if I was going to bring Superfund to Green Bay. EPA's Superfund division was conflicted when it came to the Fox River, especially with Wisconsin fanning the flames of discord. Wisconsin benefited from a reputation as one of the best states in the country when it came to protecting its natural resources. It was also the birthplace of some of the nation's first and foremost naturalists and environmentalists, among them John Muir, Aldo Leopold, and U.S. senator Gaylord Nelson. EPA, itself signed into law by executive order on the heels of Nelson's first Earth Day, respected Wisconsin's environmental progressivism—even as it was now unraveling under Governor Tommy Thompson's watch.

I figured Ken Fenner's water group, known for its willingness to flex EPA's muscles, including through litigation, might be my only chance to draw EPA into the Green Bay case. My water contacts at EPA also told me to aim for Superfund's Great Lakes coordinator or an experienced cleanup manager like Jim Hahnenberg, one of the best in the region.

A few months after arriving in Green Bay, I followed their suggestion and left several voice messages about the Fox River for Hahnenberg, but there was no response. So I kept working with Ken Fenner's group, but my successes would come in fits and starts.

In September 1992, six months after arriving in Green Bay, I heard from Fenner's boss, the director of EPA's Water Division in Chicago. He told me his division was highly interested in pursuing enforcement initiatives at three sites around the Great Lakes, and that Green Bay was among them. Partnerships with Fish and Wildlife damage assessments could be advantageous, he added encouragingly. Fenner and I then arranged a series of meetings and calls between his boss and my regional leaders in Fort Snelling. Soon, Fenner was traveling to my regional office in Fort Snelling for lively debates about how best to proceed on the Fox River in the face of DNR resistance.

But the air came out of the balloon almost as quickly. Perhaps not surprisingly, DNR didn't react well to EPA's suggestions about using federal Clean Water Act enforcement tools on the Fox River. I could easily picture Bruce Baker unloading on Fenner just as Besadny had on us.

Eventually, I doubled back to EPA's Superfund division. In November 1993, I phoned Superfund's Great Lakes coordinator to see if she might respond more quickly than Jim Hahnenberg. She called back right away, but by the end of the call, I almost wished she hadn't. She told me EPA wanted to avoid conflict with Wisconsin. She also said EPA was unlikely ever to use its Superfund authorities on the Fox River.

Despite these setbacks, I worked hard to keep my team's spirits aloft. But there were times I felt my own will and courage faltering. There were many days I'd arrive at my office and wonder how I was going to draw enough attention, even from my own team. I'd find myself staring at the floor in quiet contemplation about the fragility of the situation. Frank Horvath, a state away, was often diverted from my case to attend to other damage assessments in the region, and sometimes my Green Bay efforts spawned controversies Frank preferred to avoid. I also was competing with Matt Richmond's and Susan Schneider's busy dockets at Justice. Both were still seriously interested in the Green Bay case, but they were regularly pulled in other directions, particularly when their other litigation loomed. My case was still years from being ready for trial, and my Interior attorney continued to resent Justice's early involvement. I was honestly worried about losing my entire legal team during my first few years in Green Bay. And I continued to fret about keeping Ken Stromborg focused more on the research that advanced our case and less on the Cormorant Wars.

Day after day, I struggled with the temptation to conduct the fieldwork I loved rather than foster the broader objective of creating a damage assessment with real leverage. I could drive trucks and boats, collect data in the field, collaborate with experienced researchers, and work on those parts of the case that sparked little controversy. Or I could bend my will toward preventing bureaucratic neglect of a case that so clearly deserved national attention.

The greatest danger was allowing the paper companies' influence on cleanup and restoration to outpace ours. So on countless days after staring too long at the floor, I would suddenly stop wondering whether my case would die of neglect. Instead, I would forgo fieldwork whenever the case did not absolutely require it, and I would demand attention from Frank, Ken, Matt, and Susan—even when it annoyed them.

After Darlene achieved her graduate degree in Madison, we moved to a country house on six acres north of Algoma, a small town on Lake Michigan at the base of the Door Peninsula. A young stray dog started hanging around the property. He had a collar but no ID tag. We brought him to the local shelter in case he belonged to someone, but a man there told Darlene, "Lady, nobody's gonna claim that dog." After a week we officially took him in, naming him Brutus after our alma mater's mascot. He seemed to have inherited his beautiful coat and large, powerful build from a Bernese mountain dog and his bright gaze and herding instincts from a border collie.

Darlene and I were happily living with Brutus some thirty miles away from Green Bay when details emerged of a sinister event in the city that often haunted me during lunchtime walks in the countryside near my Green Bay office. It was not connected to me, my team, or our work, but it did relate to the local paper mill culture I was preparing to confront head-on. In 1992, thirty-five-year-old Tom Monfils had been found dead in a James River paper vat with a forty-pound weight tied around his neck. Three years later, six of his fellow Green Bay workers in the paper mill—dubbed the Monfils Six—were convicted of conspiracy and murder. The gruesome killing, followed by the lengthy investigation and trial, was a major local story that revealed Monfils was murdered soon after he'd told police that another worker had stolen a length of electric cable.

The emerging story haunted me because, at the same time, I was building a case against paper companies that would likely cost them $100 million, or even $1 billion. A murder triggered by a stolen length of electric cable made me wonder if some other thug might decide the whole Green Bay case would stall if I were to wind up dead. I knew I was neither indispensable nor irreplaceable, but it sent shivers down my spine to think about six paper mill workers willing to kill over a minor theft and feelings of betrayal.

So I spent my working days methodically trying to attract a viable team to pursue a credible case. But during lunch breaks, I paid more attention than usual to passing vehicles. I also made sure my rural address and phone number were unlisted, and I slept better at night knowing Brutus was guarding the house and property.

Back at the office, I began creating a detailed paper trail for the case, and I made certain that appropriate officials within our agency began signing off on documents that Frank and I drafted. Together, we constructed these documents carefully, with official delegations of authority flowing from the federal statutes and regulations right through the designated governmental officials and onto the signature pages of formal documents. The key, always, was to get the documents that carried the weight of the law in front of the officials who had the authority to act on them. Frank and I understood, better than most, that the full weight of the law would not fall on the paper companies responsible for the Fox River's pollution if we didn't get these details right.

The first of these documents was a big one. The 1994 Preassessment Screen and Determination officially launched the entire federal damage assessment. Frank and I now had to meet with the head of our entire region to get his signature on letters notifying the paper companies (FWS 1994).

"So . . . you're okay with signing letters identifying the paper companies as responsible under Superfund?" Frank asked hopefully. "It'll be a big deal with DNR and the mills."

"Not to worry, Frank," came our boss's coy reply. "We can kill each other later if it blows up in our faces." He gave Frank and me a cold stare

Brutus guarding the Farm, Algoma, Wisconsin, 1994. (Darlene Allen)

as we finished explaining the rationale for the letters, but he seemed on board.

After the meeting, Frank and I made plans. Frank started: "You know shit rolls downhill, right? We've got to get these right the first time."

"Don't worry," I said. "I know some EPA lawyers who promised to send me the right templates for the letter, same as EPA always uses. Plus, my dad said he'd teach me how to do searches for ownership and find registered agents for the corporations. I told you his law firm owns a title company, right? How hard can it be?"

A few months later, we sent the letters to five paper companies that we had identified, with Dale Patterson's help, as the main recyclers of PCB-laden carbonless copy paper. Leading the list were the companies commonly known as Fort Howard and P. H. Glatfelter. Three other carbonless copy paper recyclers were also identified: Wisconsin Tissue Mills, Riverside Paper, and U.S. Paper Mills. Later, we notified two additional companies, Appleton Papers and National Cash Register, which manufactured the carbonless copy paper. The seven companies would eventually become known as the Fox River Group.

Since the 1950s, these paper mills had discharged hundreds of thousands of pounds of PCBs into the Fox River. Much of that pollution was still stuck in river and Green Bay sediments. It was a very big deal. A single ounce of PCBs was enough to contaminate thousands of Olympic-sized pools above safe levels for fish, wildlife, and people. Frank and I were now pointing the weighty finger of the federal government at the companies we believed were largely responsible for the contamination.

I was amazed at how few bureaucratic hoops we'd encountered. At EPA, there would have been dozens of lawyers, managers, and secretaries proofing every word and nuance. Here at Fish and Wildlife, a couple of biologists could do all the legwork and convince the head of the region to sign off on it. Frank and I had been exceedingly careful, though. These letters were definitely going to blow up the world—the paper companies would see to that.

Once the letters were out, the story hit the press. DNR's Maryann Sumi led the state's blistering response. She finally had her chance to draft the letter she'd warned about during Fox River Coalition deliberations. She then demanded multiple meetings with Fish and Wildlife and its attorneys at Interior and Justice.

The paper companies responded with anger and a threat. An attorney and lobbyist for the Wisconsin Paper Council—the politically powerful advocate for the state's pulp and paper industry—warned that the federal move usually signaled the start of litigation. "Nine out of ten times, these things do end up in court," he told the *Appleton Post-Crescent*, where the story jockeyed for space on the front page with the newly emerging O. J. Simpson murder case (Meyer 1994). He went on to praise Wisconsin DNR for having the sense to decline Fish and Wildlife's overtures to join the federal damage assessment. A Fort Howard spokesman said the paper companies' voluntary efforts on the Fox River had been making progress, but would now be disrupted.

In an earlier letter to Fish and Wildlife, the Fox River Coalition had issued a threat if the federal government were to move forward with identifying polluters. The formal identification of responsible parties in the case, it warned, would mean "our voluntary, 'no fault' effort, will be reduced to an adversarial situation, which will likely result in the dissolution of the coalition" (Anderson 1994).

I wasn't sure if Fish and Wildlife's growing momentum would convince EPA Superfund to finally join us, or if the controversy would send them running. So I reached out to Superfund's Great Lakes coordinator again. She offered no support. EPA had not identified the Fox River as a cleanup priority. Further, she said her agency was relying on state efforts and would not invoke its Superfund authorities unless Wisconsin DNR specifically requested it. A month later, the news was more discouraging. She told me that EPA would not even consider placing the Fox River on Superfund's "National Priority List." Fortunately, I didn't know how to take no for an answer.

Now I began thinking about how to bring the urgency of my case directly to the public. This created a whole new set of problems for me to strategize about. One of the more confounding ones was the relentless though entertaining distraction of the Green Bay Packers, which enjoyed a cult-like worship in the community and were in the news nearly every day of the year. Darlene and I learned early on that the best time to avoid crowds in Green Bay was on a Sunday afternoon during a Packers game, when streets, stores, and restaurants were virtually empty—except for the crowded sports bars televising the game.

Green Bay stood apart from other NFL cities as it was North America's smallest major league professional sports market. Also unique was the relationship between the Green Bay Packers and their fans: the fans owned the team. These two unlikely facts combined to make the Packers the only publicly owned, not-for-profit, major league pro team in the United States, and among the world's most valuable sports franchises. It was a storied romance that inspired people from around the world to make pilgrimages to Lambeau Field, and brought national media attention to Green Bay every year during football season.

I had known from the start our case would have to be watertight if it were to take on the paper mills and force them to pay to clean up their costly mess. I now knew the case would also have to be compelling enough to regularly compete with the Packers for public attention. By now, the public's buy-in was looking more and more critical given that the State of Wisconsin and the paper mills so ardently opposed the Feds' involvement. That meant I needed not only to build my team but to gain public momentum for a major case I was confident would ultimately help the city's natural environment *and* the local economy thrive. But winning over the community, especially as an outsider working for the federal government . . . well, it certainly felt like a long shot for a wildlife biologist hoping to someday manage a wildlife sanctuary in Michigan's Upper Peninsula.

I was going to have to find a way to win over the public. Short of meeting with every member of the community face-to-face, that would mean persuading the local press to care as much about reporting on the contaminated river racing through the city as covering the beloved Green Bay Packers.

JOURNALISTS AND SCIENTISTS

Susan Campbell

I checked in early at the Kellogg Conference Center on the campus of Michigan State University with a few hours to kill before the reception. I hated being early and was already dreading the forced camaraderie that was sure to follow for the next several days.

Heading straight to my room seemed the best option, but I paused to consider the invitation left with the front desk receptionist. I was there for the Great Lakes Environmental Journalism Training Institute, and the organizer had left a message inviting early arrivals to drop in on a forum that would be of interest.

"I should probably check that out first," I thought, pulling my suitcase along the hallway. I was there to learn, after all. Shortly after starting work on the newspaper's environmental beat, my editors had encouraged me to apply for this fellowship. I'd been thrilled to learn I would be among the first journalists selected for the new institute, which promised lectures and workshops with more than twenty scientists, journalists, and environmental experts. For me, it was a much-needed crash course in some of the most important environmental issues affecting the Great Lakes.

I'd made it to room 100. The sign on the door read, "Endocrine Disruptors: Are chemicals threatening the reproduction and development of wildlife and humans?" The event was billed as "a dialogue between journalists and scientists." Self-conscious, I entered the room and tried to discreetly maneuver to a seat that could accommodate my suitcase and other belongings.

The mood in the room was tense, and I instinctively pulled out my reporter's notebook. Hearing references to "PCBs" and "dioxins," my ears perked up immediately. "Our Stolen Future," I scrawled on my notepad. It was the title of a new book and the speakers at the front of the room were discussing it heatedly. I glanced at the agenda I'd picked up on my way in. It identified one of the speakers as a former science and environmental writer for the *Boston Globe*, and the other as an environmental biology professor from Ontario, Canada. The *Globe* reporter was a coauthor of the book, which warned that PCBs and other synthetic chemicals accumulate in the environment and in the bodies of its inhabitants. Theo Colborn—a scientist and the book's lead author— was advancing a theory that these chemicals appeared to mimic the body's natural hormones, and were thus able to control its development and function. There was already evidence these chemicals were causing reproductive problems and deformities in wildlife, and the book introduced early evidence of similarly driven chemical foul play in people. The concept of chemicals masquerading as hormone disruptors was a radical break from the traditional cancer-centric mode of scientific inquiry. What Colborn and her colleagues warned of now was potentially far worse than cancer, however, because of its ability to affect more of the population, including the unborn.

The book, released just two months earlier, was a lightning rod for the chemical industry, which rushed to question Colborn's credentials and label her a charlatan. A small-scale version of that drama was playing out in the room now between the reporter and the professor, the latter a prominent toxicologist whose research was often funded by the chemical industry. As I watched, I recalled the backlash Rachel Carson experienced in the '60s after publishing *Silent Spring*.

I listened to the arguments and took notes. I didn't know what to make of any of it yet. What I did know was that this controversial book, its scientist author, and its powerful detractors would be an essential aspect of covering the Fox River cleanup story back home in Wisconsin.

OFFICIAL RESISTANCE STIFFENS

David Allen

The Fox River's PCB problem was more than a Wisconsin problem. PCBs from the Fox flowed across state lines in the bay of Green Bay. A little to the northwest of the city of Green Bay, a Fox River tributary flowed through the lands of the Oneida tribe, allowing contaminated fish and wildlife to move in the opposite direction—upstream into Oneida tribal territory. As if that weren't enough intersecting interests, Green Bay included waters that were subject to complicated tribal rights claimed by various Native American tribes, including the Menominee. Against this backdrop, I knew it was necessary for Fish and Wildlife to invite the states of Wisconsin and Michigan, as well as the Oneida and Menominee tribes, to join the federal government as co-trustees of the damage assessment.

It came as no surprise that Wisconsin would take no part in the damage assessment, a choice clearly forecast early on by Besadny's hostile rejection of our invitation to join forces with Fish and Wildlife back in 1992. But Wisconsin went further, staking out a position so untenable it would lead the state in exactly the opposite direction of what it intended for the Fox River. The state had a long history of opposing tribal jurisdictional claims within its constitutional boundaries. So when it came to the Fox, DNR took the reflexive position that no tribe in Wisconsin could serve as co-trustee for any damage assessment.

DNR's new leader, Secretary George Meyer, informed the head of my region that, while Meyer might not know much about federal damage assessment provisions, he knew for certain that Indian tribes could not serve as co-trustees within Wisconsin. Like Besadny before him, Meyer offered no evidence to support his claim.

Meyer cut a drab figure after Besadny, lacking his predecessor's natural charisma and political skill. Still, with his personable smile, aw-shucks mannerisms, and solid Wisconsin dairy farm roots, Meyer was well liked by many in the state and affable when he needed to be. Meyer also brought many necessary skills to his agency, having studied economics and earned a law degree from UW–Madison. He started with DNR as a staff attorney in the early 1970s before moving up to head the agency's law enforcement division from 1980 to 1993 (Durkin 2018). Some insiders who knew Meyer well said he was, at heart, a good conservationist caught between a rock and a hard place when it came to holding onto the state's top environmental job.

Governor Thompson's anger at what he considered regulatory overreaches by DNR—labeled "Damn Near Russia" and "Do Nothing Right" by conservative critics—were now legend in Wisconsin. Thompson, considering it his role to rein it in, launched a major restructuring of the DNR, a move environmentalists warned would politicize the agency (Millard 1998a, 1998b).

George Meyer didn't start out as Thompson's political appointee; he was chosen by a citizen board. What Meyer didn't know was that his would be the board's last appointment. Just two years later, Thompson maneuvered to eliminate the citizen board's power to appoint the secretary of the DNR, giving the governor direct control over the hiring and firing of the agency head. In what would come to be known as Meyergate, Meyer penned a private message to Wisconsin's attorney general. The handwritten note, obtained by the media, shed light on the pressure Thompson exerted and the tightrope Meyer likely walked throughout his tenure (Schultze 1995). Meyer revealed that Thompson pressured him to let the governor review proposed environmental lawsuits *before* they were sent to the state's Justice Department for prosecution, a request many believed was clearly afoul of state law. He wrote that Thompson also pressed him to contribute to his gubernatorial campaign (Jones 1995). When the story broke, Meyer said the incident clearly showed why the head of DNR should be free of the governor's political influence—a position Meyer would maintain even years after leaving the agency.

Meyer's heart may have been in the right place, but that wasn't enough. Neither his institutional power nor political skill was a match for those of his boss. At the time of his appointment, some in the environmental community predicted Meyer's bureaucratic allegiance to the agency might ultimately come at the cost of the state's public and natural resources. "There's a transition from being an agency person and leading the DNR, to being an advocate—and placing natural resources ahead of the DNR. We want to make sure he understands that," said a representative of Wisconsin's Environmental Decade. "George is a nice guy. Usually that's an attribute, but in this case it could be a liability" (Seppa 1993).

Like Besadny before him, Meyer could also be quick to signal intolerance for outsiders, particularly when the Feds made his tightrope walk with Thompson trickier and more dangerous. Ironically, the harder we worked to counter the governor's political rhetoric with science and the law—arguments we hoped could help Meyer resist the governor—the more Meyer dug in against us. In addition, Meyer's inflexible stance on tribal authority under Superfund was contrary to the plain language of the Superfund law, as well as to federal regulations and long-standing Interior policies for recognizing Native American tribes.

Oddly enough, all of this made my path easier. DNR, by its own reckless attitude, managed to draw attention to the Wisconsin case throughout Interior's legal ranks. In fact, as DNR escalated its poorly considered position, it united attorneys and managers in Interior faster and more convincingly than my team had managed through countless briefing papers and meetings. DNR's actions also caught the attention of Justice. Susan Schneider in Washington was more than happy to help me highlight the national implications of the tribal issue whenever anyone in the federal family got cold feet about the growing controversy surrounding the Green Bay case. In time, the more DNR fought tribal authority, the more alienated Wisconsin became from nearly every federal official—whether related to the damage assessment or not.

Meyer and his senior staff would go on to provide a series of unintended assists to my team in this way. I sometimes wondered privately if DNR officials, who so publicly and loudly opposed the federal damage assessment, ever realized that their posturing actually helped catapult the case to national prominence.

Facts on the ground also began to press my team forward. Research stemming from the $16 million Mass Balance Study of the river and bay was beginning to shine a bright light on the connection between PCB problems throughout the bay and Fox River paper mills. As the studies rolled in and the links were more clearly drawn, local environmentalists were becoming more and more agitated. For our part, we knew the information might well trigger legal deadlines for our case. It added a mountain of momentum to our motivation, and gave us another powerful reason to bring aboard senior federal officials in time.

Then Governor Thompson bypassed the U.S. Fish and Wildlife Service altogether. He went straight to the top in a brazen effort to shut down our efforts to hold the paper companies accountable. Fresh off a decisive reelection to a third term in office, Thompson was not only popular in his home state of Wisconsin but now had a big national profile—and the ego to go with it. His name had even been in the press several times as a potential vice presidential candidate. He contacted Bruce Babbitt, the head of the U.S. Department of the Interior and a member of President Bill Clinton's Cabinet, asking him to halt the damage assessment in Green Bay. Thompson wouldn't know it for months, but his power play would achieve the exact opposite result. The governor had just guaranteed that my small but growing team would finally be able to brief every level of Fish and Wildlife and Interior—all the way up the ladder.

My assignment to help prepare Interior's responses to Wisconsin's escalation gave me a rare opportunity to provide much more than pro forma internal briefing statements. I might not be invited to brief every Interior official in person, but I could write candidly about the growing controversy involving the paper companies, the Fox River Coalition, DNR, and Interior's unusually central role in the Green Bay case. I wrote directly to my team members but aimed my arguments at the senior Interior officials who were increasingly pressured by Wisconsin and the paper companies (Allen 1994b, 1995b).

I wanted to create credible rebuttals, and I wanted to give nervous mid-level managers reason to think twice when tempted to soothe company and state complaints by interfering with our case. Mostly, though, I wanted to buy enough time for the local controversy to hit Washington, DC. There, the Superfund reauthorization battle was already in full swing. The Democrats, led by Bruce Babbitt and other Clinton appointees, were fighting to preserve Superfund's key provisions, which included the Natural Resource Damage Assessment provision. The Republicans, led by Speaker of the House Newt Gingrich as well as key senators and prominent GOP governors—such as Tommy Thompson— were arguing to strip or weaken the law. I knew Governor Thompson and Secretary Babbitt would never see eye to eye on the legal and economic theories underpinning Superfund. But I also wanted to show that Wisconsin's arguments were motivated more by politics, and the companies' arguments more by profits, than by the actual facts of the site.

My plan worked even sooner than expected. My team soon had all of Interior and Fish and Wildlife institutionally behind us. We had succeeded in briefing all seven layers of my command line—leading up to Babbitt himself—plus dozens of ancillary bureaus, offices, and programs throughout Interior. For a bureaucracy as large and byzantine as Interior, this took surprisingly little time. Just four months after Governor Thompson contacted Babbitt, Frank Horvath related to me that he'd had a chance encounter with Babbitt in the halls of Main Interior, a large stately building located just north of the Lincoln Memorial Reflecting

Pool in DC. As soon as Babbitt heard the words "Green Bay," he made a pledge: he told Frank he would promptly sign a letter to advance the damage assessment if someone could just get it to his desk.

Nobody on my team, or any of the intervening layers of management, had heard yet that our agency's top official had already green-lighted the project. I could not have devised a better strategy to attract the attention and support of my entire agency.

The paper companies were also bringing their resistance directly to Washington, DC. Our letters identifying them as responsible parties under the Superfund law was the shot heard 'round the bay, and its reverberations sent a shudder up and down Paper Valley.

The paper companies' receipt of those letters finally made the case real. The letters, for the first time, put the companies on notice that they'd be held liable for the tens of thousands of pounds of chemical PCBs still buried in the Fox River—and for the untold millions of dollars needed to clean them up and make the public whole.

Official identification finally "outed" the paper companies, not only to the community but within their own circles. It meant the companies had to notify their stockholders, accountants, and insurers. It also guaranteed the companies would hire defense lawyers with Superfund expertise, and that those attorneys would come knocking forcefully on the Feds' door.

The paper company lawyers wanted to meet in DC to cut through all the politics and PR and begin negotiating with the Feds in earnest. Their negotiations would center on whether and how the companies would participate in the federal assessment and, if so, who would be in the driver's seat. The companies would want to stop or slow the process. They would want to write any assessment plan. They would want to hire any experts, conduct any work, and write up any results. In short, they would want to control the framing and execution of the entire assessment—if they failed to prevent it in the first place.

The million-dollar question for the Feds: how much would they give up to win cooperation and funding from the paper companies?

This meeting would launch one of the most consequential discussions for the entire future of cleanup and restoration at Fox River and Green Bay. This would be the paper companies' best chance to quietly lull the Feds into complacency by offering money for the case in exchange for control over the substance of the work. It was a gambit that had worked with surprising and depressing regularity at other sites around the country. It was a gambit that was already giving the companies spectacular success at limiting their exposure via the Fox River Coalition. Only a handful of people would ever hear about these negotiations between the Feds and the companies. I was not going to miss any of it. But I was about to find out it wasn't that simple.

I met Matt Richmond in Washington, DC, beforehand to brief our team in private before meeting with the paper company lawyers. As we walked to the briefing together, Matt struck up a conversation that seemed a little too scripted, considering that he and I were now on such easy terms. He disclosed that he never allowed his federal agency clients to attend meetings between defense and plaintiff attorneys on a case. Fortunately, the statement didn't catch me entirely off guard. I'd already heard rumors that Justice was worried about how Fish and Wildlife might behave in meetings with high-powered defense lawyers, which unfortunately was easy to understand. I was confident in my own sense of decorum, though, and determined to establish that I wouldn't be sidelined from my attorneys' key discussions about the case. Still, Matt outranked me within the federal government in every way that counted, so I knew I had to be careful not to overstep my bounds.

"What do you do with clients who simply walk into the room, despite your advice?" I asked. "Tackle them?"

Matt changed the subject, but I thought I saw him suppress a smile.

The briefing included Fish and Wildlife, Interior, Justice, and the Menominee tribe of Wisconsin. It wasn't long before Susan Schneider of Justice informed the rest of our team that the paper companies were sending only their attorneys to the meeting, so the agencies should do the same. This cut Fish and Wildlife out of the meeting, as Fish and Wildlife had no in-house attorneys.

I couldn't imagine sitting in another room while the federal attorneys from Justice met with the paper company lawyers and decided the pivotal question of who, exactly, would build the public's case. There was far too much riding on it. I went back to my hotel and tried to sleep. Later that night, I had an idea. Grabbing a yellow legal pad, I jotted down the specifics underlying two goals for the next day's talks with the paper company lawyers. First, we needed to spell out the key issues for the damage assessment: how could we prove liability, PCB release and transport, injuries to natural resources, economic damages to the public, and the best opportunities for environmental restoration? More to the point of this particular meeting with company lawyers: which details might we work on together without jeopardizing the government's ability to faithfully represent public interests? It would never be wise to let the paper companies determine their own liability or their own bottom line damages, but maybe we could jointly identify restoration opportunities around the bay. Second, we needed to demonstrate that Fish and Wildlife—the Justice Department's client in this case— had, in fact, a very clear idea of how to build the case, what topics to offer for initial joint efforts, and how to document progress or prove that we made good faith efforts at substantive cooperation. In short, I wanted to explain what we expected from our attorneys at this meeting.

The next morning, the agencies gathered privately to set the agenda and settle who would meet with the paper company lawyers later that day. I stopped my Fish and Wildlife colleagues in the hall beforehand to share my midnight brainstorm. Back in the meeting room, Susan Schneider knew I was up to something, but she said nothing. I still had to bring my other Interior colleagues on board, so I took them out into the hall, one by one. Our Interior lawyer agreed, and the rest followed suit.

Back in the briefing room, I noticed Susan's eye twitching. "Tread lightly," I thought. Susan stuck to her guns, explaining in her diplomatic, no-nonsense way that Justice's attorneys were expert negotiators and could be fully trusted to represent the concerns at the Fox River and Green Bay. I nodded in wholehearted agreement. Then I took out my yellow legal pad. "Fish and Wildlife and Interior are fully prepared for Justice attorneys to use their expertise in conveying several key points to the paper companies," I said, and I delineated those points, which our Interior lawyer elaborated upon.

No cracks had emerged within the team, and my midnight brainstorm paid off. Susan and the others conferred and resolved that I would attend the meeting, but without my Fish and Wildlife colleagues. It was an early and key victory in this first matchup between the Feds and the paper company lawyers.

Everybody assembled in a modest conference room inside Main Interior. It was only March but the magnolias were already in full bloom, visible just outside the tall, narrow windows that lined one side of the room. In all, there were fifteen people at the meeting: six defense attorneys on one side of the conference table, four government attorneys on the other. The Menominee tribal chairman, three Interior staffers, and I were seated behind the government attorneys, all under strict instructions not to utter a word. The paper companies' defense lawyers were dressed to the nines—five dark suits with bright ties and one red pantsuit. My first thought at seeing them had nothing to do with the case, and everything to do with the relative status of those on either side of the table: "The watches in this room are worth more than my car."

Sparks flew immediately. Fort Howard's lawyers, from the DC law firm of Beveridge & Diamond, refused to recognize the Menominee tribe as a co-trustee in the case. Susan Schneider responded, referring to the paper companies as "defendants" when she did. P. H Glatfelter's lawyer, from the Philadelphia law firm of Ballard-Spahr, loudly objected: "Is there some lawsuit filed somewhere that you didn't tell us about?" Susan apologized, though she would continue to use the term for the rest of the meeting. At one point, Fort Howard's lawyer asked me for a clarification regarding the Green Bay office's participation in the Fox River Coalition. I looked up from my green notebook as the room fell silent, and Susan and Matt swiveled around in their seats to see what I would say. I winked at Susan, then returned to my notes without a word.

When the defense attorneys finally launched into their clients' proposals, it was quickly apparent that the paper companies wanted more than to control the damage assessment—they wanted to be shielded from whole categories of liability. The lawyers hinted that the companies might be willing to accelerate cleanup projects in the most upstream parts of the river, but only if they could control the projects and limit the scope of any damage assessment for the entire site. In short, the companies sought to minimize the area to be cleaned up, prevent whole categories of damage assessment, and limit the Feds' role. If they had their way, the effect of their proposals would be to prevent an adequate cleanup and restoration.

The proposals were, of course, nonstarters, completely antithetical to our goals for the Fox River. There were ten times more PCBs in Fox River sediments downstream of the De Pere Dam than in the small hot spots the paper companies dangled for voluntary cleanup upstream. And there were more PCBs already in the bay of Green Bay than the entire Fox River. Moreover, there was nothing new here. I had already attended dozens of Fox River Coalition meetings over several years where these same ideas continually led nowhere.

The attorneys parted in a stalemate. I was relieved to have had a front-row seat to the meeting. The paper companies' lawyers were more subtle than DNR's Fox River leaders—their resistance more assured and thus harder to overcome.

After a few dozen more such meetings, I would be looking for ways to limit the ceaseless legal arguments. The Feds would be sparring with them for decades to come. It was also increasingly clear to me that Maryann Sumi, the Fox River Coalition, and the paper company lawyers were all preaching from the same book.

At EPA, I began seeing both sides of one coin: increasing engagement *and* resistance flowing from our quickening progress on the Green Bay case. EPA, Fish and Wildlife, Interior, and Justice met in EPA's Chicago office for an intense discussion about what should happen next at the Fox River. The three visiting agencies argued for EPA to join and create a united federal front on the Fox.

Afterward, I learned from Ken Fenner's shop at EPA that my team had achieved just half a loaf. Two EPA divisions supported the Fish and Wildlife damage assessment, as well as EPA's use of its Superfund authorities. But two opposed, and one of the opponents was the Super-fund division itself. I also learned that Dave Ullrich, EPA's no. 2 for the region, was watching the Fox River controversy closely. For now, Dave was cautiously sticking to the sidelines.

EPA would waffle back and forth for another two nerve-wracking months. At one point, my hope for EPA support on the Fox seemed all but lost. My strongest card—the long-standing support from Fenner's Water group—began to evaporate. Fenner even stopped taking my calls. I could picture Bruce Baker at DNR reminding him that he needed Wisconsin's cooperation more than Fish and Wildlife's. Then, rumors emerged that EPA's Dave Ullrich himself might ask Fish and Wildlife to stop the Green Bay damage assessment altogether.

The fallout from Governor Thompson's ill-fated lobbying of Secretary Babbitt, and Interior's subsequent endorsement of the Fish and Wildlife damage assessment at the very highest levels, came just in time. By June 1995, there was a seismic ground shift: I heard about executive-level discussions between EPA, Fish and Wildlife, and Justice in Washington regarding how to proceed with Wisconsin DNR on the Fox River.

I now redoubled my efforts to arm key EPA staff with critical tech-nical and legal information. I had to outrun the high-level discussions, which seemed more interested in building bureaucratic harmony than building leverage.

I also ramped up my direct engagement with the public. Controlling the flow of information about the case would be my secret weapon. I had to provide information quickly, accurately, and effectively, but in a way that preserved confidentiality and appeased my lawyers. I needed a system.

To that end, I set about implementing a series of informational con-trols to document progress and build momentum in the face of growing resistance outside my agency. I maintained an electronic database of all relevant facts that I could access quickly to refute technical misinforma-tion. My office mate Joe Moniot, a particularly meticulous and thorough biologist, helped me keep a library of relevant scientific articles that made it possible for me to add credible citations to our team's written arguments. I envisioned that together we would also assemble a public reading room in Green Bay to function as the nerve center for the case. The Reading Room would house the entire case file, with duplicate copies kept in multiple offices in Wisconsin and elsewhere in the country to give every member of the core team instant access to the substance of the complete case (Allen 2018c; FWS 2008a, 2008b, 2008c).

I was also working to gain enough trust from my team to become the unofficial public face of the assessment. I expanded on Ken Stromborg's initial introductions and began testing ideas about how to engage a much wider public. Soon, I had tempted enough journalists to talk with me that I somehow managed to develop relationships with print and broadcast media in Green Bay, Appleton, Milwaukee, Madison, and Washington, DC. Eventually, I began leading public informational meetings, lecturing at scientific meetings and university classes, and writing and distributing press releases and responding to criticism, particularly from Wisconsin and the paper companies.

As long as the core technical and legal teams agreed about strategy and substance, I was free to immediately deploy data, verbal and written statements, citations, press interviews, and detailed documentation on nearly every subject relevant to the assessment. I didn't hold back, even when high-level senior officials were unnerved by the growing controversy being fed by the paper companies and the State of Wisconsin. I also pursued goals stealthily while the stars were aligned: methodically testing scientific results, gaining support for them from the scientific community and public, and then using those results to prevent federal officials from backing down solely to appease the paper companies and Wisconsin.

With each official release, I had more momentum and leverage to speak definitively about the facts of the government's case, as well as the government's opinions about what those facts meant. I enthusiastically engaged the scientific community, the general public, the press, EPA, Wisconsin, and the paper companies with any and all legally consequential government findings. And I strove to create a sense of inevitability when the facts and the law clearly pointed to a prescribed action.

Everywhere that EPA, Wisconsin, and the paper companies looked, my growing team and I would be there, publicly explaining the facts and legal implications for the inevitable cleanup and restoration of the Fox River and bay of Green Bay.

But I would soon find that there were elements inside my own agency I could not control.

3

INNER TURMOIL AT FISH
AND WILDLIFE

THE NEW BOSS

David Allen

On June 14, 1995, I began briefing our new regional director, Bill Hartwig, about the Green Bay case. I spoke with confidence, even though
he outranked me by six levels in the supervisory chain, more grades
than that within the federal civil service system, and at least a couple
decades' worth of experience within our agency. But I knew the facts
of the Green Bay case as well as anyone, and had explored thoroughly
how Fish and Wildlife might apply the Superfund law to use those facts
strategically. More important, I knew that a senior executive like Bill
might be seduced by the opportunity to lead one of the largest Natural
Resource Damage Assessments in the United States. It was also possible
that the new regional director, fresh from leading the real estate division
at Fish and Wildlife Headquarters in Arlington, Virginia, might even
already have heard of the case before moving to Fort Snelling to lead
Fish and Wildlife's Region 3 office.

I relished the opportunity to kick off our presentations to Bill during
this rare visit to our backwater field office in Green Bay. I liked public
speaking, and I'd had plenty of practice briefing senior officials during

my previous agency gigs. Plus, I'd already briefed everyone in my command line about Green Bay, including Bill's predecessor and the presidential appointees who were still Bill's bosses in DC.

I began with slides, then closed in on the facts I thought might intrigue him as much as other senior officials who had already endorsed and funded the case. Just as I was hitting my stride, Bill held up a hand and shook his head. Bill's determined, steel-blue eyes telegraphed instantly that this was not his first encounter with the Green Bay damage assessment. With his mild West Virginia drawl, he said matter-of-factly, "David, we're taking this case in a whole new direction."

Little did I know this was the beginning of a years-long struggle to win the heart and mind of my own regional director.

I had already spent several years figuring out how to create administrative momentum within my agency, and had begun attracting a capable team willing to tackle the legal and technical complexities of an environmental case that might cost sophisticated paper companies hundreds of millions of dollars or more. Now I would have to convince a new regional director to trust my team and embrace the factual and legal realities of the case. In the meantime, I would need to keep my team engaged and on track while I dealt with this new, hopefully temporary, internal hurdle.

I would have to do so under my own power. I had no institutional or budgetary control of my own. I occupied a position on the lowest rung of my agency's food chain. I supervised no employees. I was not a contract officer, nor did I direct any budgetary line items. I would need to continue to rely on the facts and the law to persuade, and then use those tools to catalyze formal decisions by the officials who wielded the real institutional power—in this case, Bill Hartwig.

The next two years were tense. Typically, Bill kept his multitude of regional staff at bay with cold stares, a quick pace from room to room, and impatient meetings where he paid closer attention to his avalanche of emails than to the staff right in front of him. He possessed a supremely confident air in delivering regular edicts to the staff, and he was an effective decision maker, whether you agreed with him or not. Bill was, all at once, disliked, feared, and respected. He was authoritarian at times, not known for empathy, and no fool. If overly confident in some situations, he managed to correct for it later on. He didn't make many friends, but that didn't seem to bother him in the least.

Over time, I would come to regard Bill as one of the more skilled senior managers I would work with in government. My team and I managed to draw his attention often enough. When Bill's stares and proclamations failed to gain him instant control, he would remind us that he'd already cut major real estate deals for Fish and Wildlife in every state in the country, and had learned long ago how to re-deploy cooks under his command in Vietnam to the front line when enemy soldiers surged too near. Thus, Bill inserted himself into the daily leadership of the case, issuing directives and leading gatherings of the Green Bay team, calling and meeting with George Meyer at DNR, contacting the paper company chief executive officers, and drafting his own official letters to DNR and the paper companies.

In these early days of Bill's rule, he conveyed obvious disdain for attorneys and bureaucracy. But he was also naïve about the Superfund law, Natural Resource Damage Assessments, the subtle art of collecting evidence, and the history of paper company influence within Paper Valley—including, of late, the companies' direct line to Governor Thompson and Secretary Meyer. It was also clear Bill was underestimating the skill and commitment of my team, the limits of his or any regional director's control over other agencies, and the public's growing interest in Green Bay's PCB problem. Last, I was pretty sure Bill overestimated his own ability to effectively control the information and budgets of his staff.

I hedged my bets.

As I'd done from the outset of the Green Bay case, I took copious notes, building an administrative record even over some colleagues' objections. My green notebook was well known to those close to the case. I always had my notebook out, always took detailed notes, and often used my notes to create official memos documenting meetings. The more important and sensitive the subject, the more detailed the notes. Ever aware that I'd be called on to defend our case if it made it to trial, I kept notes on everyone I spoke with and every meeting I attended.

My encounters with Bill now also flowed onto the pages of my green notebook, and this made him anxious. Bill didn't want any records, accurate or not, that might limit his options. It was a relatively minor skirmish in the moment, but one we both knew had potentially far-reaching consequences down the road. As I did with anyone who challenged my note taking, I stood my ground and gave my usual response: "Let me make sure I write that down accurately in my notes so I have it right if I'm asked about it later."

The practice irritated Bill, but he accepted that he'd have to live with my record keeping.

As Bill and my team continued to test one another, a more significant conflict emerged—this one with potentially disastrous consequences for the Green Bay case. After a few weeks of disagreement over whether Bill should meet with paper company CEOs without his own government attorneys, he made a unilateral move that seemed directly out of Wisconsin's playbook: he impulsively cut out his staff and sent a solo letter directly to the paper companies, agreeing to meet them on his own to discuss resolving the Green Bay PCB problem.

I knew there was no time to dissuade Bill and no practical way to block him from going. I was also uncertain about my ability to influence him. So I set my sights on an easier but equally important target: convincing Bill to resist paper company pleas for Fish and Wildlife to abandon plans to send "Information Request" letters to the mills, as provided for in the Superfund law. The formal Information Requests were critical to the team's progress on the case. The requests would force the paper companies to produce details about their corporate structure, history of PCB releases, liability, and ability to pay for cleanup and restoration—or face criminal penalties for knowingly withholding or providing false information. My team and I had already expended enormous effort uncovering publicly available information on the companies. Now we'd devised questions to elicit details about the companies' more carefully guarded facts with the help of Information Requests.

This assembly of a "liability case" was an essential first step for any Superfund case. In Green Bay, Fish and Wildlife was in the unique position of building the case in the void left by EPA and DNR, neither of which was invoking Superfund—at least for now. Bill's predecessor at the regional office had already fired the first official shot across the bow back in 1994, when he'd signed off on letters to the paper companies identifying them as responsible parties in the case. It had been a first in Fish and Wildlife history, a job typically performed by EPA. The letters had sent the paper companies running to the ramparts and contacting their lawyers. Now, a skeptical Bill Hartwig would have to sign off on Fish and Wildlife's first-ever Information Requests. It was another major step in the case. If Bill refused, I knew there would be no practical way to build the liability case and prove its merit to Justice.

The paper companies would despise these requests. But I also knew the mills would mask their objections by offering Bill alternatives that were less intrusive, less legalistic, less bureaucratic—and that would sound reasonable to him, even clever. With few opportunities to meet personally with Bill, I strategized I'd win points with him by abandoning any attempt to dissuade him from meeting with the paper companies. So I focused on preparing Bill for a trap the companies were likely to set: convincing him to abandon the Information Requests.

The morning of Bill's solo meeting with the paper companies, he and Frank Horvath flew together on a Fish and Wildlife plane from the regional office over to our Green Bay field office. They'd had plenty of time to talk about the meeting, and about me. Frank looked even more worried than usual when he met with me one on one. It was immediately clear Bill wasn't going to grant me an audience until Frank had laid down some ground rules.

"I hope they made as many plans about how to handle the company brass as they made about how to handle me," I thought to myself.

Frank warned: "Try not to fly off the handle when you meet with Bill, okay?"

"I'm not even going to look cross-eyed at him about his goddamned meeting—he's already heard it all from the legal team," I reassured him.

If Frank had looked more worried than usual, Bill looked more annoyed than usual. I was pretty sure Frank had had to twist Bill's arm to even allow me a couple of minutes before and after the paper company meeting.

I jumped right in. "I have a hunch these guys are going to hit you pretty hard on a detail they don't like. Remember those Information Requests we told you about? It'd be a neat trick if they figured a way to sweet-talk you out of signing them."*

Bill recalled them instantly, looking directly at Frank, then me, as if to say, "I understand a lot more of this than you guys think." I was beginning to appreciate Bill's shrewdness. He didn't respond to my implicit request, but he did seem to appreciate that I didn't argue with him about meeting alone with the paper companies.

After the meeting, Bill told me the companies had, in fact, pressed him about the requests. He had agreed to delay them by six months. Braced for my disappointment, Bill started explaining his rationale. I interrupted, saying only, "I'm already on board with the delay. Let's discuss the steps for getting your signature on those Information Request letters six months from now."

Inwardly, I thought: "We now have six months to convince Bill not only about these requests but about the team and our detailed plans—which, if we play our cards right, he might just adopt and lead as his own."

At the same time that Frank and I were trying to win Bill Hartwig's support, my growing team was focused on how to produce court evidence about PCBs and the paper companies. But we weren't about to wait for a federal trial to begin disseminating the evidence. Even as we collected and organized information, we presented what we knew directly to EPA technical and legal staff. And we continued urging EPA to invoke Superfund and join with Fish and Wildlife, both to build a viable case and to help persuade DNR that government agencies were better allies than the paper companies.

To buy the team time and to preserve the case, Susan Schneider and her supervisor at Justice made it clear to EPA that it should stop thinking

---

* Bill Hartwig had delegated authority from the Department of the Interior to sign these letters, which would trigger the full weight of Superfund's requirements for the companies to respond completely and truthfully, under criminal penalties.

about disrupting Fish and Wildlife's damage assessment. Justice wanted this case. As Justice was the gatekeeper for all of EPA's litigation, this "request" carried weight.

By August 1996, my team was ready to publish the official Assessment Plan, which laid out the federal government's view of existing technical information and launched formal fact-finding efforts to build the Green Bay damage assessment case (FWS 1996, 1997). It also brought conversations with EPA to a swift crescendo. Just one month later, I learned that EPA was unofficially joining the Fox River fray. Attorney Roger Grimes and Superfund's Jim Hahnenberg had both been assigned.

In September, I finally reached Jim. He was knowledgeable and savvy and had heard about the case and controversy between Wisconsin DNR and Fish and Wildlife. I suspected he had extensive experience working with cooperative states, but probably not with agencies as hostile as DNR. Given that the Natural Resource Damage Assessment program was so new, I also figured he hadn't had much reason to work with Fish and Wildlife before, so didn't pay much attention to a random call from a small field office back in '92. I saw no reason to ask about it now.

We talked at length about the substance of the Fox River and Green Bay case. Jim was easy to talk with. Friendly, but quick to business, which I liked. And he seemed pretty fearless, a trait shared by many of Superfund's on-the-ground managers, who were expected to make consequential decisions every day. I decided to let Jim reach his own conclusions about DNR. It wouldn't take long, and he wouldn't be easy to push around. Besides, the facts of the site gave us plenty else to talk about in this first conversation. Over time, I would become very familiar with Jim's gravelly voice, easy sense of humor, and well-timed audacity. I didn't know it yet, but he was destined to become the most important figure in the entire case for transforming governmental study into real cleanup action in the river.

My job was now growing by leaps and bounds. I was responsible for building the liability case and damage assessment for Green Bay, I suddenly had real partners at EPA, and I was encountering new demands from Bill Hartwig every day. So Frank and I now reached out to technical experts with real-life damage assessment experience.

Our top choice for the job was Hagler Bailly, a science and economics consulting firm in Boulder, Colorado that specialized in damage assessments and already had access to the same economist, Dr. Rich Bishop at UW–Madison, whom I had contacted back in 1992. Hagler Bailly brought Josh Lipton into my orbit. He was the firm's most talented strategic advisor and a vital conduit to hired expertise throughout the country. He was also a former professional pianist in Boston and Paris, with delicate hands that looked like they were designed to play that instrument. Even more refined were his facial features, especially his eyes, which nearly always twinkled with mischief and intuitive exploration of possibilities that had not yet occurred to most others in the room. Josh was also a natural linguist, a trait passed to his son, who would later study medieval languages in York, England.

Of course, I hired Josh for his scientific expertise—he had earned his PhD from Cornell in aquatic toxicology and had already helped trustee agencies with some of the most successful damage assessment efforts in the country. He and I quickly became each other's sounding boards for developing complex strategies rooted in technical details but aimed at meeting legal rigor and the inevitable political machinations of Wisconsin and the paper companies.

SIZING UP THE SUPERFUND OPPONENTS

Susan Campbell

As soon as he learned I was the paper's new environmental reporter, the reporter who had trail blazed the position years earlier was eager to fill me in on the story he said would come to define the beat. He'd talk excitedly about the backstory behind the Fox River's PCB problem and the public's need to know. The stories were peppered with acronyms that made my head spin—PRPs, NRDA, RI/FS—and he would rattle off the names of the many federal and state agencies on the case. The story was both tantalizing and overwhelming.

I hoped it could simmer just a little more. I was back in the saddle at the paper, yes, but barely. I still couldn't type. The clunky first-generation voice-activated software easily tripled the time it took to write stories, and I worried it might hinder my ability to cover a story as big and complex as the Fox River cleanup.

The story couldn't wait, however. Events were happening behind the scenes and the newspaper already needed to play catch-up. The local media was largely ignoring the cleanup. When it wasn't, the press was being hand-fed stories about continued cooperation through DNR's and the paper mills' Fox River Coalition, and their progress toward a voluntary settlement to address the Fox River's PCB contamination. In October 1996, I visited the agency at the center of the controversy: the U.S. Fish and Wildlife Service. I steeled myself for the visit. These were the federal officials who were putting so much pressure on Fort Howard and the other paper mills. My colleague had described to me how, for at least the last two years, the agency had been queuing up its federal authority to push DNR to devise a cleanup plan for the Fox River and Green Bay. And he'd told me of David Allen, the point person at Fish and Wildlife who was making things happen.

These folks were bound to be intimidating. As I drove up to the Fish and Wildlife office, though, I relaxed a bit. It was an exceptionally unremarkable building, a small single-story structure that looked like a standard-issue post office set off by itself on a lonely road in an equally unremarkable part of town. I recognized a tinge of disappointment at the thought that the protagonists in this story might not be a match for the suit-and-tie executives at the paper mills. I shrugged it off. You can't judge a building by its exterior.

As I crossed the threshold, the disappointment returned. The place was even more dismal inside. The supervisor was the first to greet me. She was preoccupied but made an effort to be pleasant as she showed me around the building. She didn't seem to have much time or interest in a reporter, at least today. David Allen and Ken Stromborg emerged to usher me into a meeting room—or, more accurately, an attached garage into which the office's contents were slowly oozing. The dark, cluttered space housed a mishmash of service boats, file cabinets, and paperwork scattered alongside tables for dissecting fish and birds. My hosts pulled out an uncomfortable metal folding chair and apologetically offered a Styrofoam cup of stale, lukewarm coffee.

"It's really bad," Allen warned. I sipped it. It was undrinkable. Without question the worst coffee I'd ever encountered, and I drank bad coffee from the office coffee machine daily. At least Allen could be trusted on that point. I set my cup on the floor as there was no clear surface to set it on. In my simple skirt, sweater, and worn flats, I suddenly felt overdressed in this shabby place—and now had more than a creeping sense that this might not shape up to be the big story I'd envisioned.

David Allen, sitting across from me, didn't quite look the part, either. He was earnest, young, blue-eyed, and fresh-faced—like a former Boy Scout. "Probably a former Eagle Scout," I thought as I observed him. He didn't fit the mold of a typical bureaucrat in a government job, nor that of a fiery, tenacious prosecutor like the ones I'd covered as a court reporter back in suburban Philly. Bespectacled and studious-looking, Allen seemed to fit better on a college campus than across the table from corporate executives and agency brass. But when he talked, he spoke articulately and passionately in long, streaming sentences with perfect recall of precise facts, dates, and statistics—barely pausing to take a breath. He seemed to possess both an impatience with a world that hadn't quite caught up with him, and an abiding desire to bring that world up to speed. I would learn over time it was this latter quality that would define our relationship and form the basis of the Green Bay story the public would come to know.

Allen was a contrast to his partner, Ken Stromborg, who had arrived at middle age stout and a bit rumpled. Reserved, he mostly hung back and let Allen do the talking. Stromborg had a biting wit and radiated cynicism, looking every bit the part of a wildlife toxicologist who preferred being out in the field with wildlife rather than in an office with humans. But the laid-back demeanor and self-deprecating humor belied his deep knowledge of PCBs' effects on local wildlife. He'd also been around Green Bay longer than Allen and was well versed in the history of the local office and the larger community. The two looked an unlikely pair, but they shared an obvious in-the-trenches camaraderie.

David Allen on Spider Island in Lake Michigan, 1992. (Ken Stromborg)

Allen and Stromborg laid out the long, still-unfolding history of the Green Bay Natural Resource Damage Assessment. Since 1994, the agency had identified two Green Bay and five Fox River Valley paper mills responsible for the tens of thousands of pounds of chemical PCBs known to line the Fox River. They were working to beat legal deadlines the paper companies could invoke after the release of the $16 million Mass Balance Study of PCBs in the bay.

By the time I left the office, I had a working knowledge of the basic aspects of the story. Allen and Stromborg were clearly convincing in their grasp of the facts, their strategy, and their commitment and zeal to see it through.

But it still felt like David versus Goliath.

That feeling was underscored during my first visit to the Fort Howard paper company around the same time.

"The Fort," as it was known, lived up to its name. Situated on the west bank of the Fox River, the sprawling plant could be seen for miles, a massive steel-gray presence on the outskirts of the city of Green Bay. I was allowed through the gate and escorted into the plant to a stately conference room. Fort Howard's spokesman and several other well-dressed mill executives greeted me upon entering the room and took their seats.

The room and the men were a stark contrast to what I'd seen at my Fish and Wildlife visit. Sitting around the large, gleaming conference table, I felt small and outnumbered amid all the suits. And a bit shabby. The executives made their case, sliding one polished document after another across the conference table to bear out their points. They knew their subject inside and out, and their arguments were well rehearsed. Like their Fish and Wildlife counterparts in the Green Bay office, they seemed to relish the opportunity to indoctrinate this new reporter with their side of the story. They supplied me with copious written materials to take with me, and afterward I received a typewritten letter in the mail following up on some of my questions, together with another large stack of documents to review.

The company officials were exceedingly courteous during my visit, but somehow I left with the feeling I'd been worked over.

"THE NUMBER"

David Allen

The six-month period leading up to the planned sending of Information Requests to the paper companies was off to a rocky start. Hagler Bailly had been working under contract for months to gather historical raw data from throughout the Fox River and bay of Green Bay area, and was now laboring to make sense of all that data in light of voluminous studies already published about the site. Frank Horvath and I pushed our consultant to press on with the assessment, making sure Hagler Bailly was plugged into Dale Patterson's water quality experts in DNR and Ken Stromborg's connections in DNR's research arm.

The information was critical to figuring a preliminary dollar estimate of how much would be required to repair damages to the river and bay.

The estimate was both a necessary procedural milestone under federal regulations and an important practical step to gauge how much additional site study could be justified as part of a formal damage assessment. It was also the lynchpin fact that would define the case for the local press and public, helping both to finally conceptualize a cleanup effort that for years had been so nebulous.

Once Bill Hartwig learned the effort was underway, he demanded the team give him the preliminary estimate. But Bill wanted it for his own reasons. He wanted to use it to negotiate a quick settlement with the paper companies and DNR. I resisted. I could see Bill was relying on his long experience with governmental real estate deals. In those deals, the fair market value of land was easy to calculate, and "the number" was simply a starting point to test overlap between landowners' willingness to sell and the government's willingness to purchase. Bill needed a quick course in Superfund negotiations, and the paper companies' defense lawyers were about to teach him a lesson that the whole team—and the public—would regret. At that point, Bill didn't grasp the chasm between governmental and paper company perspectives regarding environmental risks from PCBs, and the likely costs involved in lessening those risks. He didn't realize the government would have to be able to prove, to the standards of a federal court, every element of its complicated and expensive case. He hadn't thought through the challenge of convincing paper companies to spend hundreds of millions of dollars, possibly more, on something utterly antithetical to making paper—or profits.

Tensions grew between my team and Bill about what information existed and how it could be used to eventually compel the unwilling paper companies. Bill insisted my team already knew the number for settlement and he set about trying to pry it from us for his negotiations. A flurry of meetings failed to convince him that months would be required for any of us to fully comprehend the extent, relevance, and adequacy of the existing river and bay data, and that it was foolish to assume that a settlement was anywhere within reach.

Bill convened more meetings of my team to press his case for more immediate action, and to make a show of who was in charge. I knew I had to somehow stand in the way of the reckless and dangerous path

Bill was pursuing with Wisconsin and the paper companies. At the same time, I had to assert myself to Bill as a credible authority, or risk continuing the pattern of him taking charge—essentially allowing the tail to wag the dog.

The results were mixed. For months, Bill and I each pulled the strings within our respective reach.

But I had an ace up my sleeve. I knew Governor Thompson and Secretary Meyer would eventually irritate Bill even more than my team or I did. All I needed was enough time for Wisconsin to betray my regional director.

A few weeks later, Hagler Bailly delivered the number. The Preliminary Evaluation of Injuries and Damages was a much more substantial document than typical preliminary damage estimates. And it contained a bombshell. The report figured repairing damages to the river and bay might exceed $1 billion—notably the first time any official Fox River document had predicted ten figures for a PCB fix.

About half of the estimate was for sediment restoration work that closely mirrored a sediment cleanup, a scenario that assumed EPA might remain on the sidelines and DNR might fail to produce enough leverage with the paper companies via its voluntary Fox River Coalition. The other half was for natural resource restoration work to compensate the public for the PCBs that had spread throughout Green Bay and were now beyond practical cleanup.

I knew Bill would want to keep the number and this new document mostly to himself. He would want to use it as the number for settlement negotiations with DNR and the paper companies, and also to give himself maximum flexibility to play with the figure. But I also knew the number in this document would be orders of magnitude too high for fast, easy settlement, and that the preliminary information it relied on was not enough to prove claims in court. The government was still years away from determining the actual justifiable amount needed for cleanup and restoration, and Bill was in no position to catalyze a quick deal on his own terms.

I hatched a plan. Telling no one, not even Frank Horvath, I sent a copy of the damage estimate to every federal and tribal attorney and manager working under confidentiality agreements for the Green Bay assessment. The list totaled about twenty people. Everyone on that list had a right to see the information, and each had been warned in the past not to leak materials that were properly marked—as this clearly was. I made sure to copy Bill, without showing the names of the other recipients, so the regional director would have no way of knowing who else had seen the document. This guaranteed Bill could not bury the results, or seek a lower number that might be easier to negotiate. It also ensured Bill would have to continue engaging everyone on the team, as everyone would now be armed with all the available facts.

As soon as Frank Horvath received his copy he realized what I had done and knew he'd been cut out of the decision. He didn't seem mad, but he wasn't going to offer me any cover, either. Frank was in the mood to let me squirm a little. It took only a day for him to tell me that Bill had blown his stack and was now questioning my loyalty. When I arrived for my dressing down at Fish and Wildlife's regional office in Fort Snelling, Bill challenged my decision to widely distribute such a sensitive and sought-after document, even with the confidentiality agreements in place. How could I guarantee it wouldn't wind up in the press tomorrow?

"You won't see this in the press," I said confidently, while thinking fervently to myself, "I sure hope he doesn't."

Fortunately, by the time I'd arrived at the regional office, tempers were already mostly in check—partly because I showed no fear, and partly because Frank had learned to act as the perfect foil to our boss's quick temper. With Bill, Frank was the calm, steady, fellow army officer; his was the perfect face of the team. He could explain the team's operations in ways that resonated with Bill, and he could highlight its strengths, advantages, and code of conduct, including my dual loyalties to the team and the public. Frank's diplomacy went a long way in mediating between Bill and me, smoothing over the inherent personality conflicts that could have hamstrung progress on the case many times. With Frank as my buffer, I was able to confront obstacles in the way I liked best: with battering-ram force.

Fortunately for me, everyone who received my surreptitious envelopes honored their confidentiality agreements, and the consultant's

$1 billion-plus estimate didn't make it into the press. I had gambled big and got lucky; I knew I would have done it again, though, even if things had gone the other way. I saw the public as the government's master. I believed in confidentiality systems, as long as they were used as intended. Too often, I saw them abused by bureaucrats and attorneys who exploited the veil of confidentiality to help themselves, even to the public's detriment. I was particularly riled when some mid-level bureaucrat pulled rank and tried to make me feel beholden to them, rather than both of us being beholden to the public we served. To keep things in perspective, I developed my own hierarchy of "federal Bills." In it, President Bill Clinton was a very big federal Bill, some field biologist named Bill was a very small federal Bill, and Bill Hartwig was a medium federal Bill.

My colleague Joe Moniot and I kept this at the forefront of our minds by posting a list of federal Bills on the wall of our office as dangerous humor.

THE ENVIRONMENTALISTS

Susan Campbell

Green Bay's environmental community, excited to have the *Press-Gazette's* environment beat restored at the paper, greeted my initial reporting with enthusiasm. That would change after my first major story on the Fox River cleanup saga.

The article ran in November 1996 and sought to cut a path right down the middle, telling the story of paper mill executives who feared a federal judgment might force them into bankruptcy, and of federal officials who said Wisconsin and the mills had done too little for too long. The story's front-page headline, however, took a decidedly pro-mill stance: "Fed's Role in Fox Cleanup Stirs Trouble," followed by the subheading, "Forcing Mills to Pay Could Threaten Relationship, Jobs" (Campbell 1996b).

An editorial published later that week went further, warning that the cooperative effort between the state and the mills could be undone if the federal damage assessment process was heavy handed. "The worst-case scenario is that assessments would cause catastrophic job loss and crushing tax burdens all along the Fox," the editorial read (*Green Bay Press-Gazette* 1996). "In addition, federal citations could bring costly and acrimonious court battles that would erase any hope of government and industry continuing joint efforts to help the river."

Green Bay was blessed with a tenacious environmental community, led by the local Clean Water Action Council and its executive director, Rebecca Katers. A petite middle-aged woman with large glasses and long brown hair typically tied in a kempt ponytail, Katers had schoolgirl looks and a voice her foes could easily underestimate. But she was unapologetic in calling out wrongs, uncompromising in her pursuit of environmental protection and the public's right to know, and fearless when the Fort, DNR, or anyone else tried to stare her down. No one who knew her ever mistook Katers for a shrinking violet.

An indefatigable firebrand, Katers was prolific in turning out incendiary but well-sourced press releases and newsletters, and her group had long been an aggressive check on local industry. Some of its members could also be prone to exaggeration, however, which had caused the group to lose credibility with the press. For their part, Clean Water Action members felt stung by years of pollution and the challenge of battling the mills' strong corporate public relations machine. Katers said "job blackmail" was also a factor in Green Bay, with many professionals who might otherwise donate time and money afraid to join the group for fear of losing their jobs or professional standing.

One particularly disillusioned activist had left Green Bay that September. She told me in an interview that she'd received threatening phone calls and letters, including a call at home in which the caller threatened to "stuff [her] in a vat." "I've attended national environmental conferences and it's well known that Green Bay is considered 'Stepfordville'—Apathyville—for environmentalists," she said. "It's well known that this is a blue-collar town with highly paid mill workers" (Campbell 1996c).

For some time now, Clean Water Action had perceived the *Press-Gazette* as part of the problem, as protective—even defensive—of the local mills. Now the paper's new environmental reporter appeared to be more of the same. Outraged at my first dive into the Fox River cleanup story, over the next several weeks the environmental community fought back via letters to the editor chastising the paper and me. The letter writers hit hard. "Once again the *Press-Gazette* uses job blackmail to scare politicians and regulatory agencies into dodging necessary action," wrote one, calling the article a "shameful effort to frighten paper mill workers and their families" (Manthe 1997).

"Corporate manipulation and scare tactics," wrote another (Abitz 1996). "The Fort has reaped billions in financial assets at the expense of public health and prosperity. It's about time we get the job argument straight: Fort Howard exists because of this community and its skilled laborers. Not the other way around."

The community battle lines were drawn. I was confident my story had been fair, but I was frustrated by the headline it had been given and the editorial that had followed. Worse, I worried that maybe I'd been spun by the mills in this industrial, pro-mill town, and was already losing perspective. I was also getting a taste of the paper's recent history on the cleanup issue and its distrust of federal involvement. The *Press-Gazette* had skin in the game on both sides of the debate, in terms of its geography and the players. The newspaper and its readers were in Green Bay, downriver from Paper Valley and on the receiving end of all its chemical waste. But the area was also home to Fort Howard and another mill identified as responsible for the Fox River's PCBs. Balancing the perspectives and demands of both readerships would be the paper's challenge in the years to come.

For now, one thing was certain: the voice of Green Bay's environmental community would not be ignored. But its members had a responsibility, too. I reminded the most outspoken among them that the paper was journalistically bound to cover both sides of the Fox River debate, even if that meant reporting paper mill arguments that appeared to the environmental community to have little or no merit. And I warned Clean Water Action's members to stick to the facts, which needed no exaggeration, lest they lose further credibility.

I needed them.

STALEMATE

David Allen

Bill Hartwig remained cautious about relying on the team. He continued to look for ways to negotiate directly with Wisconsin officials and paper company officers. I knew Bill lacked the authority to strike a unilateral deal and that DNR was an unreliable partner as long as the paper companies wielded influence with the governor's office. The team and I searched for practical ways to convince our regional director of this, but he was unreceptive. For its part, the team was certainly in no position to make demands. Bill was one of seven Fish and Wildlife Service regional directors, outranked only by the director and the handful of senior executives who reported directly to her in DC.

Bill continued talking regularly with DNR secretary George Meyer about how to harmonize the damage assessment with the efforts of DNR's Fox River Coalition. And he took steps to increase his own authority. Back in October 1995, Bill had added his voice to Frank Horvath's and mine to finally procure formal delegation from Interior secretary Bruce Babbitt to serve as the federal government's "Authorized Official" for the Green Bay damage assessment, the first such Interior delegation in history.

That same month, George Meyer had taken several unilateral actions of his own without bothering to warn his new ally, Bill Hartwig. First, Meyer had approved DNR's first-ever damage assessment settlement in the wake of a train derailment near Superior, Wisconsin. The settlement had relied on Fish and Wildlife data and damage assessment analyses, yet the federal government was entirely excluded from the agreement. In penning the deal, Meyer had ignored the advice of five of his own DNR divisions, which had formally recommended joint negotiations involving Wisconsin and Fish and Wildlife.

More important, Meyer now informed Bill that DNR was close to working out a deal with the paper companies on the Fox River. Bill stuck with Meyer and pressured my team for substantive analyses to support our Fox River claims in time for Meyer's imminent settlement discussions. The team continued to detail why we couldn't comply, even if we wanted to, and explained why Bill should be less bullish about his relationship with Meyer.

Throughout the rest of the year, Bill continued to look for ways to align the formal damage assessment with his negotiations with Meyer, while my team pressed onward with the details of our work.

Meanwhile, Fish and Wildlife, Justice, and EPA began working together in earnest. We launched our substantive work with a meeting in Washington, DC. We reviewed the Green Bay case's facts and legal options. We explored the possibilities of unilateral cleanup orders and listing the Fox River on Superfund's National Priorities List. In no uncertain terms, we made the case for the advantages of uniting the "federal family" for comprehensive advancement of Superfund's authorities and goals in Green Bay.

For the first time, I had an EPA Superfund audience who shared my team's vision for uniting the federal government and building technically credible legal leverage for the Fox River and Green Bay, regardless of the controversy generated by the paper companies and Wisconsin DNR. EPA's attorney, Roger Grimes, told me afterward it was the best meeting he'd attended in a very long time. I would learn to trust Roger's wisdom and perspective and would scan crowded meetings looking for his long silver ponytail. Any meeting with Roger there was more successful—and anything worth reporting would be soon shared with Roger's powerful friend Dave Ullrich. The two had worked together, as fellow attorneys, for decades on some of EPA's most consequential cases, and they remained friends and running partners long after Dave ascended to the region's highest levels.

In the coming months, Roger and Jim Hahnenberg, my new Superfund contacts at EPA, continued to be a receptive audience. Like me, however, they faced significant administrative obstacles within their own agency. Superfund resources were stretched thin. Some parts of EPA still preferred voluntary efforts over enforcement. Wisconsin remained adamantly opposed to Superfund involvement, and the paper companies continued to influence their connections in Washington, DC, as well as in Madison.

BEHIND CLOSED DOORS

Susan Campbell

"Open Doors on Water Meetings." The headline of the *Press-Gazette*'s December 30, 1996, editorial page was direct, and the forceful editorial that followed signaled a shift in priorities—that the newspaper now considered its responsibility to the public paramount in the growing pollution case (Campbell 1996e). "Members of the public have too big a stake in river and bay quality to be treated like children and told only the terms of a deal done in closed-door negotiations," it read. "Open the meetings. Tell the people what kind of deal is being struck over their water."

The editorial referred to a secret closed-door meeting held in Madison on December 20 between representatives of the state and federal governments and paper company officials to resolve how the Fox River cleanup should proceed. I had caught wind of the meeting beforehand and called to determine whether the parties would seek a cooperative settlement outside the federal damage assessment process.

The parties also had a second goal: to delay for one year the potential statutory deadline, possibly triggered by both the Mass Balance Study results in Green Bay and the Preassessment Screen and Determination, for Fish and Wildlife to file its damage claim against the paper companies. That deadline was now just a few months away. The clock was ticking.

"This would be a cooperative way out, instead of having the court decide a way out," Bill Hartwig told me in a phone interview the day before the meeting (Campbell 1996a). Hartwig said that, as part of the agreement, the mills would have to commit to some restoration work during the next year as a "down payment" on the final settlement, and to show the public that progress was indeed underway. "There's a lot of work to be done in the next three, four weeks," he said. "It's either going to make it or break it. I'm optimistic that we'll make it."

The meeting came on the heels of a letter Governor Thompson had sent to Interior secretary Bruce Babbitt in late November asking him to support a negotiated solution on the Fox.

David Allen said little when I reached him by phone, but enough to telegraph he wasn't about to put the federal damage assessment on hold—with or without the voluntary effort. "I can't possibly get this done soon enough," he said.

So not everyone was on board holding hands and singing "Kumbaya," I surmised. Some internal cracks were showing.

Rebecca Katers of Clean Water Action Council was irate about the specter of a major decision on the Fox River playing out behind closed doors with a roomful of heavy hitters pressured by industry. "This is a last-ditch effort by Tommy Thompson and his control of DNR to stop the process on behalf of the paper industry," she told me (Campbell 1996a). "They're doing this without our best interests in mind."

In the hours immediately following the closed-door session, participants were tight-lipped about what had transpired. The DNR's Maryann Sumi was the only one to respond to my phone calls for interviews, though she divulged nothing. "Discussions will proceed and I don't want to do anything to jeopardize that," she said (Campbell 1996d). What of the public and its river? "The public will be brought in and made part of this," Sumi assured. "That is everyone's intent."

I was getting nowhere. For now, I'd have to make due with whatever information I was given, however scant.

THE CONCEPT PAPER

David Allen

That December and January were devoted to creating a collaborative "Concept Paper" that would attempt to define how the Green Bay case would be settled. The paper would be negotiated by Bill Hartwig's new assistant, who had no Superfund experience; Fort Howard's general counsel; and Maryann Sumi, Wisconsin's senior attorney and advisor to George Meyer.

Like the secret closed-door session in Madison, the Concept Paper was also the direct result of a letter from Governor Thompson to Bruce Babbitt. Wisconsin hoped the Concept Paper would bring the Feds into its scheme for a speedy, voluntary cleanup outside of public scrutiny and without the leverage of potential litigation, especially under Superfund. But my team and I saw the project for what it was: a dangerous trap set by the paper companies—a trap Bill's naïve new assistant had walked right into and that Bill might not detect in time.

My team and I hated the Concept Paper, both the idea of it and the precious time it stole from making real progress on our Fox River case. My agency had been set on a meandering path of coauthoring a plan that would lead absolutely nowhere. It would serve as great PR fodder for the paper companies and Governor Thompson when it hit the press, but would give the Feds a black eye when they failed to follow through on it.

In hindsight, the Concept Paper triggered more inner turmoil within Fish and Wildlife than anything that had come before or after it in connection with the Fox River.

The fact that my team and I would ultimately oppose the Concept Paper was no secret to Bill Hartwig; the team had been arguing against it for weeks. But it was also clear our objections might be ignored. We would have to mobilize a stiff resistance to the project from within Fish and Wildlife; we'd have to create a paper trail showing Bill that the team could effectively block its implementation even if he ultimately endorsed the project.

I mobilized my entire team and we set to work detailing where the Concept Paper fell short of federal mandates. I enlisted the backing of our consultant Hagler Bailly, directing the firm's Josh Lipton to write a detailed technical analysis of the Concept Paper. I recognized, as I did so, the inherent danger of attacking a document my own agency had coauthored. Josh smelled the danger, too. He called me the night before the analysis was due and told me the disc with the file had been accidentally erased.

"You have to rewrite it," I told him. "Now." Josh tried to talk me out of it, but I stood firm.

With the analysis in hand, I gathered together all the ammunition and, to Bill's chagrin, fired off an official memo revealing there was zero support for the Concept Paper from Bill's own staff, legal team, and co-trustees. Josh's technical analysis reinforcing the point was the coup de grace. If Bill were to endorse the paper now, he would ignite a firestorm, probably even with his bosses in DC.

Hoping that daylighting the episode would discourage further attempts to derail the damage assessment case, I publicized this latest effort by the paper companies and Wisconsin. I talked to the press and environmental groups about the governor's letter to Babbitt and the subsequent attempt at "collaboration." I kept the Reading Room up to date with every shred of documentation from the project that was not eligible for exemptions under federal Sunshine Laws,* and reminded my contacts to visit often.

The latter act would earn me another special meeting in the Minnesota regional office, this one on January 27, 1997, with Bill Hartwig and Frank Horvath. It was the day after Brett Favre had led the Packers to a 35–21 Super Bowl victory over the New England Patriots, the Pack's first Super Bowl win in twenty-eight years. Bill fumed that I had shared sensitive information with the public that, for the sake of preserving his options with DNR, should have been kept under wraps. I wasn't about to violate Sunshine Laws to make their lives easier, though. Strategically sporting a Green Bay Packers hat to lighten the mood, I was able to convince them there was no practical way to block access to legitimate public information. Despite the tensions on both sides, the meeting remained calm—and everybody liked the hat.

Still, I worried we might have barely dodged a fatal bullet. I wondered how much longer the regional director would tolerate my team's interference in his ongoing efforts to strike a deal with George Meyer.

---

* The most important Sunshine Law is the federal Freedom of Information Act (FOIA), but many other federal and state laws require public access to official documents and meetings.

A SECRET DEAL

Susan Campbell

The same day that David Allen was defending himself at Fish and Wildlife's regional office in Minnesota, Titletown was having a celebration to end all celebrations. Upward of one hundred thousand fans, more than the entire population of Green Bay, lined the streets to watch the Packers' motorcade pass by the day after the team's long-awaited Super Bowl victory. Ten thousand pounds of confetti rained down, mingling with falling snow as the players rode in open-air buses through the center of the city. Another sixty thousand people waited in 20-degree cold for the Packers to arrive at Lambeau Field, three hours late because of the time it took for the motorcade to move through the adoring crowds.

I'd been part of the excitement, interviewing fans as they jockeyed through knee-deep snow to get a better view of the players, who waved and gave high-fives out the windows. On a day like this, more accurately a week like this, everyone on the staff was a Packers reporter. Back in the newsroom, however, the lines were more clearly drawn. The *Press-Gazette*'s small cadre of bona fide Packers chroniclers sat fewer than twenty feet from the metro reporters, though they might as well have been worlds away. When they weren't jetting off to cover away games, they were interviewing NFL players with multi-million-dollar contracts and names like Brett Favre, Reggie White, and Gilbert Brown. They led a rarefied existence, mostly disappearing from the newsroom with the start of the off-season in January and reappearing for training camp months later. I'd watch them saunter back into the office—tanned, rested, and ready for a new season of guaranteed page 1 stories. These were the darlings of the newsroom hierarchy, writing the stories that drove subscription rates and advertising dollars, the chronicles that readers craved. The metro reporters, meanwhile, wrote stories that offered up daily doses of legitimacy, like cooked vegetables alongside the prime rib.

I'd often muse that if even a fraction of those Packers fans were to get as worked up about the contaminated river running through their city as they did about football, they might just apply enough pressure to force a cleanup—or at least help it along. Fortunately, there had been some progress in the months since I'd started covering the Fox River story: it ranked ninth in a year-in-review survey of the area's top ten stories of 1996. Topping the list, of course, was "Green Bay Packers' success," followed by Brett Favre's painkiller addiction, but I was gratified that the Fox River story at least shared the same space.

Now the lens of the national media was trained on the Packers and Green Bay, but it would prove equally myopic. Although Paper Valley's chemical legacy was becoming as locally notorious as Titletown was internationally renowned, no one in the national media was reporting on the other "Super" brewing in Titletown's future—this one a looming federal Superfund designation that could trigger an environmental cleanup of historic proportions. Today, as I watched the confetti fall, I at least was enjoying the diversion. It was a welcome break from the growing intensity of the Fox River story, which was occupying more and more of my time.

When the Super Bowl hoopla finally subsided a few days later, I settled in for a return to the normal news cycle. But Wisconsin DNR was about to launch a startling maneuver from its own playbook.

George Meyer issued a press release announcing a $10 million settlement between his DNR and the seven paper companies targeted in the Fox River cleanup. Curiously, nowhere did it mention that U.S. Fish and Wildlife was a party to the agreement.

The settlement seemed to come out of nowhere. I knew that, since December, the DNR and Fish and Wildlife had been negotiating in earnest behind the scenes to reach a voluntary agreement before January 31—today—when Fish and Wildlife was scheduled to deliver notice of its intent to sue the paper companies as part of its damage assessment. The last I'd heard, those talks had stalled over which agency would control the cleanup. Now there was a unilateral decision between DNR and the paper companies, with no federal presence whatsoever.

It didn't make sense.

I was frustrated when I couldn't get David Allen on the phone and was directed instead to Bill Hartwig's assistant. He did little to clear the fog. The agreement was "a step in the right direction," he said, but declined to comment further as his agency had not yet seen the deal (Campbell 1997c). It was now obvious the Feds were not only left out of the settlement, they hadn't even known the state was negotiating separately with the paper mills. Something didn't smell right; the state-mill agreement seemed too cozy. Beyond that, it had the stench of a public relations ploy. The bulk of the money, $7 million, would be spent on a demonstration project to remove contaminated sediments in the most contaminated part of the Fox. Yet the rest of the money would be spent on several smaller projects that had nothing to do with PCB cleanup: a wetland restoration project in the bay, an observation deck, and upgrades to a local nature trail. The agreement also included funding for an alternative damage assessment, PCB modeling reviews, and a public relations budget—clearly all paper company defense strategies that were now embraced by the state. DNR had official oversight but little practical control, as the paper companies would hire all the consultants.

Lastly, the settlement presumed to resolve the prickly question of which agency would oversee the overall cleanup and restoration efforts: Wisconsin DNR gave itself the lead role.

Wisconsin characterized the $10 million sum as a "down payment" on a much larger cleanup. "This is a pretty significant amount of money when you look around the country and see what's being spent on other cleanups," DNR's Bruce Baker told me (Campbell 1997c). "And this is just the beginning."

Local environmentalists again were skeptical. Clean Water Action Council's Rebecca Katers said the $10 million was "a drop in the bucket compared to the overall cleanup cost" (Campbell 1997c). The environmental community pressed for the damage assessment process already launched by Fish and Wildlife to continue. It was the federal process, noted a Sierra Club spokesman, which had "brought the paper companies to the table and made them serious about getting out their checkbooks" (Campbell 1997c).

The environmentalists would have their way, at least for now. Before the day was over, Fish and Wildlife would meet its potential statutory deadlines to notify the paper mills of its intent to sue for damages on the Green Bay case.* The agency fired off a dozen notices preserving its option to litigate. The notices were directed to all seven paper companies of the new Fox River Group, so named as part of the companies' deal with Wisconsin. Copies of the notice were also sent to the head of EPA in Washington and Wisconsin's congressional delegation.

DNR UNIFIES FISH AND WILDLIFE

David Allen

The local field office supervisor burst into my office and announced that Becky Katers had called from the Clean Water Action Council. Katers had just seen a story on the local TV news that DNR had reached a secret deal with the paper companies. Katers summarized the deal as "$10 million for sediments and parking lots." A little later, I received a call from Roger Grimes at EPA who told me that Fort Howard's in-house counsel had basically admitted to the deal a day earlier. Then Frank Horvath called me and said DNR had just faxed its nine-page press release about the settlement to Bill Hartwig, fully a day after announcing it to the media.

The $10 million settlement—negotiated in secret without any input from Fish and Wildlife, or any of the federal agencies or tribes, for that matter—was a real deal.

---

* The facts revealed by the publication of Mass Balance Studies, and the date of the final signature on the Preassessment Screen and Determination, provided the leading theory for the statute of limitations for the U.S. Fish and Wildlife Service. The case would need to be filed in federal district court before the time limit expired. Notices of intent to file suit had to be delivered in advance of filing the case. Other triggers for the statute of limitations could have been argued by the Potentially Responsible Parties. The federal government and the Potentially Responsible Parties signed a series of tolling agreements that prevented any statute of limitations from being triggered during the time of the agreements, but they would not have eliminated statute of limitations that may have already been triggered before the tolling agreements.

My team and I would spend several weeks unraveling the agreement's details and figuring out next steps in dealing with the continuing machinations of the paper companies, the governor, Maryann Sumi's Fox River Coalition, and Bruce Baker's DNR. The coming months would reveal much more, however. The details would confirm our dark suspicion that the mills were angling for a dredging project only to later discredit such attempts to scoop up the dirty river bottom, and that DNR agreed only because it saw any PCB removal as better than none.

Politically, DNR had, in spectacular fashion, managed to alienate both factions within my agency and to unify us in our pursuit of the damage assessment claims against the paper companies. Practically, what it meant to my team and me was that from this point on we would have fewer problems with Bill Hartwig trusting George Meyer more than the team.

We would have to overcome other internal speed bumps along the way, but Bill soon became a steadfast and brilliant ally. He helped Green Bay leapfrog to the front of the line as the nation's top priority for Interior funding. He now personally introduced my team and me at public meetings when we presented formal results under his signature. And he went even further. Bill made Frank the case manager, me the damage assessment manager, and eliminated everyone else from the command line for the case. This realignment of duties, plus Bill's new delegation from Interior as the federal "authorized official" for the Green Bay damage assessment, cut our chain of command to just three short steps from top to bottom: Bill, Frank, and me. We would now have clearer and more complete control of our case. And we were finally all on the same page.

Critically, Bill now shared the team's vision about how to handle two *real* obstacles in our common path: open hostility from the State of Wisconsin, and paralyzing ambivalence from EPA about whether to join Wisconsin's voluntary Fox River Coalition, join Fish and Wildlife's regulatory approach under Superfund, or remain on the sidelines.

Those two problems had to be faced down before finally tackling the most fundamental obstacle before us: paper company resistance to funding adequate cleanup and restoration of the Fox River and Green Bay.

FISH FROM THE FOX: TO EAT OR NOT TO EAT

Susan Campbell

Even as Governor Thompson fought to ward off an extensive cleanup of the Fox River's PCBs, DNR fisheries experts expanded fish consumption advisories to guide anglers on how often they could safely eat fish from state waters.

The new guidelines had some unwelcome news about a favorite fish from the Fox River and Green Bay: the yellow perch, star of Wisconsin's traditional Friday night fish fry. DNR cautioned that yellow perch should not be eaten more than once a week from bay waters, or more than once a month from the Fox River.

A founding member of the local Green Bay Area Great Lakes Sport Fishermen echoed a common sentiment when he objected to the state issuing guidelines that recommended eating any fish from the Fox, even in moderation. "I wouldn't eat anything out of the Fox River," he said. "Unless you want to glow in the dark" (Hildebrand and Campbell 1997b).

EPA HITS THE BRAKES

David Allen

By 1997, my team was working closely with EPA's Jim Hahnenberg and Roger Grimes on the Fox River case. We would soon learn, however, that EPA was under increasing pressure to pull out of the case—or at least slow down.

At a March meeting, the head of EPA's Superfund division in the Chicago regional office outlined a number of hurdles to invoking Superfund at the Fox River. Chiefly, Wisconsin's resistance was highly problematic for the agency and could even affect the national debate on Superfund reauthorization, as well as EPA's budget. Forcing Superfund on an unwilling state, particularly a state known for its history of environmental progressivism, could backfire and ignite already stirred-up national passions about federal meddling, states' rights, and EPA heavy-handedness.

And there were other hurdles. The Superfund director said EPA was trying to reduce, rather than increase, the number of Superfund sites. He said the "National Priorities List" was inappropriate for large river sites like the Fox River, and that local disposal sites would not be practical there. Most important: he cautioned that his boss in Washington, DC—who led the entire Superfund program for EPA—had reported that Interior was increasingly viewed as uncooperative at the Fox River site.

I understood that the Superfund brass was telling my team to back off, that high-level political gamesmanship was afoot. My team was now up against the institutional might of the entire agency. EPA was clearly worried about Capitol Hill. EPA administrator Carol Browner, the leader of the whole agency, had recently told elected officials that her agency would never overrule a governor on Superfund, offering it as reassurance during EPA budgetary and Superfund reauthorization debates. EPA was also up against Wisconsin DNR and Governor Thompson, each powerful within their own right. The Fox River case was explosive for EPA, with not nearly enough upsides.

Dave Ullrich, EPA's de facto regional administrator in Chicago, stressed to everyone gathered in the room that no decision would be made yet.* But the regional Superfund chief's reluctance hung heavy in the air.

After the meeting, I accelerated my efforts and began working directly with Jim and Roger, and with the consultants hired by EPA headquarters to assemble the details necessary to place the Lower Fox River on the National Priorities List. And I roused another powerful ally: the public. I scheduled more public meetings in Green Bay to tout damage assessment updates, and to underscore that EPA had yet to invoke

---

* Regional administrator Val Adamkus retired from EPA in June 1997 and was elected the president of Lithuania on January 4, 1998. David Ullrich became acting regional administrator in June 1997, but he was already operationally running EPA Region 5 in the months before Adamkus retired. Ullrich was acting regional administrator until Frank Lyons was appointed to the position on April 20, 1999.

Superfund authority which would focus on human health risks relating to the contamination, and also shorten the road to cleanup.

The strategy would intensify public scrutiny about why EPA was remaining on the sidelines of what was now one of the nation's most notorious sites of environmental contamination.

4

GRAND THEFT

BEST MEETING EVER

David Allen

On April 24, 1997, three federal agencies—Fish and Wildlife, EPA, and Justice—assembled in EPA's best conference room in Chicago. It would be the most pivotal meeting of my career.

Key technical and legal staff from all three agencies was there to make a detailed case for Superfund at the Fox River in Wisconsin. But first, layers of managers from multiple divisions introduced their staff and programs. As the preliminaries dragged on around the large mahogany table, Bill Hartwig suddenly broke with protocol and interrupted the carefully scripted pageantry. He launched an unrehearsed allegorical story to his federal counterpart at EPA, Dave Ullrich. I remember the story vividly, decades later, because it was as surprising as it was consequential.

In his best storytelling drawl and with a twinkle in his determined eyes, Bill addressed Dave:

Dave, I have to admit something to you. The other day, I was walkin' down the road and I saw this truck idling on the berm. Curious, I looked inside. I probably shouldn't have, but I got in to see what it's like to drive such a big rig. Next thing you know, I have it in gear and I'm moving down the road! Fun, but I don't really know how to drive it.

Anyways, I'm picking up speed, and I'm determined to see how far down the road I can get. Problem is, we're still accelerating, and I'm starting to have trouble keeping between the lines. You probably already know this since I see you out there on the sideboard: it's your truck! I think maybe you should get in and take the wheel. Either way, though, I'm keeping my foot on the accelerator.

I just hope we don't crash, 'cause if we do, everybody's gonna want to investigate what happened to your truck.

Bill's story was met with nervous mumbling and laughter around the room. Dave Ullrich smiled nervously, too, then took the floor. Now he was all seriousness. Formally listing the Fox River and Green Bay as a Superfund site was the right thing to do in the right place to do it, he said. More than that, Dave said putting the Fox River on the National Priorities List was the only way to reach cleanup and restoration goals there. "This is the perfect one to go forward with the battle," he said, adding that his eyes were wide open to what lay ahead.

Bill said Fish and Wildlife was done waiting for Wisconsin DNR. "Period."

THE FOX GOES TO WASHINGTON

Susan Campbell

The paper companies weren't taking any chances. After their ally Governor Thompson failed to persuade Interior secretary Babbitt to call off the federal damage assessment, the mills seized on another avenue to take their case to Washington, DC: the national debate to reform Superfund.

Eight U.S. congressmen, Republicans and Democrats, sent angry letters to Babbitt accusing the federal government of refusing to work with Wisconsin and the paper mills on a voluntary cleanup. Some of the lawmakers called for the Feds to back off and let Wisconsin take the lead.

Superfund had been in the hot seat ever since House Speaker Newt Gingrich's "Republican Revolution" of 1994, with various congressional committees taking aim at the law and its Natural Resource Damage Assessment provisions. Opponents criticized it as too costly, bureaucratic, and slow. The targeted Fox River paper companies now shrewdly saw an opportunity to direct some of that ire toward their growing predicament in Wisconsin.

The letters rolled off the *Press-Gazette* newsroom fax machine one after another (Campbell 1997a). I skimmed them with a rising mix of excitement and anger as I realized the Fox River had landed smack in the middle of the national Superfund debate as poster child for federal meddling in state affairs. The faxes were from David Allen, who had just released them to the press. No need to call him for comment on this, I figured. The letters spoke volumes.

Notably, four of the letters were from lawmakers residing outside Wisconsin, among them Republican U.S. senator James Inhofe of Oklahoma. "While I originally praised this project as an example of state and local collaboration, I now see this as yet another example of the necessity of removing the federal government from the Superfund process," he wrote. Another, U.S. representative Michael Oxley, an Ohio Republican, referred to "the Department of the Interior's apparent inflexible response to the Fox River in Wisconsin." He said he'd recently learned that Superfund's Natural Resource Damage Assessment provision "had given rise to unnecessary controversy."

In joint letters, U.S. Senators Herb Kohl and Russ Feingold, both Wisconsin Democrats, bemoaned the lack of progress in discussions between Fish and Wildlife and the State of Wisconsin. Wisconsin's U.S. representatives Thomas Petri, a Republican, and Jay Johnson, a Democrat, termed the recent $10 million agreement between Wisconsin and the paper companies "the beginning of another innovative, successful solution," one "worthy of your strongest support."

Curiously, I noted that all the letter writers had been fed the same piece of misinformation. They criticized Fish and Wildlife for backing out of negotiations that had led to the secret $10 million deal between the seven paper mills and Wisconsin—negotiations Fish and Wildlife had been shut out of by Wisconsin and the paper companies.

By the time I started calling the Wisconsin delegation for comment, they were already backpedaling. Representative Johnson, a House freshman from Green Bay and former TV journalist, was the most revealing. Johnson said he hadn't meant to get involved in the congressional debate over Superfund reform. "That was why I was a little nervous about joint letters or using this to politicize things," he told me.

His instincts were right this time. The next day Johnson's mug and text from his letter ran prominently on the paper's front page alongside photos of his three Wisconsin colleagues, all under the headline "The Politics of Pollution" (Campbell 1997a).

TRANSPARENCY

David Allen

Joe Moniot faxed me the news stories while I was in Boulder, Colorado meeting with my attorneys and economists. They all wondered why I was grinning. I kept quiet. Attorneys and economists usually hate controversy. Still, as the embarrassing news stories rolled off the presses and the Wisconsin Democrats retrenched, I was pleased.

Just a week before the stories appeared, I had been copied on letters from federal lawmakers to my boss, Interior secretary Babbitt, and given a routine directive to help prepare Interior's official response. The letters arrived in quick succession, all featuring the same damning sound bytes provided by the paper companies and tying the Green Bay case to proposed Superfund reforms. I faxed the letters directly to the press without comment. Leaking? No. Disseminating public information. The press would know that the big story here was the new convergence of anti-Superfund rhetoric from Republicans, who publicly opposed Superfund, and local Democrats, whose party was defending it on Capitol Hill.

I let the letters speak for themselves.

From start to finish, the event affirmed my continuing efforts at transparency. As much as I disliked tangling with elected officials, it was worth it. Wisconsin's congressional delegation would never publicly intervene in the damage assessment again.

The day after Dave Ullrich announced to his sister federal agencies his intention to list the Fox River as a Superfund site, we marshaled our forces. It was time to take our case directly to the Green Bay public. And it was time to help Dave convince the rest of EPA that there was no turning back, like it or not.

Bill Hartwig and Frank Horvath put me in charge of creating presentations for meetings with local U.S. representative Jay Johnson and invited guests, and for the public as well. I would work directly with Hagler Bailly and the legal team to create slides and a script, but we would need to find a public spokesman. Later that day, Frank called me to report that DNR was once again taking aim at us. George Meyer had "gone ballistic" as soon as Bill explained Fish and Wildlife's plans for the public meeting.

We were proceeding, come what may.

The following week brought chaos: within my team there was a mad dash to prepare for the public meetings; others maneuvered to control whatever it was we might say. At the center of the vortex, my consultant Josh Lipton was weaving technical slides into a compelling story, and I was now sprinting toward the same public that I had, for years, engaged only from behind the scenes.

Soon, my colleagues were suggesting that I give the main public presentation. I was a civil servant, not a hired gun. I lived and worked at the site, not in Minnesota, Colorado, or Washington. I already had local connections. But could I pull it off? And did I want to step into the glare of a much hotter spotlight? It made me nervous just thinking about that James River paper vat.

By May 15, Representative Johnson had bowed out because of

growing controversy about his recent ill-advised letter to Babbitt, and DNR had declined Fish and Wildlife invitations to review the presentations ahead of time. I agreed to a dress rehearsal in front of Josh and his staff, the legal team, Fish and Wildlife managers, and public relations pros. Everyone gave me plenty of notes, but Josh's enthusiastic endorsement sealed the deal. Bill would lead the public meeting and I would give the main presentation.

The night of May 21 was a comfortable spring evening in downtown Green Bay. More than a hundred people gathered in the Brown County Library's large auditorium, waiting for the U.S. Fish and Wildlife Service's first-ever public presentation on plans for a massive cleanup and restoration of the Fox River and bay of Green Bay.

I had spent weeks compartmentalizing anxious thoughts about this meeting. Now it was here. Frank was waiting for me at curbside with a worried look on his face. I parked my red Honda Civic where he pointed, then listened to Frank's last-minute instructions and reminders as we walked into the library. It was a big crowd. I straightened my tie and scanned for familiar faces. DOJ, EPA, DNR, and people from my own field office were all there. Environmental groups, reporters, local academics, and paper reps, too. And Bill, who didn't look nervous—but whose glare telegraphed that I'd better not stumble. So far, this felt a lot like the minutes before an orchestra concert when I was playing a solo. The key was to connect with the people in the auditorium. The folks who turned out that night wanted and deserved insight, whether it was notes on a sheet of music or Josh's technical details.

Bill set the stage, then cued me. There was electricity in the air and just enough adrenaline in my body to focus my mind on my audience, and my part to play. As I slowly paced the front of the room and looked audience members in the eye, I could feel my life of fieldwork being left behind. I glanced at members of my team as I delivered the points they'd asked me to remember. I pointed at Josh's charts and graphs to emphasize the most important factual details. But I focused on the people I did *not* know in the room as I hit a crescendo on the central theme that I knew bound me together with my fellow citizens.

Everywhere you look you find the paper companies' PCBs. In the Fox River, throughout the bay, in every drop of water, there are paper mill PCBs. You can measure paper mill PCBs in the shallow waters of the Cat Island Chain near the river, in the deep waters by Washington Island, and in the northern reaches of Big Bay de Noc, a hundred miles north of here. Every scoop of sediment, every emerging insect, every fish, and every bird eating our bay's insects or fish, has measurable PCBs from the paper mills. It has been this way for decades, and it will be for decades more.

It was no shallow sales pitch. This is what most motivated me, and I was passionate about sharing it with the audience. As the presentation ended, I looked back to my team. They were smiling, even Frank and Bill. And people around the room were nodding. Maybe this was more like being the conductor than a soloist. I had finally engaged with the Green Bay community that night—directly. It energized me even more than I'd expected. Maybe I wouldn't miss fieldwork after all.

Afterward, residents lined up for their turn at the microphone. There was anticipation in the air, and plenty of frustration with the lack of progress on the river after four years of the state's voluntary cleanup with the paper mills. A member of the Menominee Indian tribe set the tone for why they were all there. "We came here tonight because we share a common interest," he said. "We love the land."

Many wanted to know the extent of PCB pollution, its effects on local fish and wildlife, and when the cleanup would occur. Others came with a simple wish. "I would like to be around to see some of the Fox River cleaned up enough so you can eat the fish," said a local resident. "The way things are going, I'm not going to make it" (Campbell 1997b).

Then Clean Water Action's Rebecca Katers stepped up to the mic and asked the question I had been hoping to hear all night. Noting that the federal damage assessment would address economic damages and fish and wildlife injuries—but not human health effects—Katers asked what nobody in the room could answer. "Where are the DNR and the EPA in assessing the human health risks?"

Now all of Green Bay could see Dave Ullrich hesitating on the sideboard of his stolen truck.

Only a month later, on June 18, 1997, Dave publicly announced that EPA was seeking Wisconsin's support in adding the Fox River to the Superfund National Priorities List. The decision had finally been settled, despite years of Wisconsin's opposition and EPA's equivocation. In a letter to Governor Thompson, Dave said adding the Fox to the list would lead to a comprehensive cleanup in the shortest reasonable time frame.

"The people who enjoy the Fox River and Lake Michigan deserve aggressive action, and we hope to move forward in partnership with the state, tribes, and local communities," he wrote. Dave noted, somewhat ominously, that if necessary EPA was prepared to move forward with the Superfund process—independent of the State of Wisconsin. Each year of delay sent another six hundred pounds of PCBs flowing from the Fox River into the bay of Green Bay and Lake Michigan, and that was under normal circumstances. A major storm could send much of the remaining ninety thousand pounds of sediment-bound PCBs into the bay in one flush.

I framed the picture Darlene took of me on our back porch the day Dave made his public announcement. It shows me drinking twelve-year old Macallan Scotch and smoking a Partagas No. 10 cigar. Both were gifts from Bill Conlon, my old friend in Ohio who now enjoyed a more extravagant lifestyle than I did. Roger Grimes, EPA's attorney, warned me not to share the photo widely because Dave Ullrich was still nervous. That was fine with me as long as EPA staff were actually about to join my inner circle—or, technically, I was about to join theirs.

For the rest of 1997 and the beginning of '98, my team and I worked closely with EPA. My goal was to transfer information from the damage assessment to EPA as completely and quickly as practical. I wanted to ensure consistency between the Fish and Wildlife damage assessment and EPA's cleanup study.

More than that, I wanted to prevent DNR from gaining complete

David Allen in Algoma, Wisconsin, celebrating EPA's announcement that the Fox River would be listed as a Superfund site
(National Priorities List), 1997. (Darlene Allen)

control of the cleanup while continuing to give in to demands from the
paper companies and the governor.

THE GOVERNOR RESPONDS

Susan Campbell

The response from Wisconsin was that EPA might just have to move forward alone with Superfund. "The last thing we need now is Washington

coming in and imposing its heavy-handed ineffective methods on Wisconsin," said Governor Thompson's spokesman Kevin Keane. "It will only get in the way and slow down the improvement of the Fox River" (Hildebrand and Campbell 1997a).

The governor himself had harsher words when he spoke to about 130 members of the Wisconsin Paper Council who gathered in early June at Appleton's Paper Valley Hotel for their annual meeting. "We have companies that want to come in and give $10 million to help clean up the Fox. They are working with the Department of Natural Resources but the Fish and Wildlife Service says, 'We want to sue you.' I mean, why?" Then, with his trademark belligerence, Thompson went on: "Those brilliant socialists in Washington, DC want to come in and screw up the works" (Murphy 1997).

PART II

THE FEDS TAKE
THE CASE

Let me embrace thee, sour adversity, for wise men say it is the wisest course.
—William Shakespeare

In the moment, each of us necessarily believes we are the hero of our own story—even those of us later judged to be villains.
—Daniel H. Wilson

5

CAN'T WE ALL JUST
GET ALONG?

THE PLAN

David Allen

In 1997, the federal agencies were beginning to close ranks in preparation for a seemingly inescapable showdown with Wisconsin, with EPA figuring out how to take back the sediment cleanup from Fish and Wildlife and returning to the norm under Superfund.

Fortunately, dozens of Wisconsin DNR experts continued their work without letting the conflict affect their results or their commitment to science, the public, and their own mandates. Dale Patterson led the way, but he was not alone. I routinely relied on DNR experts' honesty and willingness to talk. But it was becoming increasingly dangerous for these civil servants to appear anything less than devoted to Governor Thompson's demands.

My initial DNR contacts in 1992, introduced by Dale Patterson from within the agency and Ken Stromborg from my office, spread quickly to include dozens of DNR staff. They helped my team find credible evidence and use it correctly. They were important sounding boards for my team as we collected and analyzed new data. Staff in DNR's Green Bay district office knew the local scene, including the long history of paper mill discharges, as well as the mills' legal and political maneuverings. The Green Bay staff also knew many of the best opportunities for environmental restoration around the bay. Dale Patterson's shop in Madison continued to drive the very center of PCB modeling, and knew most of the best opportunities for cleanup. Researchers in Madison, Green Bay, and in the field knew how PCBs were affecting fish and wildlife. Economists in Madison had important advice about how to measure public values. PR professionals in Green Bay and Madison were adept at accentuating governmental progress without highlighting intergovernmental strife. Attorneys at DNR and Wisconsin DOJ provided sound, if necessarily informal, advice.

Superfund had already sucked all the oxygen out of the room for the Fox River Coalition. Maryann Sumi left DNR and was eventually rewarded by Governor Thompson with a judicial appointment. But the governor's remaining DNR operatives were going to be madder than hornets. I was increasingly careful to allow state staff to choose their own opportunities and methods for helping my team. Some had been fairly brazen in the past, and a few had paid a steep personal price through reassignment, official admonishment, or forced public apologies to the paper companies. Now, everyone was about to become more cautious, at least if they cared about their careers.

It was also looking like the PCB story might start to compete even more with the nightly stories about the Packers. It would be harder and harder for anyone to hide from the growing glare of the spotlight.

By the end of 1997, I knew I was at the center of something truly consequential. The paper companies had a tiger by the tail. They and their proxies at DNR had already failed to abort the damage assessment before it was born. They had also failed to lure Fish and Wildlife into voluntary complacency during their negotiations with Bill Hartwig. And they never convinced my team to offer terms for cooperation as unreasonably favorable to the companies as had the state via their Fox River Coalition. Now, EPA was jumping into the Fox River with both feet over the objection of a governor.

It was the most surprising and satisfying governmental decision I would encounter in my entire career.

I continued to focus on long-standing objectives. My highest priority remained arming EPA with enough facts, legal context, and political will to complete the Superfund cleanup in the face of direct, expert resistance from the paper companies. I would also help counter indirect opposition from DNR, whose Fox River staff continued to despise federal intrusion. Second priority: complete our damage assessment so Fish and Wildlife could fix the contaminated sediment via the damage assessment's "sediment restoration" provision should EPA fall short in its cleanup authorities. Third priority was to complete the more traditional aspects of the damage assessment, which would measure damages to the system persisting even after an adequate cleanup, mostly attributable to PCBs already in the bay of Green Bay that were beyond practical cleanup.

With EPA finally officially on board, I now began to refine my strategy for achieving all three objectives. I visualized a whole series of formal technical determinations published by Fish and Wildlife for the Green Bay damage assessment under the auspices of the Superfund law. Bill Hartwig could sign those determinations as the properly delegated "authorized official" for the federal government. I was pretty sure my team's work could win official endorsement from Michigan and the tribal co-trustees, as well—with or without Wisconsin.

Each official NRDA determination could be published in the *Federal Register* and anchor a formal public review, starting with a public meeting. More important, each determination could create a coherent and credible story about the Green Bay PCB problem based on the very best scientific evidence available, including new data produced specifically for the damage assessment. A whole series of technical determinations on every key element of the damage assessment could command attention from the scientific community and the public, for months or years, just as EPA's all-important cleanup studies came to life.

Two different but related stories were about to unfold before the public. First, the increasingly heated disputes between Wisconsin and the Feds would continue. Politics and turf would continue to dominate that storyline. However, a second storyline could begin to explain factual details, scientific principles, and legal consequences. My plan was to use the first storyline about conflict as a megaphone for the second about facts and the law. I trusted that facts and the law carried more weight than political rhetoric for finally fixing the Fox River and bay of Green Bay. I trusted that even DNR's Fox River leaders ultimately would have to recognize that. Facts and the law would also sharpen the government's arguments with the paper companies, which were always going to be the real opponents to a comprehensive and costly cleanup and restoration.

Fortune was smiling on this far-reaching scheme, at least for now. Secretary of the Interior Bruce Babbitt was firmly on board at the very top of my agency. Regional Director Bill Hartwig had full delegated authority for Interior and he was not just on board, he was on a mission. Annual budgets for the case were in the millions. Justice was now leading the legal team in harmony with a newly assigned attorney from Interior, and government attorneys from nine different offices were all pulling their weight. The technical team had increased to about a hundred members, all plugged into Frank Horvath, the "case manager" and me, the "assessment manager." I now reported directly to Frank, leapfrogging over Ken Stromborg and his supervisor in the Green Bay office. Most important: I now had the chance to conduct the entire orchestra. I was at the very center of communications between the technical team, the legal team, and a suddenly short and efficient command line. And Frank, Matt Richmond at Justice, and I had already mostly convinced the rest of the legal team, Hagler Bailly, and Bill Hartwig that going public quickly paid more dividends than waiting for a trial that might never begin. I was also at the center of communications with EPA staff just as they were building the infrastructure for the key federal cleanup study: the Remedial Investigation and Feasibility Study. And I was now the official public face of the damage assessment, rather than its behind-the-scenes emissary.

I also began a quiet shuttle diplomacy between Frank Horvath, Matt Richmond, Main Justice, and my economists to design a "draft" litigation strategy, just in case my efforts with EPA, DNR, and the public unraveled. Nobody wanted a federal trial. Being prepared for one was the best way to prevent it. But an actual trial, if it became necessary, would put Justice in charge and transform my experts into Justice's witnesses. There would always be competing trial strategies beyond my control, but the assessment work conducted now would limit the facts that Justice could pursue later, at trial.

My quiet knitting behind the scenes led to a sophisticated but unofficial negotiation and litigation strategy (Allen 2003, 2009, 2010). Only a handful of people would ever hear about it if my main plans actually worked to bring EPA and DNR completely into Superfund. We had to continue to pressure EPA and DNR to join us while we engaged paper company lawyers about the rules for participating in the damage assessment. But more than that, we had to highlight facts sufficient to catalyze legitimate settlements and lay the foundation for litigating natural resource damage claims in federal district court, with or without the cleanup agencies.

Preparing for litigation was the ultimate source of leverage on all fronts, but going public quickly, before trial attorneys faced their normal court deadlines, was key. We needed flexibility in calculating damages, preferably in ways that could win legal advantages from following the federal damage assessment regulations.*

The plan was to conduct two separate economic studies that calculated both costs and values of PCB-caused losses and restoration-caused gains, then use the emerging or final results in every context needed.

Fishing damages would be the very center of the damage assessment case because they would be the easiest to prove and a very big deal. There were a lot of fishermen in the bay and a history of decades of PCB consumption advisories throughout thousands of square miles.

---

* Due to a lack of case law, the exact benefit of the rebuttable presumption under the Comprehensive Environmental Response, Compensation and Liability Act and federal NRDA regulations at 43 CFR Part 11 is mostly untested. It might only limit the risk of summary judgment for dismissal before trial, or it might give trustee results additional deference. Trustees and Potentially Responsible Parties routinely argue about whether and how completely a "thumb on the scale" would actually materialize for trustees after successfully following federal regulations as envisioned by the statute.

Plus, studies of the economic impacts on recreational fishing resulting from consumption advisories were common and the techniques used were relatively uncontroversial. Job 1 was measuring this bright economics signal using state-of-the-art techniques and stellar experts. This centerpiece could satisfy the most cautious attorney if a trial was ever really needed.

On the other hand, fish consumption advisories were not the only kind of injury that could be proved, and anglers were not the only people affected. So the team would also measure total values and costs of all PCB injuries to every member of the public near the river and bay. Damages could then be calculated as costs or values (or both) of fishing damages or total damages (or both) for negotiations or litigation (or both). Plus, the studies would account for the whole range of cleanup options: fast or slow, complete or not, and under EPA's authorities or the trustees'.

Frank Horvath had his hands full supervising me. He said he worried my round wire-rimmed glasses, gold earring, and goatee might rub senior officials the wrong way, especially in the field-oriented, sometimes militaristic hook-and-bullet crowd that dominated Fish and Wildlife. More than that, Frank worried that my demands, particularly on our own command line, might be dismissed as too strident. So he made it his business to routinely remind me of the legitimate boundaries and essential structures of our institution.

One such reminder came when I received an unexpected package while on vacation in the middle of nowhere. It was a cell phone. It was my first, a Nokia—this was before the invention of smartphones—and it was from Frank. There was no paperwork, just Frank's official return address. It brought to mind the self-destructing tape recorder featured at the start of every *Mission Impossible* episode I had watched as a kid. "Your mission, should you decide to accept it . . ." I had turned on the phone and called its voicemail, just in case Frank had detailed a mission. But it was only a cell phone in a simple cardboard envelope arriving out of the blue. I never figured out how he tracked down my remote location or how he'd convinced FedEx to deliver there. And I never asked. The unspoken message was clear enough, if a little disquieting. Stay in touch. Always.

Frank also required face-to-face meetings in his Fort Snelling office every few weeks. There was always an avalanche of details to cover, but these meetings served another purpose. Frank was keeping me on a leash just short enough to avoid disaster. We had to stay on the same page or the whole case would blow apart. Frank was the road to institutional power; I was the network of paths to factual details. Frank steered the wheel; I had the map.

I knew Frank's judgment was sound, his advice invaluable, and I trusted his well-calibrated radar for reading others. I learned to trust his eroding patience as a critical warning signal that my battering-ram approach might cause more harm than good.

Darlene and I loved living in Ahnapee Township. Our Sears catalogue house, built in 1910 for about $1,000, sat on six acres that once had been at the center of an apple orchard and later a dairy farm. The barns now housed our boat, cars, and snow blower, as well as abandoned hay, an assortment of feral cats, and wild animals that constantly entertained Brutus. The abandoned fields were now grassland, scrub, and cedar, plus a few old apple trees. A road of rocks, taken from the fields over the decades, connected the back door of the country house to a neighbor's deer camp, just down the hill. Past the camp and a pond full of spring peepers, the Ahnapee State Trail and Ahnapee River beckoned just a quarter-mile hike, ski, or snowshoe away. Jump in the kayak, and Lake Michigan was only a short three-mile paddle downriver.

The main attraction of this home was solitude. The whole township, a little over thirty square miles, had fewer than one thousand people, the same population as in 1880. There wasn't a single traffic light in the entire county, unlike any other county in the state. You had to have a reason to travel here. It wasn't on the way to anything from anywhere. My family and I ran free out our back door whenever we wanted. Most days, only a car or two would pass by the front of the house on tiny

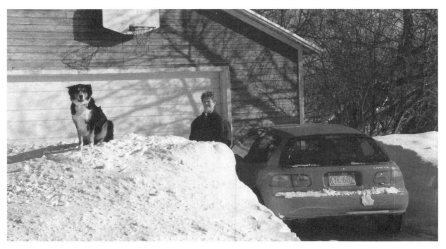

Brutus, Darlene, and the Honda Civic VX at the Farm near Algoma, Wisconsin, 1995. (P. David Allen II)

County Road M. A farm tractor or combine was more common in summer, or a snowmobile in winter.

Visiting friends and relatives marveled at the remoteness. Time moved more slowly here, and the world seemed very far away. Bill Conlon, in particular, loved visiting my rural home—he called it the Farm—because he could decompress, far from the stresses of his life in Columbus, Ohio. Bill's sporadic visits were a welcome break for me, too. He delivered a shot in the arm as my sense of isolation was growing in response to the Fox River case. Bill had taken a serious interest in the case. He asked penetrating questions and demanded context, even if it took hours to tell. As he had throughout our youth, Bill would match me—point-counterpoint—inferring meaning, spotting consequences, and challenging assumptions. He was now an essential sounding board.

Work could feel even more isolating than the Farm. There, thirty miles to the west in Green Bay, I had plenty of colleagues, but most days I didn't speak with anybody in person but Joe Moniot. My team lived elsewhere: mostly Chicago, Fort Snelling, Madison, Milwaukee, DC, and Boulder, Colorado. Ken Stromborg was around, but he resented being left behind by Bill Hartwig, and I rarely had the time or energy to keep him in the loop. The rest of the office mostly learned about the case from rumors rippling through the region, complaints from DNR, or the latest story that burst from the press.

The isolation was deeper than the physical distance from my team members, though. I was now reaching deeply within to magnify the team's reach and create real consequences for DNR and the paper companies. I was caught in the center of a vortex I had intentionally amplified and driven right into. I now held in my grasp all the strands of the case, even as the electricity running through them was nearly unbearable.

I had many reliable and capable partners at the center of the case, but nobody else wanted all that voltage at once. Nobody else seemed willing to endure the turbulence of the vortex for long. My secret weapons were a high tolerance for pain and enough discipline to channel my odd personality quirks into advantages. As always, my strategy was straightforward: follow the facts wherever they lead, channel obsessive attention to strategic details, and ride the waves of emotional resolve when opponents distorted or played unfairly. Then, try to win the public with honest persuasion.

There were times when I felt bad about the lack of compassion and empathy I often conveyed to others involved in the case and around its periphery. I knew my own severity exacerbated or even caused some of their resistance, especially from DNR and within my own agency. Frank and I likely amplified each other's intensity, and I couldn't really blame those who disliked us. Truth be told, there were quite a few people in the Green Bay matter I would have enjoyed in a casual setting, far removed from the case. But I had neither the time nor energy to spare, even for the people I liked. I always came to the same conclusion: high-stakes Superfund litigation was more like a full-contact sport than hanging out with friends. The personal stakes were also high: too much adrenaline and too little camaraderie, peaceful contemplation, or fun; too often a battering ram, too seldom a friend; too many risks of crashing spectacularly, too few chances for everybody to win. And, increasingly, too alone. I often reminded myself of the big picture, recentering myself and my role within it. The bay, the public, and the team all mattered. Somehow, I surprised myself by surviving another day, returning home to a personal solitude that made up for my professional isolation.

PCB QUEEN

Susan Campbell

Once the EPA announced the Fox River was ripe for listing as a Superfund site, news stories about an actual river cleanup gained currency. The Superfund label had instantly bestowed both notoriety and legitimacy to a topic that for several years had been coming of age. Now it was in full bloom. The endless speculation and political wagering about whether the Fox River would be proposed for listing gave way to stories about how such an immense and controversial federal process would play out, and its potential impact on the community and paper mills. By now, I was completely immersed in reporting the story. The newspaper was exploring every angle—publishing editorials, editorial cartoons, and any number of special reports in addition to the daily grind of news stories. My Fox River stories often graced the front page now, frequently with big six-column headlines that rivaled the Packers coverage—and even Brett Favre.

But for all the attention the Fox River story was receiving, it had a way of isolating me from my office colleagues. PCB Queen was now my informal newsroom title and, though said in jest, there was often an edge to it. The story had become so complex and nuanced that the metro editor's eyes usually glazed over as I related the latest developments. I began timing his responses and was dismayed to find I typically had under ten seconds to hook his attention with a story before he lost interest.

At home at night, standing in the galley kitchen of our small but quaint Tudor-style home, Tom was my sounding board, and I often relied on his innate ability to read the motivations of the various players. Since our first meeting in journalism class at Boston University, we'd always bounced ideas off one another, in life and in work. I found I needed his counsel now more than ever, given the story's ever-shifting pieces, distortions, and shadowy behind-the-scenes-maneuvering—despite my best efforts to bring them into the light.

In the newsroom, a seasoned editorial writer with a scholarly air was my other sounding board, and he stopped by my desk regularly to ruminate about the paper's next piece on the cleanup. He believed strongly in the paper's role as public advocate and took seriously the role the *Press-Gazette* and its editorials played in the debate. Though the *Press-Gazette*'s editorial page writers supported the mills' quest for a locally controlled cleanup rather than one driven by Superfund, that first editorial that had so angered the environmental community because of its perceived knee-jerk bias toward the paper mills was by now a distant memory. The paper had taken the community's pulse and would see to it that the patient—the Fox River—could access a second opinion.

Fortunately, the *Press-Gazette* editors trusted me more and more to do my own thing. While I reveled in the relative freedom, it was also daunting. Sometimes I worried that maybe they trusted me too much, that I was performing a high-wire act and could come tumbling down at any time. With potentially hundreds of millions of dollars on the line for the paper companies and all the complexities of the scientific and technical facts, a major error could be devastating. Sure, the editors supported me—but would they have my back if I published a big blunder? The thought paralyzed me at times, leading me to double-check even the facts I could recite in my sleep by now. I still had the dictation machine, but now I used it to tape marathon interviews that I regularly peppered with "Just one more question," hoping to signal to my source and myself that our call was finally almost over—even though we both knew better.

I was glad I could now transcribe my own notes, though this had become a new handicap. To guard against any claims of mistakes or misrepresentation, I voiced all my Fox River interviews into the computer, then spent hours culling through them to confirm facts and quotes before filing my stories. I was also an exacting writer, not known for punctuality. The combo often drove our otherwise easygoing metro editor to the brink. "Where's that story, Campbell?" he'd grumble across the newsroom, running his hands through his thick, dark hair in nervous exasperation. I knew that tone and gesture well—so well that in off-deadline moments I'd glance to see if his hairline was receding, worried I'd feel partially responsible if it was. Back on deadline, I'd brace for his warning: "One minute to send over whatever you have!" Heart pounding, I'd add one more sentence or make one more fact check before the inevitable "CUT THE CORD. NOW!" The metro editor would stare at his computer screen, fingers poised, waiting for the story to appear. At times it seemed I had to muster an out-of-body experience to hit the "send" key. I often wondered at such moments if I'd chosen the wrong profession.

In addition to my Dictaphone and voice-activated computer, I was helped by other new technology in the newsroom. The new Bloomberg terminal, acquired by the business department to give its staff regular access to financial news and the stock market, held an even greater appeal for me. It was the only newsroom computer with Internet access. The federal and state governments were early adopters of the World Wide Web, and often used it to post official documents for the public. It meant I could peruse the voluminous Fox River reports and studies from the newsroom now, instead of requesting and waiting for printed copies to arrive in the mail. When I spied an opening at the new terminal, I'd head over to print out the thick government reports and take them back to my desk to mark up with yellow sticky notes and a highlighter. "Tree killer," a reporter who occupied a nearby desk would taunt as the newly printed pages stacked up in the tray. "You'd think an environmental reporter would know better."

My Fox River reporting sometimes put me at odds with another newsroom colleague, one who had worked for Fort Howard before joining the *Press-Gazette* as a reporter and business columnist in the mid-'80s. His insider ties to the paper industry often paid off, and his column enjoyed something of a cult-like following in Green Bay. A ruddy Irishman with twinkling blue eyes, quick wit, and equally quick temper, he'd signal he was having a bad day by slamming the door when he entered the newsroom. I tried to keep on his good side.

On some mornings the door would slam with extra vigor. Never sure of his target on a given day, I'd feel an involuntary shudder if I'd filed a particularly charged story the night before. "The paper mills weren't breaking any laws when they discharged the PCBs," his voice boomed across the room at me on more than one occasion as he slammed that day's newspaper on his desk. There was no middle ground where the paper companies were concerned. The chasm between us was like the gulf that divided the two sides up and down the Fox River, and it wouldn't be bridged.

The paper's executive editor, Carol Hunter, was doubtless under similar pressure, though she never let on. Two of the seven targeted paper companies were in our coverage area, including Fort Howard. A no-nonsense, straight shooter who had grown up on a farm in Kansas, Hunter was a quick study and a deep thinker. Serious and reserved, she was passionate about the truth and the public's right to know. She guided the paper with a steady hand, her calm, low voice revealing a midwesterner's reserve and unflappability. She had a strong belief in community journalism and pushed hard for in-depth reporting on major local issues. Without question, the Fox River was one that rose to the top for her. In time, Hunter gave me a long leash to follow my leads and saw to it that the Fox River stories had ample space and A-1 prominence. She also pushed hard for regular in-depth coverage of the controversy, publishing serialized stories that dug deeply into all sides of the debate, the emerging science, and the public's response. Although other newspapers and broadcast media were covering the story, Hunter saw to it that the *Press-Gazette* was leading the way and devoting substantial resources to it.

I worked hard to maintain her trust. Without the executive editor's support and vision, the Fox River story wouldn't be reported as aggressively or comprehensively by the paper, or by the other local media. The public would pay the price. The *Press-Gazette* was the third-largest paper in Wisconsin, and the Fox River ran right through its coverage area. More important, the bay of Green Bay was in the *Press-Gazette*'s backyard, and the bulk of the river's toxic PCBs flowed northward from the Fox Cities to ultimately settle in the bay. The city of Green Bay was ground zero. It was no coincidence that most of the environmental activists were in Green Bay, and that the Fox Cities—"Paper Valley"— tended to sympathize with the paper companies.

If any media outlet was going to cover the damage and cleanup in a way that best protected the public's interest, it was going to be the *Press-Gazette*.

THE PAPER COMPANIES

David Allen

The paper companies were playing their part well, too well for my comfort. They had already hired many well-known experts whose background and experience helped company arguments the most. They were refining a series of clever and legitimate points that focused on key uncertainties about cleanup and restoration. If successful, they could limit how much the paper companies would have to pay to clean up their PCB mess and make the public whole, even if EPA finally brought its full authority to bear.

Fundamentally, the paper companies had refused for years to pay for significant cleanup actions in the river until somebody could prove just how much any individual action, like removing PCB-contaminated sediments from the river bottom, would reduce risk and injuries to people and the environment. Cleanup justification under the law required more than the narrowly defined engineering solutions initially offered by DNR, which focused mostly on PCB pounds removed per additional dollar spent on dredging. Instead, *successful* cleanup arguments would have to include more complete and complicated scientific analyses conducted by specific legal authorities showing how much various cleanup actions helped and at what cost.

Company experts also hammered away at potential problems that could come from digging up PCB-contaminated sediments from the river bottom. PCB discharges into the river had peaked during the 1970s, and as PCB releases declined in subsequent decades, the layers of new Fox River sediments were progressively less contaminated.

Leaving the sediments in place and doing nothing might allow this trend to continue until a natural "clean enough" cap successfully buried and contained the older, dirtier sediments. Beyond that, the company experts argued that storms and high river flows were not as dangerous as government agencies warned. Rare flooding events were the most likely way to cause catastrophic movement of Fox River sediment and spill the entrapped PCBs into the bay of Green Bay. But it was hard to predict exactly how big, and how rare, a flood would have to be to cause such a PCB catastrophe. Rare flood events did not coincide with the multitudinous river sampling days recorded in Fox River studies—and if they had, the sampling would not have been practical while floodwaters raged. That meant the question of just how big and rare a storm would have to be to flood Green Bay with more Fox River PCBs could not be easily resolved with data.

The companies also pointed to many environmental impacts beyond their own responsibility, and cast doubt about how much could be fixed by focusing solely on their share of the bay's problems. They pointed to other sources of PCBs all around Lake Michigan, and other sources along the Fox River. These included governmental sources, like agencies that recycled carbonless copy paper containing PCBs, and local wastewater treatment plants that accepted industrial wastewater for treatment. Even if forced to accept responsibility, the paper companies could use these arguments to reduce their share of the blame and the costs. They also pointed to other contamination in the bay, like atmospheric mercury from power plants and chemical DDT from widespread agricultural use, to show how a PCB cleanup wouldn't rid the bay of all toxic pollution. They highlighted how fish and wildlife populations were constantly changing because of natural factors like migration and weather. And they pointed out that these populations were changing due to other, non-PCB factors, like hunting and fishing, habitat destruction, and exotic species invasions—all to show that a PCB cleanup wouldn't eliminate every last injury to fish and wildlife. Finally, they offered up inexpensive but popular public restoration projects, like park improvements, as alternatives to expensive PCB cleanup. In short, the companies asserted that whatever benefits might come from cleaning up paper company PCBs, they were likely insignificant compared to other actions that could be much more practical—and much cheaper.

I surveyed all of these plausible arguments and wondered how I might prevent the paper companies from turning them into a sea of obfuscation stretching out in every direction as far as anyone could see. I knew that the paper companies might well succeed in befuddling the public by pressing legitimate arguments too far. So I resolved to test every one of them. I would use the best experts in the country to delve deep into the mountain of scientific data already collected in Green Bay. I would aim my impressive team at turning that mountain of data into evidence applicable under the Superfund law, and at collecting new data wherever necessary to meet legal requirements. I would prove the company arguments correct or incorrect in the eyes of the law. Ferreting out the truth was at the very heart of my strategy. Doing that well could win the support of the scientific community and the public. Doing that by the book could win with attorneys and courts. It was also the surest way to unify reluctant government agencies and force paper company attorneys and officers to ultimately confront whichever scenarios turned out to be true.

The paper companies were usually unified in their skepticism about government proposals and programs to clean up and restore the river and bay, but I noticed big differences in style when individual companies pled their particular cases. I began to think of each as a distinct personality, and this helped me navigate my interactions with them. Fort Howard was the sophisticated ringleader, the chess player always thinking many moves ahead, hiring experts and attorneys with impressive résumés, and displaying subtlety in its iron-willed resistance. P. H. Glatfelter was more aggressive, more adamant, louder—even sarcastic—and less in the mood to compromise, but also flamboyant and fun to watch. National Cash Register and Appleton Papers were more buttoned down and corporate, hard to read, hard to move, but willing to compromise if their spreadsheets suddenly showed enough advantage. The other mills seemed more like small mom-and-pop operations, open-minded but worried and trying hard to keep up with the big dogs. Together, the Fox River Group was formidable, but the partnership was fragile. I was pretty sure those personalities would lead to conflicts behind the scenes, that the eventual allocation of responsibility among the companies would drive wedges into their group quicker and deeper than any of Fort Howard's ploys to turn DNR against the other agencies. Indeed, the best way for each company to reduce its own share of cleanup costs and damages would be, ultimately, to blame the others.

Still, the paper companies would be sharpening their knives and skillfully using them to carve up the government's plans. They would reserve their best technical and legal arguments, as well as their best technical and legal experts, for the times and places of greatest impact. They would hit every official government document with volumes of criticism. At the same time, they would continue to drive wedges among the agencies by offering dangerously clever compromises during vulnerable negotiations. And they would threaten worried government managers with litigation and bad press as the alternative. No matter what happened during negotiations, the companies would continue to lobby elected officials in Madison and Washington, and they would amplify public criticism of the Feds and Superfund everywhere within their reach. They would project their influence quietly in back rooms with sympathetic bureaucrats and politicians, and loudly at meetings, in the press, and on radio and television. And their arguments would resonate far and wide. Meanwhile, paper company allies, especially those within financial or political reach, would trumpet, amplify, and expand company arguments without worrying much about stubborn facts or legal context. These emissaries would soon step up for duty: from local businesses and trade groups; from sympathetic media and paid advertisers; from local officials reliant on paper company taxes and cooperation; from people who'd already made up their minds about the evils of regulation; and from people who viewed the world only through a partisan political lens.

The paper companies were formidable adversaries. Yet I had faith that the facts could rule the day. The mills were highlighting facts they hoped could legitimately limit or alter the scope of proposed cleanup and restoration in the Fox River and the bay of Green Bay. But powerful arguments were also coming into focus about just how big the problem really was. Revealing the facts most relevant to the law was the best way to determine the cleanup and restoration answers. Revealing them directly to the scientific community and the public was the best way to ensure that governmental agencies followed the facts, regardless of how much resistance the paper companies put forth.

It wouldn't be easy. The paper companies were exceptionally skilled at this game. But EPA's Remedial Investigation and Feasibility Study could create the necessary analyses for cleanup decisions. The RI/FS, as it was called, would also carry the full weight of the Superfund law—which was the real reason the companies opposed the entire Superfund program.

I already knew I could rely on Jim Hahnenberg, EPA's on-the-ground Superfund manager, and Roger Grimes, EPA's lead counsel. However, influencing the federal agency's weighty institutional momentum would require more than careful coordination with Jim and Roger. So, I committed to deploy my team to bolster EPA at every turn. Fish and Wildlife would spend as much effort working with EPA as it did on its own damage assessment. More critically, I would aim the entire damage assessment at a very public explanation of technical and scientific facts that underpinned both the damage assessment *and* EPA's RI/FS. Attention from the public and the scientific community would carry even more weight with EPA than Fish and Wildlife's technical assistance and formal comments, and hopefully more than the litany of inevitable complaints from the Wisconsin DNR. It could also help sway skeptical paper company attorneys and officers.

In signing those first seventeen Information Request letters back in February 1996, Bill Hartwig had triggered an avalanche of documents that would eventually risk smothering the Reading Room we'd set up in our Green Bay office. The negotiations over whether—and when—any of the seven paper companies in the Fox River Group would respond to requests took months. Some of the companies claimed "confidential business information" protections, which required Fish and Wildlife to establish rigid document control procedures—and to buy a really good safe. The subsequent negotiations with the companies over the thoroughness of their responses lasted years more. By 1998, all of them had complied.

The Fox River Group companies responded to our request letters by sending information that included highly sensitive documents about corporate ownership, finances, and PCB measurements the paper mills themselves had taken over the years. But the companies now had a new strategy in mind: they would bury Fish and Wildlife with hundreds of thousands of pieces of paper. To that end, boxes of documents were routinely delivered to the Green Bay office via UPS, FedEx, and U.S. mail. If I'd been away on travel, I could usually tell by the secretaries' sly smiles that a load had arrived even before I found the latest shipment blocking the path to my desk. If I was already at my desk, I'd discover the boxes blocking my office door when I tried to leave. P. H. Glatfelter, in particular, sent box after box of documents, and the documents inside every box looked like they had been deliberately shuffled. Each box held a mishmash of papers with disparate dates, subjects, and sources. I laughed out loud when I noticed Glatfelter's own legalistic numbering schemes in some of the boxes, probably from some earlier litigation. Even these blocks of documents were in haphazard order. Where's the next document? It could be anywhere, but probably in a different box! It was a deliberate mess, and my colleague Joe Moniot and I somehow had to sort it all out.

Some paper mill reps had ventured far enough into the Green Bay office to see Ken Stromborg's "lab" and the chaos of the rest of the field office, which might have led them to underestimate my team. Plus, it was probably obvious that Fish and Wildlife was way outside its institutional comfort zone when identifying responsible parties and sending Information Requests under the Superfund law. Given all this, the paper companies might well have been counting on my local office to drop the ball. I figured this could work to my benefit, reasoning that the companies may have been more lax than they should have been in deciding what information to send and how to obscure damning details. Hence, there might well be jewels in those carefully disorganized boxes, jewels that would lead to sending the companies more pointed and revealing Information Requests, and jewels that belonged in an expertly organized Reading Room for others to see.

My team was more than up to the task of organizing the documents, making sense of them, and using them effectively. Our secret weapon was Joe Moniot. A slim, unassuming man in his fifties, Joe was easy to miss except for his attire—which was somehow attuned to a previous decade, including thick, square, metal-rimmed glasses. He was quietly relentless, almost too meticulous, and very bright. In fact, Joe's awkward, quiet demeanor hid his passions, talents, and humor well. He would have first crack at this puzzle. Joe and I sat next to each other in the highly organized damage assessment office—an island within the disorganized chaos of the surrounding field office—and both of us reported directly to the uber-efficient Frank Horvath.

For its part, DOJ had already sent its experts to Green Bay to help set up the Reading Room, and they regularly advised us on how to maximize the room's potential. The Reading Room would serve a dual purpose. It leveled the playing field for the public, giving the public and press access to most of the information shared between the paper companies and the agencies. And it shielded Fish and Wildlife staff from being inundated with the paper companies' formal requests for federal documents. Such weaponizing of the U.S. Freedom of Information Act was a popular strategy companies used to hamstring federal scrutiny. Agency responses to these requests played right into the companies' hands, as it diverted massive agency time and effort away from the very work the companies sought to slow. My colleagues at Justice taught me how a reading room could not only thwart this strategy, but also take the fun out of it for the paper companies: "Come as often as you like! Copy everything!"

DOJ also hired a former EPA engineer with expertise in papermaking, PCB releases, and federal liability cases. He was a regular, if quiet, visitor to my office, and he would be drafting the next rounds of Information Requests from Bill Hartwig to the most significant PCB dischargers on the Fox River. Plus, Hagler Bailly had brought in a company with some of the best PCB fate and transport modelers in the country.

They would help Fish and Wildlife determine the pathways taken by PCB molecules after their discharge to the Fox, and also provide technical assistance for EPA and DNR. I now focused the whole team on the onslaught of paper company documents that threatened to overtake our humble Green Bay office. The companies' shuffling and diluting of files had no chance of deterring the team from unearthing useful documents for the liability case and PCB pathway determination. Indeed, it had the opposite effect.

I had other strong motives to make sense of these files: I wanted to make it easier for each company to point the finger at the others' liability. The seven paper companies could save Fish and Wildlife an enormous amount of time and effort by helping to identify PCB release and liability information about one another. The Reading Room was about to make the Green Bay field office a very popular destination.

The Reading Room featured about fourteen government-issue file cabinets painted in various drab colors that had been scratched and chipped over the years. These surrounded an old government-issue table with some folding chairs. Each cabinet had about eight drawers that were locked with metal bars and padlocks that Joe had picked up at Menards. The whole space was wedged into the field office's attached garage, which also housed dissection tables for cormorants and lake trout, and freezers for biological samples. Within the drab space and well-worn cabinets, however, a gold mine awaited. Each drawer contained long rows of brand-new identical, neatly labeled accordion files. Each file contained exactly eight hundred pages. Every single loose page was carefully stamped with a unique page number, and the entire Reading Room was sequentially ordered by those page numbers.

After making an appointment and signing in, anyone could peruse the documents and make copies. Hard copy indexes on the table pointed to every numbered cabinet, numbered drawer, numbered document, and numbered page. An electronic relational database cross-referenced every page number with document categories, dates, page ranges,

content summaries, and status under the federal Freedom of Information Act. Thus, any member of the public could search an electronic
listing of every document in the Reading Room.

There were literally hundreds of thousands of pages. Every document
relevant to the Green Bay Natural Resource Damage Assessment was
here, except those legitimately shielded from Sunshine Laws. Copies of
official government documents and correspondence, published literature, historical documents, press clippings, and responses to Information Requests filled the cabinets and lined the shelves in the increasingly
crowded Reading Room. At the time, Google Search, launched the previous year, was yet to prove its worth. Wikipedia wouldn't be invented
for another four years, Google Scholar not for another three years after
that. Digitizing documents to CDs still cost over $1 per page.

The Reading Room, for all its comically rickety appearance, was
cutting edge.

Soon after the Fox River Group companies finished sending responses to the first round of Information Requests, attorneys for each
company began making appointments to visit the Reading Room. I
gave the first visiting attorney a personal tour. Dressed in an expensive
suit, stylish shoes, and fine jewelry, my guest made no effort to hide
a smirk as he surveyed the space and feigned admiration for Fish and
Wildlife's "mahogany cabinets." I played along and asked if he wanted
a cup of coffee, apologizing that he might find the odor of dissected
lake trout offensive. I was still unlocking cabinets when the attorney
opened one of the drawers. He pulled out a folder, looked inside, then
visibly straightened and turned to me with a look of incredulity. In an
unguarded moment the lawyer asked, "Are these all copies? Did you
Bates-stamp every page?"*

"Yes," I deadpanned, then offered breezily: "You should be able to
find everything with the index on the table, but I'll be in my office if
you need any help." I suppressed my own smile now as I wondered how

---

* Bates stamps were mechanical inking devices that increased a numerical counter by one
with each press onto a new page. Joe Moniot and David Allen stamped every page in the
entire Reading Room.

much more surprised my guest would be if he knew about the duplicate case files my team was also maintaining in Milwaukee, Washington, and Boulder.

In the coming months, multiple law firms would copy every page in the Reading Room. It wouldn't be long before the companies began turning on each other.

THE SUPERFUND LISTING

Susan Campbell

As the federal team and Wisconsin DNR sparred behind the scenes on the damage assessment, and the Feds turned increasing attention to the drafting of the complicated and consequential Remedial Investigation and Feasibility Study, EPA was pursuing an official Superfund listing of the Fox River in earnest, with the goal of announcing a listing decision by 1998.

The rumblings grew louder on both sides of the divide.

Superfund would bring both a carrot and a stick: federal dollars to aid the cleanup and stiff fines for the polluters if they refused to cooperate. While many proponents and opponents alike favored a voluntary agreement among all sides, those supporting Superfund said the time had run out on that clock—DNR and the paper companies had failed to reach a settlement after more than five years of trying. Opponents said Superfund would undo the progress that had been made, and that its stigmatizing shadow would hurt local tourism and industry. And they said all the red tape that came with Superfund would only prolong the cleanup and cost more money.

And there was something else: the ever-shifting debate in Washington over the very existence of the Superfund program. An intervention in the Fox River Valley now could make the river a poster child for reforming—or eliminating—Superfund altogether. "A lot of this, from Washington's viewpoint, is not the Fox River as much as what it might mean for Superfund reauthorization and appropriations," the DNR's Bruce Baker told me in an interview (Campbell 1998p).

The battle lines, drawn a year earlier when EPA announced it was pursuing a potential Superfund listing for the Fox, were now solidly etched. Each side was doing its best to brace for, and possibly even steer, the decision.

Governor Thompson then sent a letter to EPA underscoring his opposition to Superfund and warning it would lead to "further liability concerns, delays, expenses, and possible litigation" (Campbell 1998r). The local chambers of commerce in the Fox Cities and Green Bay were also rushing to publicly oppose a Superfund listing. County and municipal leaders up and down the river likewise began passing resolutions that urged the paper mills and DNR to reach a cleanup agreement and thereby avoid the black eye they said a Superfund designation would surely bring. Some of the rhetoric was outright feverish. The president of the Fox Cities Chamber of Commerce and Industry told the press that naming the Fox River a federal Superfund site "would suggest to people that somehow the Fox River would be the equivalent of the Love Canal" (Campbell 1998q). Further, his group issued a startling statement in which it claimed, without evidence, that the cost of cleanup could reach $3 billion—an amount that dwarfed all previous estimates.

County governments also got in on the act. Winnebago and Outagamie Counties, home to Paper Valley, both passed resolutions opposing Superfund. Winnebago was first, voting after its board was visited by a Madison lobbyist representing the Fox River Group paper mills (Kneiszel 1998). The Brown County Board, home to the city of Green Bay, was pressured to follow suit by the county executive—who happened to be the sister-in-law of the *Press-Gazette* publisher. In a 5–2 vote, the board's executive committee broke ranks and recommended that the board reject the anti-Superfund resolution (Cioni 1998). The fact that nearly 90 percent of PCBs that remained in the river were lodged in Brown County river sediment doubtless weighed heavy on their minds.

Physical evidence of the divide started popping up along the Fox River in June, when upward of fifty signs were posted at public landings warning it was risky to eat fish from the river. "It's something the Department of Health and Department of Natural Resources do not do," said a representative of the Sierra Club, which orchestrated the sign postings (Campbell 1998f). He pointed out that the DNR printed forty thousand copies of its fish advisories each year—yet sold 1.2 million fishing licenses annually.

"I never heard about them until now," a local resident said of the state fish advisories (Campbell 1998f). I found the fifty-year-old fishing for walleye the morning a sign went up in De Pere, a popular spot for local anglers. "I've just heard people talking, saying not to make a habit of it," he said.

The intertwined fates of the Fox River and Paper Valley were also drawing attention and intervention from the nation's capital. Tensions were unusually high.

Local environmental groups were spooked. They'd heard that U.S. representative Mark Neumann, a Wisconsin Republican, was planning to reprise an earlier attempt at an end-run around a possible Super-fund listing for the Fox (Campbell 1998b). The year before, saying he was acting on behalf of Governor Thompson's office, Neumann had introduced a rider to an EPA budget bill before the House Appropri-ations Committee that would give governors veto authority over EPA Superfund designations within their own states. Neumann had been called out by U.S. representative Dave Obey, a Wisconsin Democrat who also sat on the committee. The ploy was sidelined and Neumann had vowed to come back to fight another day. "The price of democracy is eternal vigilance," the Sierra Club said of Obey's wariness. "This is a good example of that."

Other legislative threats would continue through the rest of the year, including a failed attempt by Mississippi Republican and Senate major-ity leader Trent Lott to shield companies like National Cash Register, which sold its wastes to recyclers, from liability.

Meanwhile, the Fox River paper companies were taking their cue from another fray over PCB pollution. For the last decade General Elec-tric had been fighting EPA on addressing its own extensive PCB pollu-tion in New York's Hudson and Massachusetts's Housatonic Rivers. The Fox River Group and its supporters were now using GE's script, and by 1998 had even hired one of the New York consultants employed by GE to conduct PCB sampling in the Fox River. GE was also using its considerable clout to pull strings behind the scenes, enlisting a New York congressman to attach controversial riders to Senate and House appropriations bills that would ban PCB dredging nationwide for at least a year until the practice could be studied.

The pace and breadth of the Fox River Superfund story that spring was relentless, hard to navigate, and even harder to distill for readers.

A professor of public administration at UW–Green Bay who also presided over the Green Bay Metroplitan Sewerage District Commission took a big-picture view. "It's a problem of trying to deal with extreme positions. How do you come up with the middle course?" (Campbell 1998q).

> We've got to invent one because the water is the main resource we have here. We don't have mountains. We don't have seashores. We don't have palm trees. We don't have a Mediterranean climate.
> We've got water.

That fact, and Green Bay's location as an entry point to the Great Lakes, gave the matter international importance as well. The Fox River's PCBs had come up again and again at meetings between the U.S. and Canada as both nations worked to address chemical contamination in the lakes. The Fox River was a leading contributor of North America's PCB contamination.

A political science professor at UW–Green Bay who specialized in environmental policy and wrote extensively on the subject underscored the national implications of the Fox River decision. "These are the kind of issues that gravitate up to the level of the vice president or president, the congressional leadership, or the highest level of EPA—precisely because they represent such an important challenge, and the position taken can affect decisions in the future," he told me (Campbell 1998p). "Whether it's a test case or not, it's a big deal. A big deal in terms of the length of the river being considered, in terms of the quantity of contaminated sediments, in terms of costs involved."

Throughout the year, uncertainty about EPA's next move hung over Paper Valley and over all the communities through which the Fox River ran its course. Governor Thompson was still dead set against a federal Superfund listing for the Fox. Back in 1997, EPA administrator Carol Browner had reassured elected officials that her agency would never bring Superfund to a state where the governor opposed it.

Or would it?

A week before EPA's Superfund chief in Washington, DC, was scheduled to announce his decision, I was hard at work trying to sniff out some sort of clue. Jim Hahnenberg and others in his EPA office in Chicago told me over the phone that even they didn't know where the decision stood.

What Hahnenberg did know: "The black eye on the community is there regardless of Superfund. Superfund doesn't change the fact that you have a PCB problem" (Campbell 1998q).

Behind the scenes, Hahnenberg and David Allen were now bringing a laser focus to the foundational details of the RI/FS, which was always going to determine actual cleanup decisions. It was also going to finally, and hopefully soon, put EPA's overwhelming Superfund authority at the center of making those decisions.

The wait soon ended. On July 9, 1998, EPA finally announced it was formally proposing the Fox River as a Superfund site, saying it easily qualified to join the ranks of the nation's worst toxic waste sites. In a letter to Governor Thompson and Wisconsin's congressional delegation, EPA's Superfund chief wrote that the primary driver behind his decision was that the river "poses very serious human health and ecological risks which are not being adequately addressed," and that "all the waters of Green Bay and Lake Michigan exceed PCB water quality standards for the protection of aquatic life and wildlife" (Campbell 1998h).

He reiterated his concern from a year earlier: the Fox River sent more than six hundred pounds of PCBs into Green Bay and Lake Michigan annually, and many more tons could be flushed in that direction in a single major storm. He referenced studies showing that local Hmong immigrant refugees were eating the contaminated fish, as well as other

studies linking PCB exposure to immune, reproductive, and neurologi-
cal effects in humans. Moreover, he cited clear evidence of deformities
and reproductive problems in a variety of local wildlife species, including bald eagles, lake trout, and migratory birds.

He indicated he was underwhelmed by the efforts of DNR and the
paper companies to fix the problem, despite years of knowing about the
contaminants in the river and more than five years of Fox River Coalition negotiations. "There is still no commitment for a comprehensive
approach to the whole river cleanup," he wrote, adding he was confident a Superfund listing proposal "will provide the needed incentive for
the Potentially Responsible Parties to negotiate more seriously with the
state and EPA" (Campbell 1998h).

At the same time, EPA propped open the door for Wisconsin and
the paper companies to devise a cleanup plan before EPA finalized the
listing, and said it would even consider delaying the listing if it appeared
the two sides were close to an agreement.

Some of Wisconsin's congressional delegation received this last invitation with open arms, seeing in it a roadmap for Wisconsin to avoid
Superfund's stigma. The *Green Bay Press-Gazette*'s editorial board also
embraced the invitation, urging DNR and the paper companies to follow the federal road map. "Paper mill executives repeatedly have told
the community they are committed to cleaning up the river. Now is the
time for that commitment to take shape," the newspaper's editorial said,
looking ahead to two pilot dredging projects that were planned for that
fall (*Green Bay Press-Gazette* 1998). "That must occur because a Superfund listing would be a mistake."

Predictably, Governor Thompson was livid. "This is the height of
Washington arrogance," he told the press. "This is just another example of the EPA and federal government stepping in and micromanag-
ing state matters—and ultimately making matters worse" (Campbell
1998h). The paper companies fell in line behind Thompson, criticizing
EPA for ignoring the governor's wishes and saying that federal involvement would only increase litigation and slow cleanup.

For Rebecca Katers of Clean Water Action Council in Green Bay,
the news had been a long time coming. She wasn't about to offer any

sympathy for Thompson being steamrolled by the Feds. "I find his comments ironic given he's had twelve years during his administration to make something happen on the river, and they've managed to pry loose less than 1 percent of the total cleanup cost," she said (Campbell 1998h).

The EPA had bucked tradition—and made history—by declaring its intent to impose Superfund in a state over the express objections of its governor.

A thousand miles away, EPA's leader underscored that message, clearly and unequivocally, when she appeared before a New York State Assembly committee. Administrator Carol Browner was in New York to counter GE's claims that the PCB contamination lining two hundred miles of the Hudson River presented no risk to human health. "I want to set the record straight about this chemical's serious threat to public health and the environment," Browner told the committee (Campbell 1998e). "We do not have every single answer, nor every single piece of data. But clearly, the science has spoken: PCBs are a serious threat—a threat to our health, a threat to our environment, a threat to our future. To suggest, as GE does, that no action should be taken because some of the PCB studies may be inconclusive, flies in the face of every decision this country has made in the last quarter century to protect human health and the environment."

THE SUPERFUND DANCE

David Allen

By March 1998, EPA had worked out a deal with Wisconsin that allowed DNR to lead the cleanup study with EPA oversight and funding. Though the move would soon present some predictable problems, granting DNR the titular lead was the only way for EPA to prevent an escalation of the already explosive Superfund listing proposal.

One of DNR's first tasks was to hire a consultant to draft the expansive and highly consequential Remedial Investigation and Feasibility Study. The EPA's cleanup studies were a critical component of the Superfund process because they would include all the important technical details.

Chief among these: technical assessments of just how much risk the Fox River PCBs posed to human health and the environment, including the fish and wildlife living throughout the bay. The answer to that thorny question would justify exactly how much of the PCB contamination should be cleaned up—and would be the most challenging, and controversial, phase of the Superfund process.

EPA's Jim Hahnenberg insisted that DNR open up the contract selection process to the federal agencies—after all, EPA was footing all the bills and had to approve every detail. Following proposals and interviews, Fish and Wildlife and EPA recommended the same consulting company, but DNR chose a different one recommended by the paper companies. EPA went along with DNR's choice, leaving me in disbelief: the Feds were already caving to DNR even as the state continued to carry water for the paper companies. I accelerated my plans to go public with every Fish and Wildlife technical determination on the damage assessment. Opening the process to public scrutiny would be the only way for the public to have a fighting chance at a Fox River cleanup that represented its best interests rather than those of the paper companies. It was also the best way to motivate EPA to finally, and decisively, step up and take the actual lead.

At the same time, my team was coming under mounting pressure from Susan Schneider and her bosses at DOJ to help bring the State of Wisconsin into the governmental fold. So, simultaneous with damage assessment publication plans, my team and I developed a strategy of working directly with EPA, and indirectly and quietly with DNR experts in Dale Patterson's shop, DNR's Green Bay district office, and Ken Stromborg's friends in DNR's research wing. My team helped develop technical positions for the RI/FS that worked for the federal family of agencies without offending DNR's legitimate experts. Then we helped coordinate with the entire intergovernmental partnership, which included DNR's official Fox River leaders and the tribes. Very quickly, Fish and Wildlife and Hagler Bailly became key supporters of EPA as its staff pressed Wisconsin to follow Superfund procedural requirements, use technical information credibly and consistently, and coordinate with the rest of the agencies. EPA's funding and legal authority under the Superfund law were effective inducements with DNR's Fox River staff. Still, they grew increasingly agitated by EPA's oversight, seeming to view it as unnecessary meddling. They also remained unhappy with my team's involvement with EPA.

Over time, the bonds between Fish and Wildlife and EPA strengthened, but Justice remained quite concerned about Wisconsin's continued hostility. My team needed to find some sliver of common ground and try to build additional consensus from there. Our best hope to avoid litigation and maximize leverage with the paper companies was to convince Wisconsin to truly join forces with the Feds. Superfund would present the paper companies with a tremendous litigation risk if EPA and DNR joined together to decide cleanup requirements based on credible data and clear legal authorities, buoyed by endorsement from the co-trustees. I hoped that if this scenario came to pass, the state would also be more agreeable about a joint damage assessment.

Starting in 1998, my team and I began participating in hundreds of calls with EPA staff and dozens of formal meetings with EPA and DNR about the cleanup studies. We also wrote dozens of formal letters commenting on key cleanup issues, particularly related to movement of PCBs in the river and bay, Ecological Risk Assessment, and the effectiveness of various PCB cleanup options. We participated in formal peer reviews, funded by the paper companies, about PCB fate and transport in the waterway as well as risk assessment. Funded by a special grant from EPA, Fish and Wildlife even took over drafting parts of the Ecological Risk Assessment—specifically covering the bay of Green Bay—when DNR refused to look beyond the Fox River in assessing health risks to local fish and wildlife. It was another sign of undue paper company influence over DNR, but EPA was beginning to fight back. Or rather, Jim Hahnenberg and Roger Grimes were beginning to win the struggles inside EPA.

It was a cool morning in the early summer of 1998 when I left in my red Honda Civic, now sporting a caved-in hood from an earlier deer collision, for the drive from Green Bay to Madison. I had to pick up Doug

Beltman at the Madison airport, find a parking spot near the capitol, and quietly meet with a handful of DNR experts about emerging data and their relevance to cleanup decisions.

Doug had studied as a chemist and ecologist before joining EPA's Superfund division in Chicago. Now he was working for Josh Lipton as Hagler Bailly's project manager on the Green Bay case. Doug was a tall, lanky man with auburn hair. Of Dutch descent, he was originally from Holland, Michigan. He was always the smartest guy in the room—and he knew it. He could seem impatient with people whose minds didn't process information as quickly as his, and unforgiving of those who resisted his advice. A frustrated economist at Hagler Bailly once quipped to me: "I hate when he makes a beeline for my office. I think of him as the Archangel of Retribution." I knew Doug was secretly understanding, though, and even kindhearted. Doug was now one of my key experts helping EPA understand the cleanup implications of DNR's technical memoranda. The "Tech Memos," as they came to be known, were produced by Dale Patterson's DNR section, and they were all about computer modeling of PCB movement in the Fox River. There were gigabytes of data, thousands of pages of explanation, and tens of thousands of lines of computer code. And the paper companies had aimed at least a dozen of their experts at influencing the Tech Memos.

I was going to make sure EPA heard as much about the Tech Memos from my team as it did from the paper companies and DNR's Fox River leaders. Furthermore, I was going to make sure that my experts and DNR's experts were on the same page.

During one of the quiet meetings at DNR that day about some of the equations underlying the models, Doug demonstrated the importance of paying attention to excruciatingly fine details. A modeler was explaining a "sixth-order" relationship that was based on multiplying a third-order relationship by a second-order relationship. I had been hearing about the Fox River's "sixth-order relationship" for years, mostly in Fox River Coalition meetings. It was just a way of saying that the river's flow had a big influence on how much sediment, and PCBs, got moved downstream, potentially into Green Bay.

Doug whispered in my ear: "I don't know where these guys learned math, but I'm pretty sure you *add* the exponents."*

I had to work hard to not show my astonishment as the light bulb went off in my head. I had to work even harder not to laugh out loud. I checked it myself, just to make sure: "2 squared is 4, and 2 cubed is 8, so 2 squared times 2 cubed is 32," I thought to myself. "But 32 is . . . 2, 4, 8, 16, 32 . . . two to the fifth, not sixth!" Yep. Never reflexively accept a detail just because it's been repeated again and again and the speaker has a bunch of letters after his name.

These meetings were exhausting, especially for a simple field biologist. So I was happy for Doug's invitation to check out his favorite bar at the end of the day. "It's a real dive," he warned.

"Sounds great," I said.

"We can walk from here. It's just off of State Street. I used to hang out there during grad school in the '80s."

It was Jocko's Rocket Ship on West Gilman Street. This was a few years before an infamous cocaine bust on the premises. That evening it was just a dimly lit, two-story brick building with neon signs advertising Hamm's, Bud Light, and Miller Lite. Not much chance of anybody important showing up here to overhear a conversation. It looked like most of the patrons were still students without much cash. Doug and I could drink a beer and finally relax.

Doug made light conversation, making fun of his youthful appearance: "Everybody always underestimates my age."

"Same here," I responded.

Doug smiled. "I'll bet you a beer I can guess your age closer than you can guess mine."

I smiled back. "You're on."

Doug looked at me intently, leaned back in his chair, pointed, and said, "You're thirty-eight."

"Close," I replied, "I'm thirty-five. So are you."

---

* This side discussion between Doug Beltman and David Allen about adding exponents actually took place at another meeting about models on a different day in Milwaukee.

Doug laughed, "Yes! You're the first person who ever guessed right. How'd you know?"

"Well, we were both at EPA at the same time. Grad school, too. So I figured we had to be close. We both say we look young, so we both factored that in, but I'm the client so you probably aimed just a bit too high."

After a couple more minutes of banter, Doug shattered the reverie. "Ever think about becoming a consultant?" he asked. "You'd be good at it, and we're always looking for good athletes."

I had to think fast. This was dangerous territory, and every second that passed could complicate my life, even if nobody was monitoring this conversation. I knew that discussing potential employment with my own contractor could disqualify me from managing my case—at least as long as Hagler Bailly was the prime contractor. I could hear Josh Lipton's voice behind Doug's question. It would be just like Josh to explore every possible option. He'd probably suggested that Doug carefully test the waters. Of course, slamming the door too violently might offend Doug, Josh, or both. And to be sure, Hagler Bailly would probably be a pretty exciting fast lane. I was flattered to be asked, too. Plus I couldn't help but wonder how much these guys made, especially compared with my government salary . . .

"Wake up!" I shouted at myself. I realized I hadn't answered the question. How many seconds had gone by? "Jesus, am I gonna have to talk to the ethics officer and the contracting officer? No, no, I think it's only been a couple of seconds. I'm still okay if I can figure out what to say—quickly." Tick. Tick. "Damn!"

I smiled warmly. "I'm not really interested in the private sector. I really like that we civil servants have to swear an oath to the Constitution. You guys get to do a bunch of the really cool technical work, and you're on the right side of interesting cases. But you're a step removed from the public. You don't actually serve them directly."

Doug started to respond, but I cut him off with a sharp look and continued. "So, anyway . . . no. And we should probably avoid talking about this until the Green Bay case is over. You know, after I retire from the federal government in three or four decades." I figured that should make it all the way back to Josh. We finished the evening with lighter topics, second beers and, for me, no second thoughts.

GEORGE MEYER'S APRIL FOOLS' FIASCO

Susan Campbell

The interagency dysfunction that emerged in April was more than a public relations disaster—it was a confusing but revealing story that left reporters and the public with mental whiplash when it was finally over.

I'd been bewildered weeks earlier when Wisconsin DNR had announced it would host a public information meeting with EPA about the possible health effects of PCBs. The chosen setting was Kimberly, a small village in the heart of Paper Valley. The forum was meant to quell widely circulated claims by the Fox Cities Chamber of Commerce and Industry that PCBs did not pose a serious risk to human health, claims the chamber was advocating on behalf of the paper mills and in opposition to the Fox River's possible designation as a Superfund cleanup site.

Even more surprising was the fact that the state-sponsored event was to feature as its keynote speaker Theo Colborn, the controversial scientist and author who warned of the health risks PCBs pose to wildlife and people. DNR had also lined up other prominent experts, but Colborn was the lightning rod. She was the scientist I had been following since the 1996 session at Michigan State University for Great Lakes environmental reporters. Now, two years later, Colborn was hailed by many as the new Rachel Carson after introducing her theories about endocrine disrupters in her best-selling book, *Our Stolen Future*. Colborn had since gained considerable traction, especially in the Great Lakes region, where she'd done her original work with the University of Wisconsin–Madison.

Because of the Great Lakes' slow rate of recycling their waters via snow and rain, Colborn likened them to massive holding pens for contaminants like PCBs. In other words, what happens in the Great Lakes, stays in the Great Lakes—for a long time, anyway. She warned that the people and wildlife inhabiting the region were living out a large laboratory experiment in real time. Like Carson before her, Colborn was publicly ostracized by the chemical industry for her research and theories, dismissed as a hack scientist.

Despite the unlikely backdrop and the even more unlikely guest, the date for the Kimberly event was set. Colborn and the other speakers accepted, the press was notified, and news stories were published and broadcast. Predictably, some of the paper mills called Colborn a "fear monger" and objected to her scheduled appearance in Paper Valley. Soon after, in an about-face, George Meyer alerted the press that he was canceling the forum. His stated reason: the Fox Cities Chamber had retracted its earlier statement that PCBs were not a threat to human health. "There was a little bit of hardball, but we made our point," Meyer told me in a phone interview. "There's been a lot of publicity since then about how dangerous PCBs are" (Campbell 1998c). According to EPA's PR staff, the real reason for the cancellation was pressure on Meyer by Governor Thompson and former governor Tony Earl. The fact that the announcement came on April 1, April Fools' Day, only added to the sense that the speakers, the press, and the public had been played. I was literally scratching my head after my interview.

Environmental and sportsmen's groups weren't about to let the event be dismissed just because Meyer was ready to move on. Determined the public had a right to learn more about the health risks of PCBs, nearly a dozen local and national environmental and sportsmen's groups stepped up to host the forum. The organizations attempted to line up commitments from the same speakers DNR had invited—including representatives from the federal Centers for Disease Control and the Wisconsin Department of Health and Family Services—and notified the press. Recent history threatened to repeat itself. Colborn and most of the other speakers pulled out four days before the event. In the end, the only technical expert left was a professor from the University of Wisconsin–Madison's zoology department. Representatives from the Sierra Club's Midwest office in Madison rounded out the panel.

Despite the bizarre politics leading up to the event, nearly two hundred people showed up on the evening of April 27, 1998, packing the hall in Kimberly. The speakers' message about the known and unknown health effects of PCBs was ominous. "We will never know what the magnitude of the biological impacts are going to be, except that almost certainly they are going to be negative," the professor told the audience (Campbell 1998n). "And the data we have just from individual studies of PCBs alone already are showing us that the likelihood of negative impacts is pretty large."

One of the Sierra Club panelists presented research that 60 percent of women who reported eating contaminated fish from Lake Michigan were unaware of the health advisories about those fish, as were 80 percent of fishermen from minority ethnic groups. Another panelist cited separate peer-reviewed studies showing that a cohort of eleven-year-old children whose mothers regularly ate contaminated fish from Lake Michigan and Lake Erie had lower birth weights, lower reading and math scores, and lower IQ scores. "We are starting to build a large body of evidence," said the head of Sierra Club's Great Lakes Program in Madison (Culhane 1998). "The polluters can't deny they are hurting people anymore."

I took copious notes, then headed back to my office to file the story. I was pleased so many people had come out to learn about how they might be impacted by the chemicals lining the Fox River. I also made a mental note that night: here, in the heart of Paper Valley, the audience had been more concerned about whether Fox River and Green Bay fish were safe to eat than about the security of paper mill jobs.

It seemed the tide of public opinion was turning.

THE FEDS VERSUS WISCONSIN

David Allen

That first highly publicized storyline about interagency conflict continued to grow, despite monumental efforts by the Feds to join with Wisconsin.

In the spring of 1998, Frank and I decided to spend about $25,000 of our damage assessment funding to host a meeting of the entire intergovernmental partnership at Hagler Bailly's offices in Boulder, Colorado.

There, our experts could easily present all the available technical details that might be pertinent to cleaning up and restoring the river and bay.

Frank and I realigned our entire damage assessment team for the three-day meeting, inviting key personnel from all the state, tribal, and federal agencies working on the Fox River. Then we strategized with Justice about how to make the meeting appealing to Wisconsin. We offered to pay for DNR's travel. We signaled that we were briefing Wisconsin in light of the state's role as leader of the cleanup decisions. We worked hard to avoid any demands about how DNR should use the technical information provided. We rented meeting rooms near Boulder's popular Pearl Street, brought in tasty food, and highlighted the city's finer points for our state guests. Perhaps this meeting could produce a safe space that would finally bring DNR into the fold.

On a Sunday in May, I met four federal DOJ attorneys at the Inn on Mapleton Hill, where we all would stay for the next three nights and could compare notes as the meetings unfolded. Matt Richmond and Susan Schneider were still two of my closest allies; we were well prepared, and hopes were running high.

On Monday morning, the meetings and presentations started. Bruce Baker sat at the head of the tables with his jaded gaze and DNR entourage, including Greg Hill and Bob Paulson, who each worked for Baker on the Fox River project. I sat in a far corner, mostly out of view, where I could quietly help my experts adjust their presentations and conversations throughout the day, and where I could monitor the room, trying to remember my lessons from Ken Fenner at EPA all those years ago.

I needed none of Fenner's intuition, though, to sense immediately that the meeting would fail. DNR staff members were heckling my speakers, giving a Bronx cheer as one of my highly credentialed avian research scientists presented bird injury data! Down the table to my left sat my DOJ counsel; they were visibly distressed. One was shaking her head, saying, "We're losing them. We're losing them." I was in utter disbelief that professionals from an agency as storied as DNR could behave like rowdy middle schoolers in front of dozens of their peers. Baker fit the stereotype of the implacable, immoveable, cynical bureaucrat, confident in his power and having zero interest in platitudes or appeasement. But how could he tolerate such antics from his staff? I was frustrated that my own DOJ attorneys seemed worried that *my* team might somehow be at fault for failing to win over DNR. I had to act, and fast.

I stood up and walked around the table to our speaker, who was in mid-sentence in the middle of the room. I put my arm around his shoulder, smiled warmly at the group, and interrupted, "Let me help you conclude by saying we have many relevant injury data sorted and ready to transfer for evaluation by DNR." My DNR guests positively glowed with delight. One smirked and mugged for the audience. "I think you just got the hook," he announced. The DNR folks laughed and shared congratulatory looks. I smiled and waited for our expert to leave the floor before launching into a short impromptu soliloquy. Everyone on my team looked nervous. I maintained a smile, although I was worried my anger was obvious.

I outlined the entire assessment approach and its relationship to the cleanup in just a couple of minutes, figuring I couldn't hold DNR's attention longer than that. While concluding, I slowly walked to the DNR table until I stood directly in front of Greg Hill, my DNR counterpart. As I approached, I explained there were no phantom facts, only the facts my team was trying to present and discuss with DNR at this meeting. There were no mysteries about how my team was using this same information to develop credible positions under public procedures that were transparent to anyone who cared to look. Refusing to listen would change nothing. I stopped with my toes just inches from Hill's, looking down at him with disgust. Hill's face turned crimson. I adjourned the meeting until after lunch—then walked around the block several times to keep my head from exploding.

After lunch, Hill explained that he and his DNR colleagues had "heard a bunch of stuff we already knew" and had been given "reasons why Fish and Wildlife thinks it can't share information with DNR." They did not want to hear about injury to the Fox River and bay, only about strategy. I interpreted this to mean DNR wanted to hear about "the number," as Bill Hartwig had demanded years earlier, with no explanation about how those damages were calculated. I suggested we jump ahead to the evening's meeting on cleanup. DNR agreed.

The meeting resumed later that day, with EPA staff outlining Superfund requirements for determining ecological risk. They explained that early drafts of the Ecological Risk Assessment from DNR and their consultants were inconsistent with Superfund requirements. DNR's Bob Paulson argued that EPA had to provide concrete information about biological data and information at the site if the Feds wanted DNR to include it. Doug Beltman exploded: "That's exactly the information we were trying to provide to DNR when you cut us off earlier today!" Paulson answered rhetorically: "Why should DNR worry about how the state's cleanup documents and decisions might affect Superfund and the federal damage assessment if DNR has no intention of pursuing any damages in the first place?" My team took this as a clear signal that DNR remained adamantly opposed to the damage assessment, and was unsympathetic to the goal of a truly unified intergovernmental partnership.

The next day, the DNR delegation left after all the agencies had detailed the key pieces of information they needed from one another. But it was clear to me that DNR was still far from a willing partner. The Feds would continue to listen to Wisconsin's experts and take note of its official comments and complaints, but nothing had changed. We were still at square one. The next step was to complete and make public the damage assessment details ASAP and redouble efforts to engage EPA on the cleanup. DNR be damned.

Boulder had changed nothing: Fish and Wildlife's leverage would continue to emanate from its own legal progress, based on the facts and in full public view. Privately, Frank and I vowed never again to spend significant time or money wooing Baker and his team at Wisconsin DNR.

DNR REPORTS MORE PCBS, MORE POLLUTERS

Susan Campbell

A month later, Wisconsin DNR released findings percolating up from Dale Patterson's shop, probably to the chagrin of the governor. PCB discharges to the Fox River might be three times higher than earlier projections, and the list of polluters might lengthen. The agency's report estimated that total PCB discharges to the river in the last for-ty-four years ranged somewhere between 420,000 to 825,000 pounds. The new estimates were far higher than the earlier state and federal esti-mates of 250,000 pounds.

DNR's Bruce Baker said the finding surprised even his agency. The new estimate was based on "exhaustive research," he said, and from new and better data (Campbell 1998k). Many of the new data were provided directly by the paper companies, while some were pulled from confi-dential information Fish and Wildlife had procured from the companies via its federal damage assessment. Baker said the DNR also checked with sources like the state Lab of Hygiene to learn which Fox River companies had submitted water samples for PCB screening back in the 1970s, when concern about the chemicals was on the rise.

Most of the paper companies reserved comment, saying they hadn't had time to fully review the report. They also refrained from comment-ing on DNR's new roundup of likely polluters, which expanded the list from seven to seventeen, and now included several area sewerage plants that had treated the paper companies' waste.

The executive director of the Green Bay Metropolitan Sewerage Dis-trict said the district shouldn't be held to the same level of responsibility in the cleanup as the seven paper mills comprising the Fox River Group. The district was found to have discharged a relatively small amount of PCBs to the river when it treated pulp waste for two paper companies in the late 1970s and early '80s.

Although the sewerage plants and newly named paper mills were indeed believed to be less culpable than the paper companies that made up the Fox River Group, Baker said any or all of them could be called on to help share in the cost of cleanup. "If there's litigation, the companies have said they would turn around and take legal action against all the contributors they could find" (Campbell 1998k).

SUPERFUND GOOD FOR THE PRIVATE SECTOR

David Allen

In 1998, U.S. senator Herb Kohl's environmental staffer called me with an opportunity. After the standard pleasantries, she got right to the point: "Listen, I just heard a presentation to the Appleton Rotary Club. The Fox Cities Chamber of Commerce and Industry was offering some thoughts about the federal damage assessment. Any interest in offering a different perspective?" I could almost hear her smiling over the phone. I tried to imagine the chamber's worried rhetoric at the Rotary meeting—probably something about paper mill closures and federal threats to Paper Valley's very way of life. I didn't need to overthink this one. "Count me in. It might be fun to present right in the paper mills' backyard."

I soon had billed my talk as "The Green Bay NRDA and Why CERCLA Liability Makes Sense for the Private Sector" (Allen 1998a).* I figured an audacious title might hook an Appleton audience of business leaders. The Rotary organizers must have agreed because they doubled my allotted speaking time to forty minutes. When I arrived, the room at the Paper Valley Hotel was packed.

I covered all the usual points about Green Bay and the damage assessment, but my main focus was one inescapable fact. The residents of Appleton had only three viable choices: live with the PCBs in their river, use tax dollars to clean them up, or let Superfund's liability approach work as intended. This last option would make businesses cover their own cleanup costs, which would also increase the efficiency of the market. "Do you really want to champion taxes and government bailouts just because the responsible businesses are local?" I asked rhetorically. "Are you really ready to accept paper company arguments about PCBs if it means leaving them in your backyard for another hundred years?"

Afterward, several people continued the conversation with me at the back of the room. They seemed intrigued that a Fish and Wildlife agent

---

* CERCLA is the official acronym for the Superfund law.

was willing to engage them directly and on their terms, rather than lob yet another passionate plea to save cormorants.

DEBATING THE SCIENCE OF PCBS

Susan Campbell

The potential human health effects of PCBs would take center stage in Wisconsin's Paper Valley once again. The stage would still be in Kimberly on the Fox River, but this time, some of the nation's leading PCB experts would serve as the principal actors. Within days of proposing Superfund for the Fox, EPA reached out to Theo Colborn and two federal toxicologists to bring the latest in PCB research to the heart of Paper Valley. It would be the third invitation in three months for the senior scientist with the World Wildlife Fund, but the third time would be the charm.

The paper companies lined up three scientists of their own for the event, scientists known for their opposing views about PCBs' potential to harm human health. Among them was John Giesy, the renowned Great Lakes environmental toxicology professor from Michigan State University who had trained so many successful PhD students. Giesy was now working for the paper mills, and was an outspoken critic of some of Colborn's theories.

I was excited to see Wisconsin queuing up as a locus of the evolving public health debate on PCBs. I wasted no time in lining up phone interviews with Colborn and Giesy for a story and Q&A piece. Colborn's book had triggered a major policy response from the federal government, prompting funding to expand research on endocrine disruption, and leading Congress to call for the screening of one hundred thousand chemicals in the environment to search for estrogenic or other hormonal effects. For his part, Giesy now served on the National Academy of Sciences panel on endocrine disruptors, which was expected to issue a consensus statement on the issue later that year based on its review of studies. Given the reputations of the two scientists, I was eager to interview them both. But my pulse quickened as I dialed Colborn's number and waited for her to pick up. Colborn's prescient book and its warnings about the effects of chemicals on wildlife and people had been one of my earliest introductions to the environment beat. I'd interviewed plenty of big names in my reporting career. Yet I found I had a special regard for this wiry, hip, and energetic grandmother turned scientist who had earned a PhD late in life, then managed to turn the scientific world on its head while confronting some of the world's most powerful corporations.

Colborn was a straight shooter and talked fast. The interview lasted about forty-five minutes, and I was thankful for my tape recorder. Colborn quoted studies and statistics and never shirked from questions about the criticisms levied by her detractors. I asked her to answer critics who argued that PCBs' effects in animals don't automatically translate to the same effects in people. Colborn noted that the PCB effects worked similarly "whether it's a human, a domestic animal, wild animal, or laboratory animal" (Campbell 1998d).

Posing the same question to Giesy, who was analyzing chemicals in local fish tissues for the Fox River Group of paper companies—and giving them advice—I found the first part of his answer in line with Colborn's. Whenever effects in wildlife are observed like those seen in the Fox River and bay, "you should sit up, take notice, and say, 'That is something we should watch for and protect our human populations,'" he said (Campbell 1998d). "Absolutely."

But for Giesy, it was a question of sufficient exposure. Was the local human population exposed to enough PCBs from the river and bay to justify concerns? "It is not very useful if the risk is fairly marginal—which it probably is for the population living around the Fox River—to raise expectations to the point where you can't fulfill them," he said (Campbell 1998a).

Giesy and Colborn would take their respective messages to the public. On the night of July 27, more than 150 people converged on Kimberly to hear them square off against one another and their colleagues. I was there early, excited to finally see Colborn in person as well as Giesy and some of the other experts I'd been interviewing for months now. As before, I was pleased to see people turning out in such high numbers on a warm summer evening in Paper Valley to hear a bunch of scientists debate the particulars of PCBs.

Scientific data and studies dominated the prepared speeches, but there would be heated exchanges, too. Each speaker hoped to use the emerging science on PCBs to their own advantage, but there was also plenty of money and politics motivating the rhetoric. The anticipation was palpable as one by one the scientists took their place at the podium. At the front of the auditorium on a large screen flashed image after image of animals that were impaired by PCBs in the environment. "This is the individual to whom we should be directing our concerns and our attention," Colborn concluded as the image of a human fetus appeared on the screen (Campbell 1998m). "Every baby born in 1998 will be exposed to these chemicals for 266 days in the womb."

Giesy said that whatever risk PCBs pose to people resulted from people eating contaminated fish, not simply from the chemicals' presence in the water. "Unless they are a major consumer of large carp from the most contaminated areas, it is going to be very difficult to show any difference in exposure between the people in this area and other areas," he said (Campbell 1998a).

An EPA scientist noted that the Fox River's PCBs spread far beyond the river's banks, its fish, and Lake Michigan. The chemicals are carried in the air and in the bodies of migrating fish and birds as they make their way around the world, he said. PCBs had even been found in seals, polar bears, and the breast milk of Inuit women in the Canadian Arctic.

A state DNR modeling study was cited that showed PCB levels in Fox River fish were declining, but so slowly that if no cleanup were undertaken, 150 years would pass before it would be safe to eat a large walleye from the river every week.

But Giesy said there were ways to reduce local people's exposure to PCBs other than throwing all or most of the cleanup dollars at removing PCBs from the river. One option he suggested: a bounty system in which the state would exchange a clean fish for a contaminated fish, paying the angler a $10 incentive. "We can't change how toxic PCBs are," Giesy said (Campbell 1998a). "All we can do is manage the resources—either the populations of people and animals, or what is out there in the sediment. Normally, the answer is a combination of both."

EPA's answer: We prefer cleaning the river and making the public's fish safe to eat.

TRAGEDY STRIKES

David Allen

As 1998 was coming to a close, we prepared for a systematic publication of all our voluminous damage assessment results. It was time to start using the megaphone born of agency conflict to direct attention to the real story about the unfolding facts and the law.

It was clear we could not rely on Wisconsin for any official leadership or support on any part of the damage assessment. Furthermore, Fish and Wildlife and EPA had to continue locking arms to prevent the paper companies from unduly influencing DNR on the official Superfund cleanup document, the Remedial Investigation and Feasibility Study. Fish and Wildlife now had teams of experts assigned or hired for every topic needed for the entire damage assessment, and for many of the topics needed for the cleanup studies. At the same time, Fish and Wildlife was weaning itself from the informal help of willing DNR experts behind the scenes. If the case went to trial, the governor could too easily block access to state officials, and attempts to circumvent him would be dangerous for the DNR experts Fish and Wildlife would likely need the most. Thus, by September, my team and I had everything lined up to finally begin taking our assessment results to the public. But fate would deal us a card we never anticipated.

A small two-engine plane crashed in a cranberry bog in central Wisconsin at 7:45 the morning of September 16, 1998, less than an hour after taking off from Dane County Regional Airport in Madison. As it attempted an emergency landing, the plane snapped trees and gouged a scar in the earth measuring ninety-five by sixteen feet, charring vegetation along its path before coming to rest among foot-high grasses. The plane was en route to Siren, Wisconsin when the pilot reported a problem to the air controller and announced plans to divert to the nearest landing site, Volk Field Air National Guard Base. "Minneapolis seven four Quebec, we're gonna return. We're gonna go into, ah, Volk," he transmitted. "We got some smoke comin' outta this thing."*

The pilot, a seasoned veteran with 14,800 accumulated hours of flying, was given clearance to land at Volk, about sixteen miles away. At 7:40 a.m., however, he transmitted what would be one of his last communications. "Four Quebec, okay and, ah, I guess you could declare it as an emergency. We're not gonna fool around. We got some sm . . ." His voice cut off.

A witness reported hearing an aircraft fly overhead, about six hundred feet above his shop, and seeing dark smoke coming out of the aircraft's centerline before the plane crashed one and a half miles away. A second witness described black smoke pouring from the plane's back end before impact. Both witnesses reported that the plane's landing gear was up during the descent.

All three passengers on board the six-passenger 1973 Beech Baron 58—the pilot and two other employees of the State of Wisconsin—were killed. One of the passengers was Dale Patterson, forty-nine, on his way to a routine meeting in the village of Siren.

I was in Madison when I learned of Dale Patterson's death, attending a two-day meeting about lake trout studies for the damage assessment with Frank Horvath, Ken Stromborg, Josh Lipton, Doug Beltman, and various government fish experts. The following week, I was at a Minneapolis meeting with DNR's Bob Paulson and some of the experts behind the $16 million mass balance study of PCBs in Green Bay to determine how to use the data in Superfund's RI/FS. During this time, I also talked regularly with Dale's staff about the Tech Memos.

Everybody was busy. There was no time to talk about Dale. But it was more than that. Nobody knew *what* to say, what to think.

It was crazy *not* to talk about the sudden loss of someone so central to what everyone was working on. But it also felt somehow inappropriate

---

* Plane crash N4574Q accident description, https://www.planecrashmap.com/plane/wi/N4574Q/.

to discuss such deeply personal human events while working on something as dry and mundane as study plans or data. Plus, the whole interagency warfare just seemed trivial next to this real catastrophe, so tragic
on both a personal and a professional level. I was going to miss Dale's
knowing look, almost a smile, when he showed me the latest gem of
scientific evidence he'd uncovered. I was *really* going to miss seeing the
obvious affection bestowed on him by his staff. I could hear the emotion
in their voices when I talked with them. A couple of times, somebody
would try to put something into words about Dale, but it just felt hollow
and inadequate.

I checked my voicemail: "This is Susan Campbell at the *Press-Gazette*.
I'm trying to reach David Allen for a story about Dale Patterson's death."

I'd been avoiding reporters all week, but I knew I couldn't avoid this
one. I trusted Susan, and I hoped she had started to trust me. It was
hard for me to think of this as a story, but that didn't mean it wasn't one.
And it wouldn't be fair to give Susan the cold shoulder just because I
didn't know what to say.

I picked up the phone. "Hi Susan; David Allen."

"Dave! Thanks for calling back. I was hoping to talk with you about
Dale Patterson."

We talked for a while about the details we knew. Then Susan asked
a question that made my blood run cold. "Given Dale's long-standing
credibility and his apparent willingness to follow the science even if it
made his bosses' lives uncomfortable," she started, then hesitated. "Well,
I was wondering if you think there's any possibility of foul play."

A cacophony of thoughts flooded my mind. I knew, instantly, that
this question was the real cause of some of the awkwardness of talking
or thinking about Dale's sudden death. I knew there were no good reasons to suspect foul play. I knew conspiracy theories were dangerous
drugs for paranoid and weak minds. But I also knew how troubling
Dale's expertise and integrity might have seemed to some of the goals
of powerful men trying to spin the Fox River case. I decided to use the
same approach that I pursued on the Green Bay PCB case: follow the
empirical evidence.

"Well, I can't think of any shred of evidence that points in that direction," I answered matter-of-factly. "Plus, it seems like it would be such a dangerous and criminal plot that no smart politician would consider it. And, whatever you think of their policies, we have pretty smart politicians in Wisconsin."

I was satisfied with my response and with Susan's quick agreement—but sweat was dripping off my brow as we hung up.

DREDGING FOR ANSWERS IN KIMBERLY

Susan Campbell

The specter of a Superfund listing and an RI/FS to rid the Fox of PCBs raised more questions and potential uncertainty. How would the river be cleaned, and what assurances were there that the cleanup itself wouldn't uncover and potentially stir up and spread the contaminants?

These were legitimate questions, and the paper companies saw in them an excellent opportunity to influence the answers and, right along with them, political and public opinion.

Two pilot dredging projects were envisioned and planned on the river, the perfect vehicles to probe these questions and gain a hands-on perspective of the future cleanup. The projects were as different as night and day, at least in terms of what mattered most. One was small and well defined, the other large and part of a seven-mile, nearly continuous bathtub of PCBs. One had manageable concentrations of PCBs that made it easier to test dredging techniques, the other the highest concentrations in the river. One was upstream in Paper Valley, the other downstream near the bay of Green Bay. One was funded and controlled by agencies whose mission was environmental protection, the other by companies whose missions were paper and money.

By the end of November, DNR and EPA were poised to launch the first effort, referred to simply as Deposit N. This, the smaller of the two projects, would test hydraulic dredging in a three-acre section of riverbed near the village of Kimberly, in the heart of Paper Valley. The project would remove twelve thousand cubic yards of PCB-tainted sediment from the riverbed, enough to cover a football field to a depth of six feet.

PCB levels in the sediment there measured around 45 parts per million, relatively low compared to the levels measured in sediment downstream near Green Bay, where even more PCBs had collected over time. The agencies were funding the $4.5 million project to help determine the effectiveness of precision hydraulic dredging, future cleanup costs, and the potential impacts of dredging to people and the environment.

Most of the more than one hundred local community members who turned out for an agency open house and tour of the site said they had little concern about the project. "It's a necessary evil," said a resident from nearby Little Chute (Cole 1998). "You always hear about this stuff in New York and the canals. Now it's in your backyard."

The agencies hoped to have the Kimberly work completed and the results in hand well before EPA's final Superfund listing for the Fox scheduled for the following summer, and well before the RI/FS, whenever it might reach completion. A DNR project manager was relishing the project's launch in the days before the first load of contaminants was due to be sucked from the riverbed. "It's been seven years that I've been working on getting one of these pilot dredging projects going," he said in a press interview (Bruss 1998). "This will give people a chance to see what we have been talking about."

Community members were far less confident about the larger of the two pilot projects, however. That project, funded by the paper companies and targeting a slice of the river's highest PCB contamination, had residents scratching their heads at another public meeting—this one hosted by DNR and the paper companies.

A Fox Valley Sierra Club member worried that data from the company-funded project could be construed to say whatever the paper mills wanted it to say. The president of the local Wolf River Watershed Alliance was similarly concerned. He cited a video the paper companies had circulated to the media earlier in the year that showed dredging scattered more contaminants than it removed. The video, it turned out, showed a dredging method typically used for navigation projects with clean sediment, not cleanup projects like the one planned for the Fox.

"Now we're supposed to trust you people?" he asked, incredulously. "I don't trust you at all! What you're going to do is get in there and stir things up, and when you've screwed things up enough, you're going to say it doesn't work" (Campbell 1998j).

DAMAGE ASSESSMENT RESULTS BEGIN
David Allen

On the night of December 10, 1998, in Green Bay, I publicly unveiled our first damage assessment report documenting PCB injuries related to fish in the Fox River and the bay. The report laid one of the foundations for my agency to determine how much could justifiably be spent to restore the bay and make the public whole. That value, I reminded attendees at the Brown County Library, could range anywhere from tens of millions of dollars to hundreds of millions.

For now, our 198-page report confirmed the validity of Wisconsin's and Michigan's fish consumption advisories, in place since 1976 to protect anglers from ingesting PCBs from the fish they caught in Wisconsin and Michigan waters (FWS 1998a). PCBs had been documented in the bodies of thirteen species of Fox River fish, twenty-three species of Green Bay fish, and six species of Lake Michigan fish. The presence of the contaminants led to losses by sport and commercial fishermen, losses my team and I would now tally as part of our ongoing damage assessment.

"Virtually every sport fish that can be caught in Green Bay has had a fish consumption advisory on it at one time or another," I told a relatively small audience that night (Content 1998). "The contamination is widespread—meaning a long time, a large area, and a lot of species."

COMPETING FOR THE PUBLIC'S EAR
Susan Campbell

The first-floor conference room of the *Press-Gazette* was a critical stop for the various players in the Fox River case. The room was stately, with a soaring ceiling, rich wood-paneled walls, and tall windows on two sides looking out on the bustling corner of Walnut and Madison Streets. The iconic 1924 building occupied a central perch in downtown Green Bay, located next door to city hall, one block from the Brown County Courthouse, and four blocks from where the Fox River split the city's east and west sides. Like the building that housed it, the *Press-Gazette* served as a crossroads of sorts for the large cast of characters who came through its doors to plead their cases with the editorial board.

These sessions gave the *Press-Gazette* editors a direct, unfiltered view of the arguments that would fuel the newspaper's Fox River editorials. I was invited to sit in on these meetings, too: it was an opportunity to ask questions and write a story afterward if anything newsworthy came up. I was often uncomfortable in these meetings, sitting in the same room with my sources and editors. It was a collision of two worlds, similar to parent-teacher conferences in grade school, though I wasn't being graded now—at least not overtly.

Early on, I spotted an inequality in these encounters. Men and women in expensively tailored suits, especially paper company CEOs and their PR strategists, attracted a full-court press of editors seated around the large conference table. So, too, did visits from high-level agency representatives from the state and federal governments. It was a different scene, though, when the environmental groups visited. During one of these visits, I sat there awkwardly at the table with a lone editor for a few minutes, until dispatched for a quick run to the newsroom to round up others. I was unsuccessful.

One editorial board meeting visit fell somewhere in the middle. In late August, three representatives visited from the Green Bay Remedial Action Plan's Science and Technical Advisory Committee, better known as the RAP STAC. They were experts who arguably knew as much about the Fox River and bay of Green Bay as anyone else, and they said they were being left out of the loop when it came to deciding the future of the waterways.

For ten years, the committee had offered uniquely local expert opinions about studies of PCB problems in the river and bay, including the monumental $16 million Mass Balance Study that had helped make Green Bay among the most-studied water bodies in the United

States. Many committee members also advised the Fox River Coalition when it was formed in 1992, and much of the committee's work was now relevant and available to DNR and EPA as part of the Superfund cleanup process.

Committee member H. J. "Bud" Harris, chairman of natural and applied sciences at UW–Green Bay, worried that the current polarization between the federal government and paper companies was sidelining the scientific arguments and risking further gridlock. A member of the environmental group Fox-Wolf Basin 2000 complained that the government was leaving the committee and its collective expertise out of the process. "As this moves forward, our concern is that the decisions on what happens on this river are going to be made by lawyers—and they're going to be based on dollars," he said (Campbell 1998o).

The federal Superfund process might be too rigid a hammer to allow for local flexibility, the committee members told the editorial board. And a decision led by the paper companies was equally troubling, they said. Most of the seven paper companies responsible for the pollution were based outside Wisconsin, including Fort Howard, which a year earlier had merged with James River Corp. and transferred the Fort's headquarters to Illinois.

In other words, paper company executives "don't fish on the Fox River," the local experts warned.

Looking ahead to the next calendar year and the two pilot dredging projects, the *Green Bay Press-Gazette*'s executive editor predicted that 1999 "will likely be a pivotal year" for the long-running Fox River cleanup story.

In her December 27 column, Carol Hunter drew a line in the sand on any further delay of addressing the river's widespread PCB contamination. "I've agreed with paper mill representatives who've argued that a determination on how to clean the river should wait until receipt of data from pilot dredging projects," Hunter wrote. "But then it's decision time. Delays would add credence to accusations that the mills have been stalling all along" (1998).

6

MAKING THE CASE

RACE TO THE FINISH LINE

David Allen

I saw 1999 as the year that would make or break Fish and Wildlife's leverage to truly unify the intergovernmental partnership and finally place EPA's Superfund authority at the center of decision making— ultimately compelling the paper companies to act. Budgets were peaking but could not last much longer. Assessment studies and data analyses were nearing completion on all fronts, but that information could easily be superseded, especially by new data collections ordered by the paper companies. I was keenly aware that my ability to influence EPA with a mountain of evidence and expertise would be greatest just as cleanup decision documents—specifically the Remedial Investigation and Feasibility Study—were being designed and drafted. A U.S. presidential election was also on the horizon. No matter who won, there would be new Interior officials to brief in 2001, and they might not be as enthusiastic as Interior secretary Babbitt.

So, Frank and I pressed all of our experts relentlessly, and began queuing up official documents for Bill Hartwig to sign. We also began scheduling public meetings and official comment periods for each document that would be released. Bill was now leading the charge in concert with the team, and his famous impatience had become a key asset for completing the barrage of work on time.

Bill and the legal team had signed off on two early technically straightforward determinations about restoration project criteria and fish consumption advisories back in late 1998 (FWS 1998a, 1998b). The complicated and weighty injury determination for birds affected by paper mill PCBs was scheduled to come out next, in May 1999. This determination was central to Fish and Wildlife's long history of scientific study in the bay of Green Bay, and it would mean finally resolving the Cormorant Wars.

PUBLIC COMMENTS POUR IN ON SUPERFUND

Susan Campbell

Amid the snow and cold of early February in Green Bay, I decided to pay a visit to the local Brown County Library. Just a short walk from the newspaper's office, the library was one of several along the Fox River where public comments on the cleanup were available for public review. I was ushered to a table and shown stacks of volumes.

EPA's publication of its intent to pursue a Fox River Superfund listing had launched a sixty-day comment period, inviting the public and anyone else watching the case to weigh in with their opinions. The public responded in numbers EPA had never seen before.

"Dear EPA, this is my first letter to a government agency," wrote one of the more than seven thousand residents who sent in comments about the Fox River. "Please add my name to the other citizens who wish to support a Superfund cleanup."

The Green Bay woman, who signed as Mary Rose Paul, was one of the majority—4,865, to be exact—of petitioners and letter writers favoring Superfund (Campbell 1999e). Her letter joined the thousands of others that were now bound in sixteen volumes. Reached by phone at his Washington, DC, office in early February, an EPA spokesman told me that most sites proposed for Superfund generate only about twenty comments. The most EPA had ever received for a site was sixteen hundred comments, submitted in the early '90s about mine sites in Utah.

Months earlier, EPA's Jim Hahnenberg had advised that while his agency would accept all manner of comments about the Fox, the most relevant would be those addressing the technical merits of the proposed listing. It "doesn't relate to emotional or political considerations," he'd told me in an interview. "It's a scientific and engineering evaluation, and we ultimately have to make our decision on the basis of what is protective" (Campbell 1998g). Later, as the comments kept coming: "A lot of people seem to believe it's a vote," he said. "It's not" (Campbell 1998l).

The comment period might have been meant to elicit technical comments, but thumbing through them now, I saw these comprised only a small percentage. Most took the form of petitions circulated by Becky Katers and the Clean Water Action Council in favor of the proposal, and by Appleton Papers and the United Paperworkers International Union against it. But there were plenty of other thoughtful letter writers who had been moved to write personal accounts of what it was like to live in the shadow of the paper mills. I settled into my chair. It would be a long afternoon, but an engrossing one full of one-sided introductions to the many folks who quietly made up the backstory of the Fox River conflict.

One resident, Mitchell Miller of Green Bay, recalled seeing fist-sized clumps of paper sludge floating in the Fox River. "Fort [Howard] paper company needs to be made to pay their large share of the cleanup," he wrote. "Other mills on the river need to give back some of the billions of dollars of profits they have made over the past decades" (Campbell 1999e).

Another letter writer, Betty Fierros, who was born and raised near the Fox, wrote of the ineffectiveness of Wisconsin's fish consumption advisories. "People are warned not to eat the fish they catch, via a sign in English only—even though there are many Mexicans and Hmong people here who do not necessarily read English and whose main diet is seafood" (Campbell 1999e).

Boyd Young, the president of the powerful United Paperworkers union was one of the minority writing to oppose Superfund. A big-dollar cleanup could directly harm Fox Valley employment, he warned in comments he also forwarded to President Clinton, Vice President Al Gore, and EPA administrator Browner. "We believe the effect on public health caused by a substantial rise in unemployment in the area would be considerable" (Campbell 1999e).

After spending the afternoon among the volumes, I asked the library aide behind the counter if anyone else ever came in to read this stuff—sincerely hoping the answer would be yes. Oh, they come in regularly, I was told, though of course some spent more time than others. "When people ask to look at it we say, 'Oh, God.' It's so hard," the aide said, motioning to all the stacks that now had to be lugged back to their protected space behind closed doors.

More, much more, was on the way. DNR and EPA were ramping up to send the library boxes of studies that could be used in the RI/FS to address the extent and sources of the Fox River's chemical contamination, as well as the various cleanup scenarios and potential risks.

DAVID FINALLY SEES A PAPER VAT

David Allen

By 1999, DOJ's expert—a former EPA engineer with expertise in paper-making, PCB releases, and federal liability cases—had the paper companies' full attention. With Justice's blessing, he had begun sharing the long-awaited and potentially damning draft estimates of PCB releases with the members of the Fox River Group. The estimates were based on each company's answers to increasingly specific Information Requests signed by Bill Hartwig, and informed by dozens of meetings with DNR staff in Dale Patterson's section and Fish and Wildlife's experts.

As I had predicted when the Reading Room first opened, the paper companies were now jumping at the chance to share their own analyses and expertise with us, especially when doing so served to point the finger at one another.

By now, each company had conducted its own exhaustive searches in the Reading Room and in its own internal files, to find and highlight every shred of information that implicated the other parties. DOJ's expert was more than happy to receive this information as it gave him leverage to demand more thorough answers. It also gave him entrée to the mills' sprawling facilities along the Fox.

I usually tagged along on these visits. I never realized my fear of encountering the James River paper vat where Tom Monfils was killed, but I did see countless noisy machines in rooms with towering steel ceilings and endless concrete floors that seemed longer than a football field. I tried to conceal my nervousness whenever I walked by one of the clanking, humming, or steaming contraptions. They looked plenty dangerous, and I wasn't remotely inclined to ask the watchful mill workers—most of them clad in hard hats, safety glasses, and heavy steel-toed boots— whether any of this equipment resembled the infamous paper vat of the murder. I was struck by the sheer size of these plants, some of them so immense they resembled small cities. Standing within the actual belly of the beast was much different than mailing out Information Requests to paper company addresses from the comfort of my Green Bay office. This was tangible and eerily real. At times, I found it hard to imagine that the owners of even one of these massive plants might ultimately be held accountable for its role in fouling the Fox River.

For their part, paper company officials didn't always embrace these on-site visits, and at times they took pains to impose safeguards aimed at preventing the DOJ expert and me from learning too much. National Cash Register and Appleton Papers were a case in point. Their attorneys and officials agreed to our visit to their paper-coating facility in Appleton, where PCBs had been used in carbonless copy paper starting in 1954. They assigned a tour guide and warned that nobody else in the plant was allowed to speak with us. The tour started off according to plan. Once inside the Appleton plant, we were met by the spokesman, who began leading a carefully guided tour to the newest paper machines in the cleanest part of the mill. Our DOJ expert, a large, engaging man with an easy sense of humor, wasn't a fan of guided tours, however. He had something else in mind and made a beeline for the oldest paper machine in the plant. The spokesman and I could barely keep up as he strode across the floor, looking intently at the machinery and floor drains. He knew exactly where he was headed. He casually struck up conversations with some of the mill workers, putting them immediately at ease with his depth of knowledge and obvious interest. Despite the edict from upper management to keep quiet, the workers answered freely.

I kept a poker face, but I saw the spokesman break into a sweat.

PILOT I ERROR: "EXACTLY WHAT THE PAPER MILLS WANT"

Susan Campbell

That winter brought into focus major concerns about dredging the Fox River.

The agency test project at Deposit N in Kimberly that began in late November had been curtailed by the onset of winter's cold and ice on the Fox River, neither of them strange phenomena for winter in northern Wisconsin. Yet the project had paused with less than half of the targeted PCB hot spot removed.

DNR publicly announced the pause in early February and simultaneously released an interim report by the engineering firm hired to monitor any movement of PCBs from the dredging. Those results showed that nothing was released from the project, DNR's Bruce Baker assured me, "and if there was anything, it's very, very minute quantities" (Campbell 1999b).

Although the government-led project at Deposit N would be completed successfully the following season, the paper companies weren't yet convinced. The question of whether dredging might stir up and spread the PCBs was central to their argument that the best cleanup approach might be to simply leave the contaminants in place; the companies were in no hurry to embrace information to the contrary. An Appleton Papers representative called the results "premature." His company was funding additional PCB monitoring, and he said they were awaiting the consultant's more extensive results.

Clean Water Action Council's Rebecca Katers was aghast when I reached her the day of DNR's announcement. Extracting just part of the hot spot and leaving the rest of it exposed in the riverbed "is exactly what the paper mills want," she said (Campbell 1999b). Looking ahead to the much larger and "hotter" project planned that spring at "SMU 56–57" near the Fort Howard mill in Green Bay, which would be funded and controlled by the paper companies under the earlier state-company deal, Katers was more than skeptical. She was worried. "If they do that kind of project there, we're in real trouble," she warned.

DNR's Bob Paulson was also worried. He'd told me of looming problems with the upcoming project only a couple weeks earlier. Public pressure had just forced nearby Winnebago County to slam the door on its landfill accepting any sediment containing PCB levels of 50 parts per million (ppm) or more. The hot spot outside Fort Howard had PCB levels measuring up to 700 ppm—the highest known concentrations along the Lower Fox River. With no local landfill in sight now to accept the riverbed's high-level PCB waste, Paulson said the Fort Howard project might have to be cut in half before it even started. The closest available landfill now was near Detroit, and it would charge a fee three times what Winnebago County would have charged to haul and dispose of the waste. Paulson said a smaller removal project might make the DNR's planned "bull's-eye" engineering approach at Fort Howard—extracting only the highest concentration of PCBs—impossible. "We'd have to look at the size of what the project would be, based on that disposal cost, to see if you can really safely go into that part of the river and not leave something worse behind," he told me in an interview (Campbell 1999c). "If it means you could only dredge through this one area and expose 300 ppm and you've got to stop, that's not good." Paulson suggested one option: the paper companies could pony up more money. The companies were footing the bill for the $7 million pilot project near Fort Howard, and funds for the project made up the lion's share of the $10 million secret deal they'd struck with DNR back in January 1997.

I immediately reached out to Appleton Papers' representative, who told me unequivocally that the companies wouldn't spend more on the project. DNR had chosen the site near Fort Howard, he noted, not the paper companies. Furthermore, he said, the PCB deposit there wasn't the companies' first choice because it held about one hundred thousand cubic yards of contaminated sediment—and the companies had known it couldn't all be removed with a budget of just $7 million. "Removing half of it was our goal. Do we have to put in another $7 million to remove it all?" he asked rhetorically (Campbell 1999c). "That's kind of foolishness. That would be nice, but this is just a demonstration project."

This time, the *Press-Gazette*'s editorial board lost no time in calling foul on the paper companies. "Time and again," the newspaper's January 31 editorial began,

> executives from Fox River paper mills have sat across the table from us explaining the importance of a pilot project that they said would prove to doubters—environmentalists and the U.S. EPA among them—how committed they were to attacking the environmental and health hazards posed by river contaminants.
>
> Now, the mills appear to be saying that a scaled-back river project is OK, despite serious reservations about that approach expressed by the state DNR. (*Green Bay Press-Gazette* 1999a)

The newspaper noted it had opposed a Superfund designation for the Fox and defended the mills in their push for a local solution. The pilot near Fort Howard, so long championed by the mills, must now proceed as planned even if that meant the mills would be forced to kick in more than the $7 million they'd budgeted for it. Downsizing the project "would be a serious mistake," the editorial warned. Such action would only "further undermine the mills' credibility in the community."

Appleton Papers fought back, taking its message straight to the Green Bay community via a full-page ad in the *Press-Gazette* the following Sunday headlined "The River as We See It." The top third of the page featured a lovely aerial view of lush treetops and a winding Fox River (*Green Bay Press-Gazette* 1999b). This was no tourism ad, though. After highlighting Appleton Papers' history as a responsible corporate citizen, the text launched into the ad's real purpose: defending the importance the two pilot dredging projects would play in determining ultimate cleanup goals for the river and the community.

"We feel the best solution will be determined by scientific fact, not politics or conjecture," the ad asserted. "We're confident that the two demonstration projects, as well as scientific modeling results, will give us the facts we need to do what's right for the river." The text then veered into more familiar territory: a threat. "The economic drain of an enormous river cleanup could impact the future of the Fox Cities for decades to come. Expansion, jobs, and supporting industries all could be affected."

Appleton Papers was willing to pay its fair share of PCB-related cleanup costs, according to its ad, but basing all future actions on "reliable scientific facts" was the "most effective way to get the job done with as little adverse economic consequence as possible."

ENDING THE CORMORANT WARS

David Allen

As my team and I pressed on with determining the scope of PCB injuries for our damage assessment, we knew we had to finally determine whether the co-trustees could prove in a court of law that PCBs caused crossed bills in cormorants, as well as a host of other bird injuries. By now, the oft-published photos in the press of the disfigured cormorants had made them nearly synonymous with PCB injuries to local wildlife, at least for much of the public. My team had to know whether we could actually confirm this connection for the purposes of our case. If the paper companies were made to address crossed bills in birds, their lawyers would most certainly contest it in court.

We assigned consultants, outside experts, and frontline laboratory and field researchers, but I took dramatic action myself. I planned a direct assault on Ken Stromborg's office to take possession of his cormorant files.

Ken was the Oscar to my Felix in our own real-life version of *The Odd Couple*, and nothing highlighted our differences as much as the manner in which we organized our individual workspaces. I checked the office schedule and picked a week when I knew Ken would be away on vacation. In my most innocent voice I asked him if it'd be okay to finally, after years of asking, look through his cormorant files for the case while he was away. Ken agreed, but I worried my friend didn't realize what was about to hit his office. When the appointed week arrived, I steeled myself and surveyed the mounds of paperwork.

This was going to be a lot like searching through P. H. Glatfelter's disorganized, disheveled responses to our Information Requests. Cormorant files could be anywhere in those mounds. But once I was over the threshold and moving within the stacks of paper, I was systematic and relentless. For five straight days I worked, ripping some eight thousand pages of cormorant-related documents from the office. In the process of mining, I accidentally destroyed the "geologic record" of Ken's paperwork, the depth of pages within the mounds serving as his primary clue for determining a document's relative age. When I was finished, I stacked all the remaining papers—from every project Ken had ever undertaken—into orderly columns. Each column stood about five feet tall and was arranged neatly in a corner of the lab. I then braced for the inevitable storm.

Ken howled when he returned to the office. "What did you do?! How am I gonna publish this stuff now?" We both knew there was nothing I could do to appease him, so I gave a quick apology and made an even faster retreat. It was a risky move for which Ken barely forgave me, and only many months later. By then, the information had more than proved its worth, however.

In April 1999, Josh Lipton, Doug Beltman, and I led an intense discussion about the issues at the center of the Cormorant Wars, as well as about injuries to birds more generally. We knew we had to bring Tim Kubiak into the fold to see if the team could credibly describe the relevant science without reigniting the controversy between Tim, who said PCBs were to blame, and Ken, who said the PCB theory lacked sufficient evidence. The team also knew we could not place Ken and Tim in the same room because of their now-infamous mutual dislike. Instead, we relied on two government experts to represent Ken, a husband and wife who were two of the best avian field researchers in the country. The couple had a command of the scientific literature equal to Tim's, and were just as organized. They had been working on my team for years, and with Ken for decades—one had actually been Ken's passenger when the small plane they were flying ran out of fuel and crashed into the bay of Green Bay as they chased cormorants. Ken trusted them both, as they shared his research perspective on avian field studies. Just as important, the whole team trusted that "Ken's experts" cared more about scientific credibility than about any kind of advocacy, including taking sides in the Cormorant Wars.

We led a team of government lawyers, government specialists, and hired consultants to systematically review all the key data and literature, species by species. Tim usually favored language that implicated PCBs as the cause of injuries; Ken's experts were more cautious and more convincing about the underlying science. Every time an argument threatened to evoke an angry rebuttal from Tim, one of Ken's experts would pull key papers from a briefcase. Tim would read and relent, even when it came to crossed bills in double-crested cormorants, though he did not seem happy about it.

One evening after an arduous day of arguing, several of us were out to dinner with Tim, who began orating about bird injuries. He was a large man, and as he spoke, his body language demanded more and more space. Near the end of the meal, Tim's usually soft-spoken voice crescendoed into an impassioned speech. Finally, he proclaimed angrily: "Say what you want about cormorants, but nobody fucks with my terns!" It was an acknowledgment that he would not fight the team on cormorants, but also a vivid performance that convinced the rest of us we wouldn't want to rely on Tim as an expert witness in court.

The next day, Frank and I worked with Hagler Bailly to finalize decisions that capped weeks of discussions with specialists, consultants, managers, and attorneys. By day's end, everyone was exhausted but satisfied that we had crossed critical thresholds with our full assemblage of technical and legal expertise.

By now, I had been working closely with Josh and Doug for years. We trusted one another and had just accomplished the impossible: a Fish and Wildlife bird injury determination that apparently would not be opposed by either side of the Cormorant Wars. We had systematically

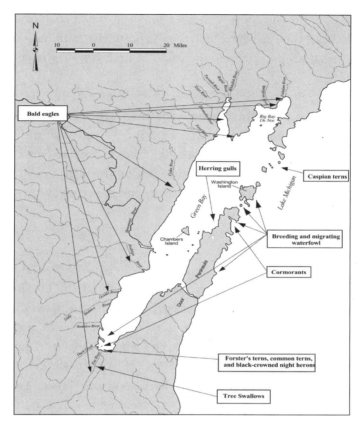

Locations of studies of PCBs in birds, by species. (U.S. Fish and Wildlife Service, Injuries to Avian Resources determination, May 1999)

unraveled the leading theories that linked PCBs and crossed-billed cormorants.* We had weighed the scientific literature, conducted field research, and run multiple lab experiments spanning several years using wide ranges of PCB concentrations, including some that were orders of magnitude higher than any found in the bay. Lastly, we had tested the

---

* Multiple laboratory experiments over several years failed to produce any crossed bills even with very high concentrations of co-planer PCBs, PCB mixtures, and PCB extracts from Green Bay fish that mimicked cormorant diets. Furthermore, multiple years of intensive field studies at Cat Island, the cormorant colony with the highest PCB concentrations, failed to show any crossed bills. The actual cause of crossed bills was never determined.

reliability of our own expert witnesses. Crossed-billed cormorants were out of the case, though reproductive injuries to cormorants—as well as deformities and reproductive injuries to other birds—remained just as solidly "in."

The team took a few hours off over beers. We laughed. We joked. As the night wore on and the alcohol took hold, we even cast a hilarious movie, choosing which film actors we wanted to play all the interesting, maddening, and outright peculiar characters we had come to know through our four years of working together on the Green Bay case.

It was a much-needed release as we prepared ourselves for what was to come.

Before a crowded auditorium in Green Bay in May 1999, I laid out the results of known PCB injuries to birds throughout the Fox River and Green Bay. The findings, which capped years of study, would finally answer the public's questions about the grotesque bird deformities found on the bay, other health effects, and whether the local game birds were safe to eat.

The solemnly titled Injuries to Avian Resources, Lower Fox River/ Green Bay Natural Resource Damage Assessment would be the third of eight documents, released over a twenty-four-month period from 1998 through 2000, presenting Fish and Wildlife's damage assessment results to the public (FWS 1999a). Notably, this was the first of six Fish and Wildlife damage assessment documents bearing information of enough consequence to warrant both a public meeting and an official public comment period.

I would mark the occasion by granting interviews with ten area media outlets, staffers for U.S. senator Kohl and U.S. representative Petri, and technical representatives for the Fox River Group of paper companies. The megaphone was even louder than I had expected. Print, radio, and TV reporters now all wanted in on this story about how PCBs affected birds and what that meant for cleanup and restoration in their community. And for once, people all around town were actually talking about damage assessment results—not about the war between Wisconsin and the Feds. Sure, it had required plenty of advance work with the press and stakeholders to explain why the scientific and legal details mattered. But it was gratifying to see so many people who were more than interested: they were hungry to understand more about what was happening to their river, bay, and Lake Michigan, and what they could do about it.

I now highlighted how the co-trustees had eliminated one of the most notorious local injuries from our case—crossed bills in double-crested cormorants—but had established that plenty of other injuries were, in fact, caused by paper company PCB releases. I pointed to the unacceptably high levels of PCBs throughout the river and bay system, as well as in most of the waterfowl that lived there. I summarized the waterfowl consumption advisories aimed at protecting people, mostly recreational hunters, who ate waterfowl from the river and bay, and showed how PCB levels in many waterfowl species throughout the bay exceeded federal Food and Drug Administration levels for safe human consumption.

Beyond this, I showed that nearly every bird species throughout the river and bay area was exposed to PCBs and that, in turn, the chemicals caused harmful health effects in a handful of the dozens of species studied there. Forster's terns had lowered reproductive rates, as well as physical deformities like crossed bills and poorly developed bones and bills, and behavioral abnormalities such as nest abandonment. Common terns also had lowered reproductive rates and physical deformities. Double-crested cormorants and bald eagles both had lowered reproductive rates, though bald eagle reproduction was also affected by the chemical DDE—a breakdown product of the pesticide DDT.

In summary, the co-trustees had found the scope of the injuries from PCBs alarming. All of the river and bay waters exceeded the federal standards set to protect fish and wildlife. All of the fish in those waters were exposed to PCBs, as was the wildlife that fed on them. Most had too many PCBs in their bodies to be eaten safely by people or wildlife, and some creatures experienced a range of disturbing health effects. The PCB contamination of the Fox River and bay of Green Bay was complete. It was wall to wall.

Notably, DNR's Fox River staff didn't bother to attend the meeting, discuss the findings, or respond during the official comment period. Still, I was pretty sure Wisconsin was now watching my agency intently.

PCB PROBLEMS STACK UP FOR RESIDENTS

Susan Campbell

It was a breezy morning in early June 1999 when I rang the doorbell at Bill Acker's home, situated on a small cove along the bay's southern shore near the mouth of the Fox River. The former paper industry engineer regularly contacted me and others involved in the case to float ideas about potential cleanup methods and technologies for the Fox River. Highly intelligent and possessing an insider's view, Acker approached the contaminant problem with an engineer's zeal, a passion for protecting public waters, and a persistence some found annoying. He was also an eccentric.

He'd invited me to his home this day to share his most recent revelation: a personal complaint about how the PCBs impacted him as a private property owner. Acker's wife came to the door and ushered me straightaway to the basement where, she said, Acker was working in his office. Descending the stairs, I was dumbfounded. The brightly lit basement held a labyrinth of files stretching in every direction and nearly touching the pipes that hung from the basement ceiling. Acker yelled out a cheery "Hello" from somewhere within the organized stacks and came rolling over, flat on his back on a small scooter he propelled by his feet. He moved about with surprising dexterity and speed for a middle-aged man. Acker clearly knew the maze well, rounding the corners with ease before careening down the final stretch to where I stood waiting. He got up, adjusted his glasses, and proudly gestured toward his subterranean library. "This is what I've been talking about." He'd wanted to show it off for a while. After working for eleven years as an engineer at a paper mill, Acker now ran his own engineering consulting firm. These files comprised the tools of his trade. I marveled at his unique filing system and promised myself I'd get out of the office more often.

But the real show, at least for today's purposes, was outside. Acker led me up the stairs and out behind the house, where a new picture window overlooked an altered shoreline. He pointed to where zebra mussel shells had crept up about two hundred feet from the water's edge and piled in mounds, some as high as six feet, along the shore outside his home. The small shells crunched loudly underfoot with every step we took. There was no sand here, no dirt. A barefoot stroll along this beach would be about as pleasant as walking through cut glass.

The zebra mussels, an invasive aquatic species first confirmed in the bay in 1993, had done much to change the bay's ecology. Most notably, the thumb-sized filter feeders had cleared the water, which had upsides and downsides environmentally. For Acker, a clear downside was the fact that the decomposing bodies in all those shells harbored toxic PCBs. He noted that researchers from UW–Green Bay had found concentrations in the mollusks' fat ranging from 2 to 12 parts per million, with the highest concentrations along the bay's southern shore, where Acker and his neighbors happened to live. University of Wisconsin–Sea Grant officials had told him the situation wouldn't improve appreciably and the mussels were bound to continue stacking up. As they did, Acker said, he and his neighbors would be responsible for digging out their cove. Figuring that about a thousand tons of the shells had accumulated there in just the last four years, he estimated it would cost about $3,000 in tipping fees alone to dispose of the shells at the local landfill. But there was a bigger concern. Although there were no laws governing disposal of PCB-tainted mollusks, Acker worried the day might come when he and his neighbors could be held liable for whatever they dumped. The paper companies, he said, should be made to pay that cost as part of whatever damage settlement arose from the cleanup.

After my visit, I called DNR's Bob Paulson. He agreed Acker had a growing problem on his property. "As long as there are PCBs in there, he's right to contact us," Paulson said (Campbell 1999j). "If he does it and we find out later it's a problem, we could make him go clean up whatever farm field he spreads it on." I knew a state committee was already at work debating what level of PCB-contaminated soil might be safe enough to spread on Wisconsin farm fields and other open lands, a fact that many environmentalists found worrisome in its own right.* But Paulson said DNR had no authority to include PCB-related damages to private property owners in any cleanup plan for the mills. "Where do you draw the line?" he asked. Paulson pointed to another avenue for Acker to try to recoup his costs: Acker could sue the companies on his own.

Surveying the piles of contaminated shells outside Acker's home and knowing that PCBs were accumulating similarly in other places all along the bay, in its wildlife and, potentially, in its people, I felt overwhelmed. It was just a taste of what the community was up against, and what federal scientists like David Allen were struggling to assess in figuring out how much the paper companies ultimately should be expected to pay.

TRACING PCB PATHWAYS

David Allen

August 30 was the date of the next landmark public meeting in Green Bay, this one to roll out the latest piece of the federal damage assessment. Bill Hartwig had just signed another official determination, the PCB Pathway Determination for the Lower Fox River/Green Bay Natural Resource Damage Assessment, that specifically detailed where the Fox River's PCBs originated, and where they landed (FWS 1999d). I had talked up the study beforehand with the local papers, radio stations, and TV news to bring as much transparency as possible to the research, which confirmed key facts underpinning the history of the Fox River and Green Bay's PCB contamination.

Chief among the facts I shared with the audience that evening: about 660,000 pounds of PCBs had been released by paper manufacturing and recycling facilities owned by a handful of companies whose corporate

---

* Wisconsin Department of Natural Resources website, Zebra Mussel, https://dnr.wi.gov/lakes/invasives/AISLists.aspx?species=ZM&status%20%3C%3E%20OBSERVED&groupBy=County.

structure and ownership had changed over the years, the same companies now represented by the Fox River Group. What happened to all
those PCBs after their release into the Lower Fox River? That was the
next big question, and an equally contentious one for the paper companies. The companies were loudly claiming that their own computer
model showed the PCBs were buried and immobilized in the riverbed
beneath clean sediment.

I said the data told a very different story, however—a damning one.

The Fish and Wildlife research showed PCBs hitching rides on sediment particles from the riverbed and being ferried out to the bay on
water currents. Indeed, the data showed that the Fox River was the
dominant source of PCBs to all of Green Bay, and that birds and fish
throughout the system were exposed to those same PCBs via the food
chain. The waters, sediments, and living organisms all showed the same
pattern of contamination. The bay was like a giant bathtub in which
the average currents flowed counterclockwise. PCBs traveled from the
mouth of the river at the southern end of the bay 120 miles up the east-
ern shore of the bay, past Wisconsin's Door Peninsula and Michigan's
Garden Peninsula, and then 120 miles back down the bay's western
shore. Although PCB concentrations in Green Bay had declined since
the 1970s, they were still alarmingly high because the chemicals were
designed to break down so slowly.

And more of the contaminants kept pouring in from the Fox River.
The same data showed that the bay of Green Bay was a major source of
PCBs found in Lake Michigan. Nobody was quite sure, even among my
team of experts, just how far the Fox River PCBs traveled once out in
the main part of Lake Michigan or how many of the lake's PCBs traveled
via global air transport to places like Lake Superior and the Arctic.

I explained to the audience that my agency's findings were rooted in
the enormous PCB data sets that had been collected for the earlier Mass
Balance Studies of the Fox River, bay of Green Bay, and Lake Michigan,
as well as new PCB data, mostly from fish, collected by Fish and Wildlife
using methods identical to those in the earlier studies. I summarized
the mass balance models created by DNR and EPA, and showed additional modeling by Fish and Wildlife. I pointed to plume and mixing

studies for the river and the bay, sediment cores pulled from deep in the river and bay, spatial and temporal patterns of PCBs throughout the system, and PCB congener patterns (the relative concentrations of the 209 individual PCB chemicals) throughout the system.

The data were comprehensive and technical for a local audience composed mostly of laypeople and news media. But the findings themselves were unequivocally clear. "All our lines of evidence point in the same direction," I said (Campbell 1999f). "Our conclusions are simple, straightforward, and robust."

ARC OF A REPORTING CAREER

Susan Campbell

In the first week of September, Tom packed his bags and headed to DC to work at *USA Today*. It was the beginning of a four-month internship at the paper. After dropping him off at the airport, I began settling into life alone for the first time in more than a decade. We had decided more than a year ago that Tom should apply for the internship; it was offered to Gannet newsrooms on a rotating basis, and many reporters and editors vied for the chance to work at the company's flagship paper. We'd agreed early on that job decisions should favor Tom's career because if we had children, I'd be the one to get off the career track. Plus, it was exactly the wrong time for me to leave the Fox River story. Much as I would have liked to jet off to DC to work at *USA Today* for a few months, it would have blunted the *Press-Gazette*'s Fox River coverage just as the story was peaking.

The internship had seemed a long way off—and not even a sure thing—when we first discussed it. I had nearly forgotten about it until months later, when Tom mentioned after work one night that he was heading to *USA Today* at the end of the summer. I'd been thrilled for him but had also felt a pang of jealousy. I'd felt it again this morning as he left, suitcase in hand, but had pushed it aside. I'd agreed to keep the home fires burning, and knew I had plenty to keep me busy in the coming months.

Soon after Tom left, however, there came a recurring and awkward question from friends: "Why don't you and Tom have children?" It came out of the blue, and it stung. Older friends with children told me I was in danger of missing out; others seemed to interpret Tom's DC stint as a separation of sorts—a sign, perhaps, that we were coming apart at the seams as a couple.

My desk mate, a smack-talking, middle-aged divorcée, asked me my age one day and when I told her, she declared me "tirty-tree and a turd." It was a playful nod to a stereotypical northern accent, and we both had a good laugh. But it did get me thinking about my age. I wasn't getting any younger, and suddenly thirty-three seemed much older than the twenty-seven I'd been when I arrived in Green Bay. "You're not a spring chicken anymore," another colleague needled when a young reporter, about ten years my junior, was hired. Somewhere along the line, I had crossed over from being too young to be taken seriously to being "older." When had I actually peaked? But there was that bigger question Tom and I managed to avoid for years: what about children? We'd been married ten years. Starting a family had always been a possibility, but we were in no hurry to become parents. It seemed a poor fit for a couple of reporters working unpredictable hours, and downsizing to one newspaper job from two would be hard to manage financially. There were too many people on the planet, anyway. So we'd punted, and mercifully, most people had stopped asking. Until now.

But there was also this: my hand injuries had given me an early window onto the fickleness of the business world, and a sneak peek at what life might be like in the twilight of my career. I had learned I was disposable, valuable to an employer only as long as I could produce something. Once that utility ceased, because of injury, failing health, or perhaps simply being over fifty, my value would also cease—or at least wane significantly. I saw it in the newsroom, and heard stories from colleagues about hitting salary caps and other insults as they marched closer to retirement age. Reporting—or almost any career, for that matter— seemed inherently unsustainable and unfulfilling to me for the long term. At the same time, as I watched my own parents age, I had come to value family more and more.

And so I wrestled inwardly, though there was never much time for deep introspection. The Fox River had taken center stage for more than three years; now the issue was raging. I couldn't quit now, just as things were starting to come to a head. It seemed self-important and silly to let a news story dictate when to start a family, and Tom and I both acknowledged the absurdity. Still, we'd punted.

And now Tom was in DC.

PAPER COMPANIES AND GENERAL ELECTRIC

David Allen

I was worried about an upcoming public meeting arranged by the paper companies and General Electric. It would bring a panel of scientists to Green Bay for two days of exploring how best to address PCB cleanups, not just locally but nationwide. The inquiry was yet another instance of the Hudson River case reverberating in the Fox River Valley. Congress had ordered the study in response to a call by General Electric, which continued to fight a multi-million-dollar Superfund-driven cleanup of PCBs in the Hudson. The company vehemently opposed dredging as a solution in New York, and wanted to bar EPA from moving forward with PCB dredging anywhere in the country until a scientific review was conducted. Congress had complied by ordering, in conjunction with EPA, the National Academy of Sciences to appoint a panel to study the human and ecological risks of various PCB cleanup methods, and develop guidelines for how such cleanups should be handled. A New York representative whose district happened to include contaminated stretches of the Hudson River had added the order as a rider to the EPA's funding appropriation.

I suspected GE and the Fox River Group would want to maximize the opportunity to highlight only the drawbacks of dredging, and minimize the risk of any counter arguments that might play into the governments' hand. I decided to help meet the challenge when the panelists came to town. Outside the formal proceedings, I invited panelists, John Giesy among them, on a Fox River field trip aboard my boat. I didn't say much,

David Allen in his twenty-four-foot trawler in Sturgeon Bay, Wisconsin, Lake Michigan, 1994. (Darlene Allen)

but I made a sincere effort to laugh at Giesy's jokes and show a keen interest in whatever he had to say. Giesy needed no encouragement, though, as he held forth for most of the day, including on topics well beyond his expertise.

Amid the boatload of information I absorbed from my trek was a singular gem: I thought the paper companies might have a loose cannon on their hands in Giesy.

SCOPE OF THE CLEANUP

Susan Campbell

Wisconsin DNR was noticeably absent from the National Academy of Sciences' hearings in Green Bay, which featured presentations by Fish and Wildlife, EPA, and the public. Some of the academy's panelists were disappointed that dredging and natural recovery were the only two options presented during the two days of hearings. "I feel like people are walking around with blinders on," one of them told me (Campbell 1999i). A Sierra Club spokesperson had predicted just such a narrow polarized debate when the visit was announced earlier that summer. Although the panel had been tasked with reviewing all sorts of remediation tools—among them sediment capping, source control, and natural recovery—she'd told me that, given the GE connection, "There's kind of an implicit focus on dredging" (Campbell 1999h).

The Sierra Club had voiced even more reservation about the visit because two of the panelists were involved directly with the Fox River cleanup. One of them was John Giesy, the Michigan State University scientist who had debated Theo Colborn on PCBs, and whom the mills had now hired to conduct an Ecological Risk Assessment of the river. The Sierra Club worried that this panel of potentially biased origin and makeup would have a major ripple effect on PCB cleanups—and not just for local waters. "The panel's recommendation could have a very significant effect on both the fate of the Fox River and on sediment cleanups nationally," Sierra Club warned (Campbell 1999h). "They will essentially, through their recommendations to Congress, dictate how EPA addresses contaminated sediment."

The question of which cleanup method would be used in the Fox River remained unsettled for now, but at the end of October came news that the potential scope of the cleanup had expanded significantly. Wisconsin DNR agreed to comply with a federal request to include the bay of Green Bay in the state's potential cleanup scenarios. Given the known PCB contamination there, EPA had requested that all fifteen hundred square miles of Green Bay—including its waters, sediment, fish, and wildlife—be factored into the state scenarios.

Jim Hahnenberg told me the new DNR studies could well show that removing or capping the PCBs in bay sediments would not be feasible, a point DNR had argued in initially deciding to leave the bay out of its cleanup scenarios. "But in order to make that determination, we have to go through a rigorous scientific analysis," Hahnenberg said (Campbell 1999a). "You can't just do it by gut feel."

Behind the scenes, Hahnenberg had agreed early on with Fish and Wildlife that the federal RI/FS had to include the bay because the risks there were so much greater than in the river alone. In other words, the cleanup studies' risk assessments for human health and the environment would need to incorporate the bay to justify cleaning up the river.

Eventually, DNR's resistance on this point forced Hahnenberg to contract with Fish and Wildlife to draft the Ecological Risk Assessment of the bay. It was yet one more instance of Fish and Wildlife shepherding a damage assessment that would lead the Superfund process, instead of the other way around.

ASSESSMENT RESULTS ACCELERATE

David Allen

I had been watching the *Lelond La Fond* since I moved to Algoma in 1993. It was a fifty-two-foot, all-steel fishing tug. Built in 1942, it still plied Lake Michigan waters, departing daily from its dock along the Ahnapee River. And it was still bringing in fish most days, even in winter. I loved watching this steel-topped, black-and-white beauty putter past the old fish shanties, past the red lighthouse, and into the rolling waves of the lake.

Needless to say, I was thrilled when Fish and Wildlife's local fisheries chief asked me if I wanted to go out on that boat with its owners to bring in lake trout for the damage assessment study. I had first met the local fisheries chief when I had arrived in Green Bay in 1992. He was in the midst of a career devoted to, among other things, restoring Lake Michigan's lake trout population. He and I had been talking about studying lake trout for the damage assessment since 1993, and now those studies were well underway.

I liked the boat even more from the inside. The aroma of diesel fumes and fish entrails mingled with the blue cloud of cigarette smoke from the chain-smoking captain. The old six-cylinder diesel never skipped a beat, even when the superstructure's portholes dipped below the lake's surface in heavy rollers. The crew was after lake chubs that day, in addition to the lake trout catch commissioned by Fish and Wildlife for the study. Large powered rollers spun in the gill nets as the crew collected

David Allen kayaking on the Ahnapee River in Algoma, Wisconsin, passing the *Lelond La Fond* commercial fishing boat, 1992. (Darlene Allen)

the lake trout. Calling from an old black rotary-dial telephone that hung on a steel bulkhead, the crew reported back to shore about its catch.

I could hardly believe I was being paid to tag along on this joyride. I didn't have to get my hands dirty, or even take notes. I just had to stay out of the way.

Lake trout nearly become extinct in Lake Michigan in the early 1950s because sea lamprey invaded Lake Michigan from the Atlantic Ocean through canal systems (Eschmeyer 1957). The parasitic eel-like lamprey uses a suction-cup mouth to clamp onto fish, and a file-like tongue that scrapes through flesh to feed on their prey's bodily fluids, often killing them in the process. I learned that since the collapse of commercial fishing for lake trout in the 1940s, decades of sea lamprey control had failed to bring about a natural recovery of lake trout in Lake Michigan (Holey et al. 1995). In fact, lake trout eggs in Lake Michigan were notoriously unsuccessful at producing viable young that could survive into adulthood (Jones et al. 1995). There were two leading theories about why this was so: PCB contamination, or thiaminase from alewives that broke down vitamin B_1 in lake trout (Berlin, Hesselberg, and Mac 1981; Mac 1981; Fitzsimons 1995).

Lake trout would be a very big deal for the Natural Resource Damage Assessment if it turned out PCBs were behind their continued reproductive failure. Lake trout were a top-of-the-food-chain predator, and one of the most important species in Lake Michigan. The species was also hugely popular with recreational anglers, and historically the dominant fish for commercial fishing (Knuth et al. 1995).

Frank and I dedicated large sustained budgets and attention to study the lake trout question. The research itself fascinated me. One of the scientists had invented tiny needles from specialized glassware that he used to inject PCBs into individual lake trout eggs without damaging them. Field teams had traveled to multiple states and Ontario for eggs and adult lake trout. They had developed methods to bathe the eggs in thiamine solutions. Frank and I also sat in on numerous scientific discussions at meetings dedicated to the lake trout studies to determine which hypotheses and experiments should receive attention and support from our damage assessment.

Adult lake trout and eggs were collected from hatcheries and various wild populations—including those I had helped collect aboard the *Lelond La Fond* in Algoma—and brought to the lab. There, we fertilized and treated the eggs, and tested for thiamine, PCBs, and other chemicals. We also tested the viability of the eggs and the recently hatched fish. Next, we used statistical analyses to compare the eggs' PCB concentrations versus egg viability, then similarly compared the eggs' thiamine concentrations versus egg viability.

The field studies and lab experiments both worked. Our results showed clearly that thiamine deficiency in the field caused the lake trout's reproductive failure, not field concentrations of PCBs (Tillitt et al. 2005).

Further study showed that PCBs could cause some of the harmful effects to the eggs, but only at concentrations much higher than those measured in Lake Michigan at the time of the experiments. This prompted us to analyze historical data of PCB concentrations in Lake Michigan lake trout. The PCB concentrations had indeed been higher in the past, when the paper companies were still actively releasing the chemicals and in the years that immediately followed. Based on our analyses, however, the concentrations were not high enough to cause such harmful effects on the eggs after 1980, when the Superfund law was passed. The timing was important because Superfund would have made the paper companies liable for such injuries.

The co-trustees could now eliminate lake trout injuries from our case. In particular, we were careful to keep lake trout injuries out of economic studies that measured public preferences and values at the heart of our damages calculations.

The findings would admittedly limit potential damages but, as it turned out, they were great publicity for the case either way. I would also soon find that these results earned my team credibility.

Fishing the Great Lakes can be a bit of an extreme sport. Fresh water isn't as dense as salt water, so the wind can whip up big waves in a short time—and they're steeper and closer together than ocean waves. My father and I witnessed waves over twenty-five feet a few times from shore, such as the ones that sank the legendary SS *Edmund Fitzgerald* during a November storm on Lake Superior in 1975. We purposely fished in barely manageable eight-foot waves a few times, as long as the wind was already subsiding and especially if Bill Conlon was along to help me egg my father on. I never forgot the time, when I was a kid, when a front screamed across Lake Erie while we were out fishing twenty miles from port. By the time we made it back, the waves were eight to twelve feet and built to twelve to sixteen feet soon after we docked. The pressure system drove a seiche—a phenomenon where water is pushed to one side of the lake at the same time waves are building—that raised the lake level about eight feet in just a few hours. The docks and ramps were buried in water, and the waves crashed over most of the lakeshore roads.

All to say: open-water Great Lakes anglers are really serious about their fun. And they have the equipment to prove it.

I started fishing the Great Lakes when I was three years old. Back then, my family used a fifteen-foot Lyman, made of wood in the 1950s, with a thirty-five-horsepower Evinrude. In that boat, Lake Michigan's Big Bay de Noc at the north end of Green Bay looked positively fierce

The Allens' first Great Lakes boat, circa 1960s. (David F. Allen)

even with waves of two to four feet, which happened often. It was worth it, though, because the big lake had northern pike, smallmouth bass, and walleye swimming its waters.

By the end of the 1960s, the salmon introduced into Lake Michigan by the Michigan and Wisconsin DNRs were beginning to take hold. That meant fishing in deeper water, with down riggers, and longer expeditions into open waters. And that meant a bigger boat with a newer motor. So my grandfather bought a seventeen-foot fiberglass Sportcraft, and my father bought a Bearcat fifty-five-horsepower motor. That was an investment of thousands of dollars, even before buying the down riggers and bigger trolling tackle. Those purchases spawned one of the biggest family controversies in my memory. But a couple of trips a day on the big lake calmed everybody down, particularly when the big coho and Chinook salmon started filling the coolers.

Then, in 1972, my father found a deal: a twenty-one-foot Lund with a 140-horsepower Mercruiser for a little over $5,000, including the trailer. Now, with two Great Lakes boats, we were really set.

It was during the 1970s that PCB advisories began accompanying fishing licenses, especially for big salmon in Lake Michigan. By the end of the 1980s, my whole extended family continued to fish the big waters, but we took great care to avoid eating the most contaminated species and to avoid parts of the less contaminated fish that had the highest PCB concentrations. Nobody ate the thirty-two-pound Chinook that my grandfather caught. Nobody under the age of fifty ate any fish over twenty pounds. PCBs gravitate to fat, so the smaller fish were cleaned to remove as much skin and fat as was practical, and the fillets were zippered to remove the fatty lateral lines. Then the bright orange pieces were grilled so that even more fat would drip away. Some of the younger women and the kids, facing greater health risks from PCBs, didn't even eat these.

But everybody kept fishing.

In the 1990s, the reality of Lake Michigan PCBs really hit home when I started working in Green Bay. Still, nobody in my family stopped fishing. And everybody still wanted to eat the fish. It was time for a bigger boat to reach cleaner lake trout twenty-five miles out on Lake Superior. Another $29,000, this time for a 1992, twenty-three-foot Sea Ox with a two-hundred-horsepower Mercruiser and a trolling outboard. It didn't take long to find the Lake Superior lake trout. Even on Lake Superior, though, nobody ate the really big lake trout. They had PCBs, too, mostly from the air after evaporation from places like Lake Michigan. But the small lake trout, which hadn't lived in the water long enough to take up many contaminants, were mostly clean—and delicious.

Eventually, the smaller Lake Superior lake trout and Lake Erie walleye became my family's primary Great Lakes targets for fishing. The PCB consumption advisories on Lake Michigan were a driving factor in our taste in fish. To accommodate this, my family moved up to an even more capable boat for the really big waters of Lake Superior: a $136,000, twenty-five-foot Grady White with twin 150-horsepower Yamaha outboards.

I heard countless versions of my own family fishing story from other Green Bay and Lake Michigan anglers via my work on the damage assessment's economics studies. I learned that Lake Michigan anglers are just as avid as my family. They buy really big boats. They buy really expensive tackle. They travel from Wisconsin, Michigan, Illinois, Indi-

The Allens' fifth Great Lakes boat, 2015, with Frank Horvath on the left. (P. David Allen II)

ana, Minnesota, Ohio, and more distant states. They fish even when the weather makes them look crazy for doing so. They hate PCBs and fish consumption advisories even more than they hate coming up empty after a long day on the lake.

But they do not stop fishing. And they do not stop looking for safe ways to eat their fish.

On November 8, 1999, I led Fish and Wildlife's next key public meeting. This time, Bill Hartwig had signed three official determinations: Injuries to Surface Water Resources, Injuries to Fishery Resources, and Recreational Fishing Damages from Fish Consumption Advisories (FWS 1999c, 1999b, 1999e). The facts told a startling story all on their own. My job was simply to deliver them, then get out of the way.

I highlighted the fact that surface waters throughout the Lower Fox River and bay of Green Bay exceeded the injury threshold to protect fish-eating wildlife, a threshold established by EPA and the eight Great Lakes states. In fact, this threshold was exceeded in every single water sample in the entire assessment, and by ten to one hundred times in most Fox River samples. The PCBs circulating in these surface waters also led to the fish consumption advisories, the same advisories that studies showed were often missed or ignored by subsistence fishermen, recreational anglers, and their families who ate fish from the river and bay.

I now laid out Fish and Wildlife's surprising finding about the demise of the iconic lake trout, explaining that both field and lab studies had clearly shown that thiamine deficiency—not PCBs—explained the lake trout's reproductive failure in Lake Michigan. I announced that lake trout injuries, therefore, were eliminated from the case.

It was an honest admission that those following the case closely, supporters and detractors alike, hadn't expected from federal cleanup proponents. During the public comment portion of the meeting, a retired chemical engineer from one of the local paper companies approached me and expressed his appreciation for Fish and Wildlife's candor and transparency. He wouldn't be the last.

The Fox River paper companies' PCB releases couldn't be linked to reproductive failure in lake trout, or to crossed bills in cormorants—at least during the era of Superfund. But the contaminants caused plenty of other serious problems in the Fox River and Green Bay, and I was about to home in on the one that mattered most to the community.

Notably, the PCB contamination had prompted Wisconsin and Michigan to issue consumption advisories for nearly every species of fish valued by anglers in the river and bay from the 1970s to the time of the federal damage assessment. Fish and Wildlife had now confirmed that PCB levels in many fish species throughout the river and bay exceeded the level set by the federal Food and Drug Administration as safe for people to eat. My team had also confirmed that every species of fish throughout the river and bay was exposed to PCBs. The chemicals, in turn, had caused harmful health effects in at least one of the species studied there: walleye registered higher rates of liver tumors because of paper company PCBs.

It was finally time for me to talk about the number, or at least one of the numbers. The public was going to learn the first of what would ultimately be several bottom lines for what PCB damages to the Fox cost in terms of dollars.

"This isn't the only element of damages, but it's certainly one of the most straightforward and most important," I told the audience. "To cut right to the punch line, we think this study of recreational fishing damages is the most concrete and rigorous evidence to date that the PCB problem really is important to the general public."

I started with methods, detailing how those met rigorous academic and regulatory standards. I explained that this first study about damages focused on how fish consumption advisories affected present-day anglers in the river and bay, and was exciting because it was brand-new research. Anglers' reaction to fish consumption advisories was a relatively easy signal for economists to measure. The study assessed how anglers traded between three factors related to their individual fishing habits: boat-launch fees; catch rate for the species they targeted; and the severity of consumption advisories among those targeted species. My team found that consumption advisories mattered more to anglers, on average, than did their own catch rates. The results were striking. "It really shows dramatically how important the PCB problem is to people," I said. "People who are currently fishing actually would rather have the consumption advisories lower than increase the speed with which they can catch those fish."

I then went through the numbers, driving home the study's key determination: PCBs from the paper companies had caused at least $100 million in damages. That figure included a bunch of caveats, however. The number represented only the losses for active anglers, not the rest of the public. The number was only for fish consumption advisories, not for the rest of the injuries caused by paper company PCBs. And the number assumed that EPA and DNR would clean up the Fox River as quickly and completely as practical, thereby shortening the duration of future fish consumption advisories. I concluded that every day of delay, and any part of the cleanup left undone, guaranteed a bigger number.

The vice president of the Green Bay chapter of Walleyes for Tomorrow was in the audience that night. Local anglers were due some sort of compensation, "there's no question of that," he said. But he couldn't say whether $100 million was too high or too low to compensate for their losses. "You can't put a dollar amount on how much the fishermen or the environment have lost because of this. You really can't," he said. "We lost" (Campbell 1999g).

He was right that it seemed an impossible reach to even try to calculate the incalculable. Yet my team had done just that, at least in terms of figuring damages beyond each angler's private losses. And that didn't include losses experienced by other members of the public, the rest of the PCB injuries to wildlife, or the cost of cleanup.

SUPERFUND GAINS POPULARITY

Susan Campbell

More than a year after EPA announced it was pursuing a Superfund listing for the Fox River, an overwhelming majority of the Green Bay community was backing it. A survey of local residents released in October found that most favored a Superfund-led cleanup, and a majority, 65 percent, believed the seven paper mills responsible for the PCB contamination should pay for it. Conducted by the local St. Norbert College Survey Center, the phone survey had polled 424 random people aged eighteen and older of varying education and income levels.

The survey center director was surprised to find that 70 percent of Brown County residents supported a Superfund listing for the Fox River, despite the negative connotation the Superfund label held for so many. He surmised that the survey reflected the public's frustration with an issue that had been around for years with no real progress toward resolution. "EPA's justification for putting it on the priority list was that nothing was getting done," he said. "Maybe that's in the public eye right now: that this thing's been around and a problem for a while, so why not take a major step to cleaning it up?" (Campbell 1999k).

CALM BEFORE THE STORM

David Allen

During 1999, Bill Hartwig had signed off on five key official determinations—in May, August, and November—on behalf of the federal government and its co-trustees. Each document launched an official public review that started with a public meeting on the technical results of the federal studies.

The two Fox River storylines, one about relevant facts and the other about interagency strife, were now feeding each other. Three levels of government—federal, state, and tribal—now vied for control of cleanup and restoration decisions. The struggles among agencies played out before an increasingly rapt public audience. The press, academia, and interest groups, which had been aware of PCB problems for many years, became increasingly fascinated by the emerging drama. How would cleanup and restoration decisions actually be made? Who would make them? What would be done? And especially, who would pay for it? The conflict between DNR and its natural governmental partners in Wisconsin and Michigan made even bigger news than the typical disagreements between government and responsible parties at sites like the Hudson River in New York.

My team and I relied on the now-intense interest of the public and scientific community to guarantee scrutiny of our work. We took advantage of the bright light provided by Wisconsin's and the paper companies' campaign to discredit our efforts. We used that bright light to ensure that a very large audience engaged us directly. We were confident that the general public and the scientific community would give us a fairer hearing than the emissaries sent by Wisconsin and the paper companies. We were also confident that all that scrutiny from the public and the scientific community would sharpen our arguments for court, should it come to that.

EPA leaders were also paying close attention. They were now requiring Wisconsin DNR to draft the Remedial Investigation and Feasibility Study—the EPA's official cleanup studies—in harmony with the technical results emerging from Fish and Wildlife's damage assessment. This was often done over DNR's objections. Gradually, EPA prevailed over Wisconsin on nearly every major technical issue, with support from Fish and Wildlife, the tribes, and eventually the State of Michigan.

The damage assessment results continued to provide most of Fish and Wildlife's significant leverage. My boss Frank Horvath, my lawyer Matt Richmond, my consultant Josh Lipton, and I continued to quietly strategize and harmonize the legal and technical issues. Privately, Frank and I also steadfastly kept our vow to each other: no more big meetings on Fish and Wildlife's dime to persuade Bruce Baker. Wisconsin DNR would either be convinced by the facts and bow to public pressure, or be left behind. I would learn soon enough, though, that forging a bond with Wisconsin would prove as elusive as ever. The winter of 2000–2001 would give rise to the most heated, most public, and most pointed battle between Fish and Wildlife and DNR in the entire history of the Green Bay cleanup and damage assessment.

7

ESCALATION TO THE BREAKING POINT

DNR DROPS THE BALL

David Allen

After their secret deal with the paper companies, back in 1997, it took DNR a couple of years to hammer out the details of an actual dredging demonstration project. In June 1999, DNR's Bob Paulson gave an update in Chicago to the other agencies about how that project, at "SMU 56–57" next to Fort Howard, was going. Tensions were high. EPA was in the process of launching its Superfund authorities for the entire river, and the federal government was deeply concerned about the paper companies purposely trying to demonstrate how badly a dredging project could go. Federal and tribal concerns only seemed to strengthen Wisconsin's resolve to press ahead in an attempt to show *any* form of on-the-ground progress, consequences be damned.

Five months later, those fears turned to dread. In a November conference call, DNR announced to the other agencies that dredging would cease in December with less than 40 percent of the project completed. Money was running out—and so was time, as winter approached.

By February 2000, Paulson began revealing data to the other agencies that showed the paper company–funded project being conducted downstream by Fort Howard was now a bona fide environmental disaster. PCBs in the surface sediments were now 280 parts per million, a couple of orders of magnitude higher than when the project began.

DISASTER

Susan Campbell

It was a sobering moment when I realized that at no time in recent history had the rollicking, roiling Fox River presented more danger to the public than it did right now.

It was early November 1999, and the DNR was holding a press conference to announce that cost overruns, project setbacks, and winter's onset were about to put an abrupt halt to the dredging project at the river's hottest hot spot, the one funded by the companies under the secret state-company deal. The project had started September 1 and the goal had been to remove eighty thousand cubic yards by Thanksgiving, but project officials now admitted that only about twenty thousand cubic yards had been removed so far. Moreover, only $2.5 million or less remained of the $9 million the paper mills had agreed to pay for the project. That was enough to fund the work through the season's end, but it was anyone's guess whether there would be money left to resume work at the site in spring. More money was unlikely. Fort Howard had already kicked in an additional $2 million once it was clear that project costs would exceed the $7 million they'd originally budgeted.

The pace of dredging had now increased to twenty-four hours a day and some of the equipment on site had been doubled to try to make up for lost time before operations shut down for the long Wisconsin winter. DNR's project manager told reporters that workers were sealing off areas at the site to prevent the exposure of high-level PCBs in the surrounding sediment after the dredging wrapped up. "What we're trying to do is make sure we leave the least amount of exposure we can, knowing that we're probably not going to get all of it out this fall" (Campbell 1999d). "Is that going to be a significant risk? I don't know," he said in answer to a reporter's question. "That's open to interpretation, I guess."

News of the extent of the damage and potential for calamity finally broke the following March, when DNR reported that dangerously high levels of PCBs had been exposed in the Fox River and called on the mills to complete their dredging project.

On its face, the project had been intended to show the effectiveness of dredging and disposing of Fox River PCBs. But the mills had hoped to prove just the opposite. By the time the paper companies abandoned the project, the dredging had removed less than 38 percent of the goal. Worse, like ripping a scab from a wound, the dredges had scoured away the top layers of the riverbed in places before aborting the project. This had exposed PCB concentrations of hundreds of parts per million—hundreds of times higher than the cleanup standards DNR and EPA eventually would set for the river. These measurements, more than six times the federal standard for hazardous waste disposal, dwarfed the original PCB concentrations of 2–5 ppm found in the site's shallower sediments.

Now, with spring on the way, the contaminants were exposed and poised to sweep downstream into the bay with the next flooding.

The widely publicized DNR report also shared data showing that in areas where it was completed, the project had succeeded in its goal of reducing PCB concentrations. But the Fox River Group put its own spin on the data, telling the media the results proved their long-standing position that dredging actually spread the river's PCBs. The mills dangled some misleading math to show this. They averaged the high PCB levels from the incomplete areas along with the much lower totals of the successfully completed areas. The result? PCB levels "rose" to an average of 75 ppm throughout the site after dredging. The mills then dug in against completing the project. Instead, they pushed publicly for capping the remaining contaminants in place, an option most experts opposed because of the area's natural volatility. I caught the sleight of hand and reported it, hoping other media would do the same and call out the mills' misinformation. But the paper companies had successfully exploited the media's and the public's blind spot when it came to science; the companies would go on to grow those seeds of deception into a full-scale campaign against dredging.

On March 21, the Fox River Group hired a public outreach director and launched a five-week TV campaign on all four local network stations. The thirty-second ads, aired during newscasts and prime time, aimed to bolster the mills' argument against dredging as they awaited the results from a much-vaunted peer-reviewed study of how PCB-tainted sediments move along the riverbed. The peer review, funded by the paper companies, looked at two models. The first model, used by EPA and DNR, showed PCBs and riverbed sediment moving from the Fox River into the bay. The second, developed by the paper companies, showed that PCBs in the riverbed don't move (Campbell 2000g).

By now, the Green Bay community was distressed and angry about the exorbitantly high PCB levels in the Fox now laid bare. Rebecca Katers likened the situation to "the equivalent of a major toxic PCB spill," and called for immediate EPA intervention. She called out the paper companies on their endgame. "Polluters should not be allowed to use this badly designed project as a precedent for the rest of the Fox River cleanup," she told the media, "or as a nationwide example of the failure of dredging" (Campbell 2000b).

The Green Bay Remedial Action Plan's Science and Technical Advisory Committee, which had studied Fox River pollution since the 1980s, also weighed in, sending a letter to DNR urging that dredging be completed as soon as possible. "These concentrations," the committee wrote, "represent a substantial increase in the potential environmental risk" (Campbell 2000f).

Soon the talk would turn to a key emergency tool at EPA's disposal: an "Act now, ask questions later" policy that gave the agency authority to order an emergency cleanup in the event of an immediate and substantial risk. If the polluters refused, the agency could perform the cleanup itself and sue the polluters later for cleanup costs.

The real hammer: EPA could also charge the polluters punitive damages totaling triple the cleanup cost, and fine them up to $25,000 per day of violation.

TURNING DISASTER INTO OPPORTUNITY
David Allen

I saw a silver lining.

Bill Hartwig was now enthusiastically committed to fixing the PCB problem in the Fox River, and his patience with DNR had evaporated. EPA was now inextricably committed to river-wide cleanup, and staff there was tiring of the paper companies' undue influence with Wisconsin. DNR was still rankled by the intrusion of Superfund and the Feds. But the agency was also clearly worried about the environmental consequences of the monstrously failing demonstration project and the fact that DNR alone bore official responsibility for the project's authorization and execution.

Meanwhile, the paper companies were still proclaiming that dredging always costs more, takes longer, and fixes less than agencies claim. I sensed that the paper companies were in danger of overplaying their hand, however.

I saw the failed project as a potentially lethal pinprick in a seven-mile stretch of buried PCBs that could suddenly explode from the river into the bay of Green Bay: a genuine emergency. Indeed, it was just the kind of emergency the Superfund law was made for. At any time now, a major storm could loosen and mobilize the once-buried PCBs, and after the floodwaters began to tear away at those contaminated sediments, more and more would swiftly flow downriver all the way to the bay. I knew the pinprick would need immediate surgery, but that it should also be extensive enough to cure the patient—achievable only by extracting all the adjacent grossly contaminated sediments. That might mean removing the entire continuous PCB deposit in the last seven miles of the river, reaching all the way from the De Pere Dam to the bay of Green Bay. I saw an amazing opportunity to tackle 90 percent of the PCB problem in the entire river—and tackle it now, not after more years of arguing with Wisconsin and the paper companies.

My path was clear. For the next few months, I would focus on convincing EPA to perform the surgery: an emergency response under Superfund to force dredging of the river below the De Pere Dam. I checked in with my team to make sure my scheme wasn't foolhardy. Everyone was on board. In February, I called Jim Hahnenberg at EPA, and we brought in EPA attorney Roger Grimes. Soon, Jim, Roger, and I had DOJ worried about impending litigation over hugely consequential unilateral orders, and mid-level EPA managers worried about potentially crushing workloads.

I hedged my bet by roping in Bill Hartwig. In theory, Bill could issue his own unilateral order, with EPA's concurrence. Without a doubt and without delay, he could issue a letter to EPA recommending unilateral orders, offering to invoke his own authority, and explaining why. Lastly, aware that transparency would be key to securing the public's support for the emergency unilateral order, I gave interviews to the *Green Bay Press-Gazette* and the national publication *Inside EPA*.

By March, Roger, Jim, and I had catalyzed an emergency governmental meeting in Chicago to address the failed demonstration project. Representatives of Wisconsin DNR, Fish and Wildlife, Justice, and EPA's key Superfund staff were there, as were representatives of the National Oceanic and Atmospheric Administration and the tribes.

Greg Hill took the hot seat for Wisconsin. He explained the history of the demonstration project: the Fox River Coalition had originally identified the site as a top priority based on PCB levels and erosion potential, but the coalition disbanded once Superfund intervened. The site had started with PCB concentrations measuring 2–5 ppm at its surface, but those levels rose to over 700 ppm in deep sediments. Thus far, only 1,325 pounds of the 3,000–3,500 pounds of PCBs targeted for removal had been dredged from the site. Then Hill dropped the bomb: the whole project had been designed to see how much could be removed with $7 million. It was the amount agreed to in the sweetheart deal DNR had struck in secret with the paper companies back in January 1997.

Hill's summary was met with stunned expressions around the room. Everyone was astonished DNR had agreed to such a project. Wisconsin had made no attempt to tie cleanup actions to risk reduction or injury prevention. In fact, the agency had taken few if any precautions to ensure it would leave the site in better condition than when the operation began. DNR had been as unconcerned about how much might actually be accomplished within the Fox River Group's budget as it was about how to weigh dwindling funds against environmental outcomes as the project progressed. Further, DNR had failed to prepare for, or apparently even anticipate, the paper companies' predictable arguments that dredging would actually make conditions worse. And, of course, the agency hadn't bothered to consult with the other agencies or the public.

I guessed that DNR might have figured a penned deal at the time was worth more than any eventual consequences. If so, it had been a gross miscalculation.

In the room now with Hill and the other agencies, I almost felt sorry for Hill as the attendees pummeled him with questions and opinions about how project goals and operating procedures would now have to be radically altered. The original plan of dredging to a predetermined depth would have to be abandoned; dredging all the way down to clean clay might be needed now to avoid leaving PCB concentrations at the surface that were higher than at the project's start. The potential sloughing of adjacent soft, contaminated sediments into the newly dredged hole at the hot spot was an obvious problem. This might require dredging contaminated sediment from the entire river below the De Pere Dam or, at the very least, constructing some sort of long, sloping cap. And that might have to be redredged as part of later solutions for the entire site. Ironically, DNR might find itself vulnerable to litigation by the paper companies because it had authorized this action without due diligence. Risk reduction was key now, not simple-minded mass removal. But the partners in the room worried about an even bigger problem: high river flows in the spring could easily be disastrous for the bay—and beyond to Lake Michigan and all the Great Lakes.

I finally asked Hill, point-blank, if DNR intended to oppose unilateral orders by EPA to address the emergency. Hill answered that George Meyer preferred giving the paper companies an opportunity to respond to a voluntary order. Right on cue, EPA attorney Roger Grimes asked me if Fish and Wildlife might be willing to issue its own unilateral order. I confirmed: yes, Bill Hartwig was willing. Our Interior lawyer noted that our agency would need EPA concurrence. Bill Hartwig's new assistant,

Charlie Wooley, said our agency would need technical assistance from EPA. DOJ's Matt Richmond said Fish and Wildlife would also need access to EPA's federal contractors. Through it all, I took notes in my green notebook and hoped everybody realized I was taking their caveats as permission to drive forward with a Fish and Wildlife unilateral order.

Assignments followed. DNR would provide cost estimates for a second dredging pass with contoured slopes and an engineered cap. EPA would craft language for a unilateral order. Fish and Wildlife and the legal team would research legal options for joint orders and EPA concurrence. Out of left field, as if DNR suddenly embraced the river-wide Superfund process, Hill wondered aloud if the paper companies might delay the cleanup studies for the entire river by fighting the unilateral order at the hot spot. I left the meeting wondering if I might hear George Meyer's head explode when Hill reported the results of the meeting. I also wondered if signs of bureaucratic panic within the federal government would reach my desk in Green Bay before I even returned. Finally, I sincerely wished I could be a fly on the paper companies' wall when they read the eventual letter from Bill Hartwig—which I was already eagerly assembling in my mind.

The next day, Jim Hahnenberg called me to report that his regional Superfund chief was thinking about capping instead of dredging. Luckily, EPA headquarters had already confirmed sufficient money for emergency dredging projects. Further, EPA's Dave Ullrich and his boss Frank Lyons were pressing forward to have a unilateral order in place by April 15—and no negotiations with the paper companies, at least for now. With help from my team, I started drafting Fish and Wildlife letters and unilateral orders for Bill Hartwig to sign. A few days later, we had a draft letter ready to be sent from Bill to Lyons, his counterpart at EPA. It urgently called for a unilateral order from one or both of them to finish cleaning up SMU 56–57. The letter also recommended not stopping until the emergency was addressed, even if that meant cleaning the whole last seven miles of the river.

For the rest of March, I pressed everybody I could reach to launch unilateral orders against the paper companies. At the same time, Bruce Baker announced he was having discussions with the paper companies about releasing them from natural resource damages liability in exchange for addressing the emergency voluntarily. Realistically, DNR had no authority to release the companies from federal, tribal, or Michigan liability, but it could certainly make everybody's path forward much trickier.

Roger Grimes was quick to reject Baker's latest ploy, and EPA moved forward with its own Superfund authorities. The scene that followed was all too familiar, however. DNR fought everybody, seemingly blind to the continued erosion of its own credibility. Fish and Wildlife was focused on creating direct leverage over the paper companies despite the mounting controversy. And EPA was trying to figure out how to wield its considerable Superfund authority without crossing DNR or Fish and Wildlife.

Bill Hartwig came through for the team in late March: he signed the letter to EPA recommending a unilateral order to begin emergency dredging in the Fox River. I made sure the public and the press knew all about it. In April, Bill signed another letter to the Fox River Group of paper companies. He now had everybody's complete attention: a senior executive, and the government's authorized official for natural resource damages, was openly calling for unilateral action that could lead to immediate cleanup of most of the PCBs in the Fox River.

I soon heard that George Meyer and the outside counsel for P. H. Glatfelter of the Fox River Group were outraged with Fish and Wildlife. More pointedly, Fort Howard's outside counsel was not only upset with my agency, he warned that continued Fish and Wildlife resistance would lead to more deals between DNR and the paper companies. Foreshadowing indeed. It wasn't long before Bruce Baker was announcing meetings between Governor Thompson and the paper company executives. Fish and Wildlife had struck a nerve—and hard. Good, I thought.

In May, EPA held firm to its emergency dredging order and Fort Howard began compromising. EPA and Fort Howard were now on course for an "administrative order on consent," but by the book and under the Superfund law (EPA 2000). There would be no secret deal and no early settlement of natural resource damages, regardless of Wisconsin's complaints.

Then, Appleton Papers offered $70 million in exchange for an agreement not to sue the company for seven years. That stunned many skeptics, including Bruce Baker. Here a single paper company was offering more than double a cleanup request Baker had made to Congress, back in 1994 as part of DNR's voluntary and ill-fated Fox River Coalition process, and in exchange for nothing but a delay in federal lawsuits. I was gratified my team's leverage was beginning to bear fruit, but I also worried many would be too eager to take the deal. In fact, I thought Appleton Papers was clever to offer so much. Blunting the government's growing leverage at this critical moment amid the demonstration project chaos might actually succeed in furthering paper company goals.

Also in May, Wisconsin finally agreed, at least on paper, to join the damage assessment by signing onto the Feds' third damage assessment addendum (FWS 2000a). My team and I viewed this document as our last best hope for opening a candid technical discussion with DNR that might convince the agency to finally embrace the federal damage assessment results. Dale Patterson's passing had left a huge hole in the team's coordination with DNR experts, however, and DNR now seemed more determined than ever to prevent Fish and Wildlife from completing its assessment.

Later in May, Bill Hartwig reported that George Meyer had finally agreed to decouple natural resource damages from the demonstration project emergency. I wasn't buying it, and I didn't think Bill was either. "Fool me once, shame on you," I told myself. "Fool me a hundred times . . ."

THE FIX

Susan Campbell

Fort Howard finally blinked. Company executives announced on May 25 that it would finish the failed pilot project rather than contend with an emergency cleanup order from the EPA. Fort Howard's agreement with the EPA and DNR would finally put an end to the potential hazard and public relations nightmare that lay just beyond the paper mill's discharge pipe into the Fox River. The Fort had initiated the pilot project in concert with the other six paper companies as part of their secret agreement with DNR, but it would be Fort Howard alone that would fix it. In return for the fix, the State of Wisconsin and EPA agreed to release Fort Howard from state and federal cleanup liability at the SMU 56–57 cleanup site, though not elsewhere on the river (Wilson 2000).

Unlike the original state-company pact, this plan wasn't doomed to fail. The agreement set a cleanup goal for the site, rather than a dollar figure to determine the project's scope. The new plan was that PCB levels at the site, currently measuring up to 310 parts per million, would be reduced to just 1 ppm. To accomplish this, Fort Howard agreed to dredge the fifty thousand cubic yards of contaminated sediment that was left untouched after the initial project had been forced to shut down the previous winter. The contaminated sediment would be disposed of at a Fort Howard landfill just west of Green Bay designed specifically to hold PCBs (Campbell 2000e).

The agencies praised Fort Howard for stepping up when the other six paper companies had dug in against dredging, offering instead the temporary and risky remedy of capping the contaminants in the riverbed.

Not surprisingly, Rebecca Katers was in no mood to celebrate when I reached her that day. Katers criticized the fact that a pilot project might turn out to be the only remediation work done on the river's hottest hot spot. Additionally, all the decisions regarding the site, such as the cleanup goal and the decision to landfill the PCBs, had been made in private negotiations with the paper companies. "The public was supposed to have input on those discussions," she said. "This sets a precedent for the rest of the river" (Campbell 2000e).

A month later, interference from Washington, DC, once again threatened to stall overall cleanup progress at the Fox River. Language was added to a U.S. House of Representatives bill that was headed to the Senate. EPA was directed not to order PCB dredging "or other invasive sediment remediation technologies" anywhere in the U.S. until results from the national study of cleanup technologies—still several months away—could be incorporated into the agency's policies (Campbell 2000c).

The report, from the National Academy of Sciences study that had sent panelists to Green Bay less than a year earlier, wouldn't be out until fall. How long it might take for EPA to incorporate the study's results after that was anybody's guess.

EPA administrator Carol Browner condemned the bill, which was used to fund her agency and included a number of other anti-environmental riders. "The nation hasn't seen this kind of anti-environment, anti-public health assault by the U.S. House of Representatives in several years," she said (Campbell 2000c).

EPA said the legislation would stall cleanup progress not only at the Fox River, but also at twenty-seven other sites around the country. Even so, it appeared to maneuver carefully around the emergency Fort Howard hot spot fix, and apparently would not interfere with voluntary settlements (Behnke 2000).

NEVER SAY DIE

David Allen

Meanwhile, EPA and DNR were in tense negotiations regarding a litany of issues about cleanup. At Fish and Wildlife, my team continued to feverishly prepare arguments on three fronts. First, we sought to influence EPA to pursue its unilateral response powers to address the failed demonstration project near Fort Howard before they had a bigger disaster on their hands. Second, we argued for continued rigorous EPA oversight of the cleanup studies for the whole river. Third, we pressured DNR to finally join our damage assessment, including signing off on the extensive work already completed and published.

Critically, we argued that the emergency near Fort Howard should not compromise a comprehensive cleanup. Nor should any cleanup sacrifice the hard-fought damage assessment or the restoration required to make the public whole.

At the same time, Fort Howard continued leading efforts to arm Wisconsin against FWS's damage assessment, particularly related to restoration options and economic damages. Fort Howard also continued offering concessions on cleanup in exchange for Wisconsin embracing paper company alternatives to our damage assessment. DNR continued to support Fort Howard's efforts, despite the bucket of new leverage the emergency provided the governmental agencies.

So, during the summer of 2000, my team worked furiously on the damage assessment details. We needed to integrate all our previous findings about PCBs, injuries, and damages with the new information about restoration and damages. We set a deadline of October 25 to complete the nation's first Restoration and Compensation Determination Plan (RCDP)—the lynchpin of the federal damage assessment that would form the technical basis for our restoration proposal and damage estimate. We assumed we'd have to publish the results without Wisconsin's endorsement, but we also saw this as our best opportunity since 1989—when DNR launched its ill-fated damage assessment program—to convince Wisconsin to finally join us.

I focused during these months on my priorities. I was careful not to take any action that might endanger completion of the RCDP by October 25. I worked feverishly to share the results as soon as they emerged, making them directly available to the scientific community, local stakeholders, and the press. It was important that everybody expected the final results in October. I also convinced the State of Michigan to join the assessment and to formally endorse the final document as another co-trustee. I hoped to include the Michigan public, equally invested in Green Bay and Lake Michigan from their location on the north end of the bay and opposite side of the lake, and intensify the pressure on Wisconsin to follow suit. At the same time, I still hoped to convince Wisconsin that the detailed damage assessment results were sound. I would even try to convince DNR's Fox River leaders—especially Greg Hill, Bruce Baker, and George Meyer—that they were better off working with Fish and Wildlife than against us. It was fine with me if they truly only cared about practical cleanup.

In June, I began my gambit with Bruce Baker and Greg Hill. Meeting in Milwaukee with seventeen staff from multiple agencies, I started by explaining the assessment results that mattered most to DNR cleanup plans: the highlights of Fish and Wildlife's published conclusions about

PCBs and injuries to water, sediment, fish, and wildlife, all of which could help DNR draft their cleanup studies.

I used no notes so that I could look DNR staff in the eyes and be alert to objections. There were no substantive disagreements with our pathway and injury results, but Greg Hill suddenly interrupted. He was clearly agitated, and I wondered if I might have accidentally slighted some DNR study or mischaracterized a data set. Hill then sidetracked the proceedings onto a whole new topic. Describing his father with admiration and emotion, he said he was willing to take *his father's* advice on the Fox River case because of his age and lengthy experience. He pointed out to the group that I was considerably younger than Hill, let alone Hill's father. I now found myself in an uncomfortable place; I couldn't think of a practical way to conceal my age.

"Greg, I think maybe I bungled my presentation about all these studies and data," I said. "Let me try another angle to see if I can just lay out the plain information without any comment from me so you guys can see if we missed something or have anything wrong." I continued where I'd left off in my earlier summary, but with greater emphasis on the other agencies—including DNR—that had contributed to the impressive corpus of Green Bay information.

The outburst had been so surreal that I was relieved when, during a break, a DOJ attorney pulled me aside to marvel at Hill's bizarre display and compliment me for keeping my professional cool. It had really happened.

Near the end of the day, Bruce Baker concluded that the agencies were 80 percent in agreement on pathways and injuries, but Wisconsin was more interested in cleanup than restoration. I countered that, since not a single disagreement had been raised on *any* pathway or injury issue, the agencies were realistically much closer to 100 percent agreement. Further, as Fish and Wildlife's pathway and injury conclusions directly supported Wisconsin's rationale for cleanup, I suggested it made sense for Wisconsin to now formally endorse the co-trustees' pathway and injury determinations. Baker affirmed that Wisconsin had no plans to further investigate PCB pathways and injuries, and that endorsement might indeed be possible. A good sign, I thought.

The next day, still in Milwaukee, outside expert economists joined the meeting, including Dr. Rich Bishop from my team. Also present was an economist from Arizona whom the paper companies were funding for Wisconsin DNR. Fish and Wildlife had hired Rich, a professor and the department head in agricultural economics at UW–Madison, because he had published in the relevant natural resource economics literature and enjoyed a stellar national reputation. (As a bonus, he was probably older than Hill.)

Rich had been directly involved with my team in conducting primary economics research for the Green Bay damage assessment. So I had him explain, in detail, our approaches and results. None of my team had ever heard of DNR's hired gun from Arizona, who, I noted privately, looked even younger than me. DNR's expert was skeptical about Fish and Wildlife's use of a widely known economics method called "stated preference." It modeled hypothetical choices among options, even those with no known market value. For example, most Americans express an honest willingness to pay for smog control in the Grand Canyon even if they never visit there. The DNR expert simply did not believe in stated preference modeling, including when local residents made hypothetical choices among various Green Bay injury, damage, and restoration scenarios. The economists traded thought experiments, but DNR's guy was unmoved about the fundamentals of the Fish and Wildlife studies. Indeed, Superfund defendants always hate stated preference economics studies because they're the only way to measure many public losses. Eliminating this kind of study from damage assessments eliminates whole categories of damages, a fact not lost on Superfund defendants. Thus, it was easy to see why the Fox River paper companies were paying this guy from Arizona to oppose every stated preference study on the planet on ideological grounds. What was appalling to me was to see Wisconsin DNR so eager to amplify his advice.

Their expert was much more optimistic about the paper companies' results and the data they produced. The paper company study had relied on a different but also widely known modeling approach called "revealed preference." It modeled actual choices in existing markets. For example, people drive further and spend more to reach better fishing sites. It was the only approach the DNR expert believed could work. He suggested that the agencies exchange data and models. I was cautious about turning over all my team's work before it was completed, knowing that the paper companies were funding DNR's attack. Hill agreed to share the paper companies' work with Fish and Wildlife, since that work was already complete.

In the coming weeks, I spoke regularly with my team and DNR about how to resolve our differences. But Hill wanted to see Fish and Wildlife's detailed economics data and models, and little else. I offered to fund an independent review of all of the economics work by the paper companies and Fish and Wildlife. I offered to use experts for the review who would be picked jointly with DNR. I also pressed for ways to prevent DNR from sharing Fish and Wildlife's preliminary data with the paper companies until the studies were complete, and sought access to the paper companies' completed models and results.

In July, the DNR expert traveled to Boulder to meet in person with my team and me. There was still no convincing him that our approach had any merit. The visit wasn't a total loss, though. I had come to learn that the best insights are often revealed in unexpected ways. In this case, it was over lunch. One of my Hagler Bailly economists sat next to him and casually turned the conversation to his life and experience. The expert was eager to talk about himself as several of my team members and I quietly listened. He said he had only a master's degree. He had mostly worked for industrial clients who were responsible parties at Superfund sites. He had never published any studies. He had never worked on any studies that attempted to value natural resources that were not traded in markets. He had, however, raced rented Ford Mustangs while traveling. It was an unusual qualification to highlight.

ANOTHER SECRET DEAL

Susan Campbell

I received a major tip from David Allen. George Meyer was cutting a unilateral deal in Sheboygan, another Wisconsin PCB site on Lake

Michigan, located about an hour south of Green Bay. A company there had once been a major source of PCBs to the Sheboygan River. Wisconsin had just secured $5 million for natural resource damages that would be tacked onto a cleanup, which EPA had estimated could cost $41 million (Klas and DeKeyser 2000).

According to Allen, Bruce Baker had helped negotiate the deal along with George Meyer and two staffers for Governor Thompson. Wisconsin was thinking about using the damages, along with a $41 million cash-out for cleanup, all for dredging. Meyer had blindsided his own DNR staff, who had been working at the site for more than two years with other agencies.

I started calling my contacts right away. Fish and Wildlife was furious, worried about what Meyer's latest action might portend for the Fox River. "It isn't what we had expected," said Fish and Wildlife's representative in Fort Snelling (Campbell 2000h). It was a major understatement. He said the state and federal agencies had been scheduled to meet with the company later that week to begin talks on a unified claim to restore the Sheboygan River and harbor. Instead, he and his colleagues learned that Meyer had met privately with the company and offered a separate settlement for damages to the state's natural resources.

David Allen called it "a troubling pattern" when I interviewed him on the record (Campbell 2000h). "What George Meyer has done in Sheboygan is completely consistent with what he's done at other sites."

I called George Meyer next. It was unusual for him to handle press calls about the Fox River, yet today I reached him directly. Meyer wouldn't discuss his offer. He was bristling. "It's highly unprofessional what they're doing," he said of Fish and Wildlife's public statements (Campbell 2000h). Meyer said there was no correlation between his action at Sheboygan and his dealings with the Fox River paper companies. "There is an agreement between the Fish and Wildlife Service and the Wisconsin Department of Natural Resources to work in tandem on the Fox River, and we're doing that," he said. "There's no such agreement with Fish and Wildlife to do that on the Sheboygan River."

Fish and Wildlife said Wisconsin's settlement would leave the agency trying to tease apart which natural resources fell strictly within federal jurisdiction—a tangled web when species cross state boundaries, for instance, a migratory blue heron eating a PCB-contaminated frog that lived out its life in a Wisconsin pond.

David Allen said it was just that sort of quandary that had led Fish and Wildlife and every Great Lakes state except Wisconsin to reach standard agreements for joint damage assessments. He noted that Wisconsin DNR had declined to participate in Fish and Wildlife assessments for two other sites in the state, and had resisted working cooperatively on the Fox River since the early 1990s. "If George Meyer believes he can show a federal piece of a duck, or a state piece of a fish, we're open to both the technical and legal arguments he wants to present," Allen said (Campbell 2000h).

As I hung up the phone, I couldn't help thinking that Allen might actually relish such a debate.

TURNING UP THE HEAT

David Allen

The *Press-Gazette* story ran on Saturday. Tempers flared. The next day, Bill Hartwig's new assistant, Charlie Wooley, reached me at home.

"David, work's on the phone." Darlene shouted up the stairs.

"It's the weekend. Tell 'em I'll call back tomorrow from the office. Wait, who is it?" I shouted back down the stairs.

"Charlie Wooley . . ."

"Don't hang up! Coming . . ."

Shit, that was way too fast, I thought to myself. Never had one of the five senior-most people in a region of a thousand Fish and Wildlife staff called me at home. Especially on a Sunday.

Darlene looked a bit amused as I rushed down the stairs, until she saw my face. Now we both looked worried.

I took the phone and tried to catch my breath. "Hi, Charlie! What's up?" I asked, as if I didn't already know.

"Hi, David, sorry to bother you at home on a weekend . . . but I just read your quotes in the paper."

"Wow! I didn't even know you worked on weekends."

"David, I'm really worried about this. You *can't* be talking about George Meyer by name."

Charlie was deeply concerned that I was tangling with Wisconsin's chief environmental officer. The conversation was brief and to the point. By the end of it, I had agreed not to call out George Meyer by name in subsequent interviews—as long as Charlie agreed not to squander our agency's leverage on the Fox River case by appearing overly conciliatory about Wisconsin's actions at Sheboygan.

Privately, I was actually quite troubled about Charlie's level of discomfort with me. And I suspected he was unaccustomed to staff offering conditions for meeting his terms. I enjoyed a good amount of freedom in my public handling of the case. I didn't want to lose any ground, especially now.

Once again, it was Bill Hartwig who would run interference for me. During my next meeting in Fort Snelling, Bill went out of his way to joke with Charlie about my lighting fires and keeping Wisconsin honest while Bill was away. The Sheboygan story had broken while Bill was on vacation. It was a clear signal that I had permission to continue applying pressure, as long as it increased Bill's leverage.

Later that July, I sent Greg Hill a letter (Allen 2000b). It was my usual battering ram. I reminded Hill that DNR had rejected the Fish and Wildlife offer to pay for an independent third party to evaluate the competing economics approaches. I reminded him of his promise to transmit the paper companies' data and models. I reminded him about trustee confidentiality provisions, including some that carried criminal sanctions for purposeful disclosure. And I reminded him of DNR's verbal commitment to endorse the federal pathway and injury determinations.

The rest of July and early August were eventful for me as several key Fox River storylines reached their conclusion. In July, EPA issued its order to finish cleaning up the botched dredging project next to Fort Howard, successfully averting a potential ecological disaster, even if it did not launch an immediate cleanup of the entire lower river. DNR formally joined the federal damage assessment—on paper. And an Appleton Papers agreement-in-principle eventually went through at $40 million in exchange for a four-year delay in federal litigation against the company.

In August, Greg Hill transmitted Wisconsin's blanket endorsement of our pathway and injury determinations, as published by Fish and Wildlife over the previous two years.

CHANGE IN THE AIR

Susan Campbell

I awoke one morning with a splitting headache, my worst in recent memory. Hours later, the sun and August heat were building outside the closed bedroom blinds in my room. Nothing could calm the throbbing in my head, and the thought of heading into the office later that afternoon seemed impossible. The weekend police beat was back after several years' hiatus, except it now included all the newsroom reporters, so my shifts were infrequent. Tonight would be my first time back.

As I lay in the darkened room, unable to sleep off the headache, a slideshow of grim memories played out in my mind: a small, dilapidated house on the city's west side draped in yellow police tape after a fatal shooting; a family huddled in the street late at night, wrapped in blankets against the cold as they watched their home devoured by flames; the bloated bodies of teenagers laid out on the shoulder of a highway on a Friday night after a horrible car crash. These were stories I'd covered during my earlier time on the police beat and I found the memories hard to shake—especially at times like this when sleep eluded me. The truth was, I was more comfortable covering the political shenanigans surrounding the Fox River cleanup than the raw life-and-death stories that made up the daily life of a community. I got ready for work and hoped there would be no drama tonight.

Thankfully, there would be none, at least on the police beat. By the time I left work that night, my headache had cleared and I felt almost buoyant. It was midnight and the moon was bright, almost magical. I looked across the *Press-Gazette* parking lot at city hall, and thought of the police beat and all the city council meetings I'd covered there during my first year in Green Bay. So much had happened since then. After four years of writing hundreds of stories about the Fox River saga, the cleanup finally seemed headed toward some sort of resolution. David Allen had been rolling out one study after another from the ongoing federal damage assessment, all leading to October when he would finally unveil the long-awaited compensation plan for the Fox River. EPA was gaining momentum with its cleanup documents, which would eventually be published with DNR in 2001. There was now an agreement to address the epic failure at the PCB hot spot outside Fort Howard. My Fox River stories had won awards for the paper and earned me respect from the community and my colleagues. I paused to reflect and revel in the moment. I relaxed and breathed in deeply.

I was overtaken by nausea. What was that smell? It enveloped me. The familiar rotting-cabbage paper mill odor was wafting in from Paper Valley. But there was something else intermingled with it. Leaning heavily against my car, I sensed the other odor came from the bay. It was the swampy, stagnant smell of decaying algae, and it hung thick in the humid night air. I had never been bothered by it before. Not like this, at least. I slid into my car and slammed the door to shut out the smell.

On the way home, I stopped at a drugstore and bought a pregnancy test.

FORT HOWARD PLAYS DNR

David Allen

I discovered in September 2000, a month before publishing the restoration and compensation plan that would be the lynchpin of the federal damage assessment, that Fort Howard and Wisconsin had been just as busy with their own priorities as my team had been with ours. Fort Howard led a settlement discussion with representatives of DNR and my team at the regional Fish and Wildlife office in Minnesota. The Fort revealed a new pact with Wisconsin that was as brilliant as it was jarring.

An advisor to Fort Howard's president explained that the Fort was inviting us to join in on a new settlement between Wisconsin and Fort Howard. The Fort's inside counsel laid out the background for my team and the assembled governmental lawyers. Fort Howard recognized only Wisconsin as the lead for the Fox River damage assessment, he said. He continued that they were more receptive to the damage assessment process than the other paper companies, and had not been part of the national coalition lobbying against dredging. Fort Howard, he noted, had not only acquiesced to Wisconsin in conducting the failed SMU 56–57 project outside its mill, it had been cooperative once it started. The fact was, he said, that during the last year, Fort Howard had focused on twin priorities: reaching a deal that could satisfy EPA and DNR on the emergency cleanup at the same time as resolving the company's potential liability for natural resource damages.

Fort Howard's outside counsel from DC provided the punch line for why the Feds should join the settlement. He claimed they designed their natural resource damages proposal to address multiple ecological and human endpoints all at once. He gave reasons why Fort Howard's allocation for liability should be less than 10 percent of the total damages, an amount he said was actually far less than was being offered in their proposed settlement. My team and I saw that this was not just a gimmick. Fort Howard had all its ducks in line. The company had already drafted a judicial consent decree for the federal court and already had endorsement from DNR managers and experts about the quality of its proposed restoration projects. The company had technical support from the paper companies' economics studies, and Interior's lead damage assessment lawyer in DC had publicly confirmed that Interior always preferred early settlements. Finally, the Fort's lawyer pointed out that Wisconsin had now settled Fort Howard's damage assessment claims. This left the other agencies with a simple choice: settle now, or litigate later and wrangle with legal problems like statute of limitations, jurisdictional questions, and federal liability.

The Fort then handed us a draft consent decree with all the agencies added to the settlement. They offered flexibility to their proposed September 30 response deadline, now just nineteen days away.

Greg Hill immediately voiced DNR's enthusiastic support for all Fort Howard's proposed restoration projects, and Bruce Baker said George Meyer also favored the projects. Baker concluded by admitting that DNR, the Wisconsin Department of Justice, and Fort Howard already had struck their deal.

Brilliant. So much for George Meyer's assurances that Wisconsin would never cut another unilateral deal at Fox River.

My team quickly rejected the offer. The restoration proposal was the wrong scale, even if the proposed projects had merit. Plus, the federal government would gain nothing by joining the agreement as it would bring about no additional restoration. I reminded Fort Howard that Fish and Wildlife would be publishing its own results in just a month, and we would rely on those results to evaluate real settlement opportunities.

Quietly, my team and I were impressed by Fort Howard's continued mastery of Wisconsin. We also marveled anew at DNR's continued willingness to give Fort Howard and the other companies so much leverage against the other governmental parties.

Later, lawyers at the Wisconsin DOJ said the deal with Fort Howard was struck the previous May, right after George Meyer had assured Bill Hartwig he would decouple damages from the emergency cleanup of the failed Fort Howard dredging project. That also meant the deal must have been penned three months before Meyer complained to the press about Fish and Wildlife's purportedly baseless concern that the unilateral Sheboygan deal might foreshadow another at Fox River.

"The lady doth protest too much," I thought to myself now, recalling Meyer's defensiveness about Sheboygan.

Throughout the rest of September and into October, my team and I continued to meet with Wisconsin about the upcoming Restoration and Compensation Determination Plan. We would keep on schedule to publish it October 25, come hell or high water.

FRIDAY THE 13TH

Susan Campbell

The pregnancy test was positive. That was the good news. The bad news was that my newfound sensitivity to odor had become a continuing theme. The assault on my nose was unpredictable and random. If odors were represented as colors on a spectrum, my world had shifted to a sickly yellow tint. The shift was subtle, but enough to make some familiar odors unfamiliar, and others intolerable.

The industrial city of Green Bay offered plenty of opportunities to discover new and disturbing smells. But there were two odors that brought on a feeling of nausea and, unfortunately, the bay remained at the top of that list. The second was coffee, another of my loves. Tom had taken to grinding and brewing his morning coffee in the basement because I couldn't stand the smell of it in the house. Dealing with this new aversion to the bay wasn't as easy, however, but I did my best to avoid going near it whenever possible. It was a cruel irony, as if my own senses were now rejecting the very thing that had drawn me here in the first place.

Heading back to the newspaper one afternoon along a route I'd driven countless times before, I was suddenly overwhelmed by the familiar odor of scented dryer sheets coming from a local manufacturing plant. I quickly rolled up the car window—and knew in that instant it was time to go. All at once, the familiar smells of Green Bay—the decaying algae in the bay, the sulfur smells from Paper Valley mills, the scented dryer sheets from yet another industrial factory—gave rise to an irrational urge to flee. How I didn't know. Maybe something would happen. It had to.

When I walked into the newsroom, Tom signaled that we needed to talk. Something was up. When we met downstairs in the break room, he was anxious. "The *Journal Sentinel* called and wants me to go down to Milwaukee for an interview," he said under his breath. "What do you think?" I surprised him, and even myself, with my gusto: "Go!" This was it: the exit plan. Tom worried I wouldn't want to leave Green Bay or the paper, especially with the Fox cleanup still a question. But I shared the revelation from my drive to the office only moments earlier. As for the Fox, the issue was on its way to resolution. Fish and Wildlife's damage assessment continued its rollout to the public, which would lead to an official price tag for damages and ultimately substantive negotiations on cleanup. I had faithfully reported the story's politics and infighting all the way to the brink of a solution. It would be another reporter's job to cover the cleanup.

Truthfully, I was tired.

More important, we had a baby on the way. We hadn't figured how that would play out with our positions at the *Press-Gazette* and hadn't yet broached it with our editors. The *Journal Sentinel* would solve that problem. There, Tom would earn enough that I wouldn't have to work full-time. I could stay home with the baby and freelance write—a dream of mine that dated back to my days at Boston University when I'd first decided to pursue journalism. To that end, I was already floating around a manuscript in hopes of nailing a book contract. Leaving the *Press-Gazette* would give me time to finally focus on that. The prospect of the *Journal Sentinel* job sounded better and better the more we talked it over, discreetly, in the break room.

For now, deadline awaited. "Don't blow it," I told Tom, only half joking, as we headed back up to the newsroom. "You have to get that job."

There was a full moon on Friday, October 13, 2000. The date marked an occasional overlap of a moon phase and date that many consider unlucky—unusual enough that it wouldn't happen for another fourteen years. I was only a little superstitious, but more than a little worried about what this day might hold. My first ultrasound was scheduled for that morning. The nurse's indelicate reference to my "advanced maternal age" had surprised and maybe even offended me at the first appointment three months earlier. Recalling it now unnerved me as Tom and I headed to the doctor's office. But there would be good news: the baby was a girl, had ten fingers and ten toes, and already seemed to have mastered how to wave. In other words, she was normal.

More good news awaited us at home. I checked my email and found an offer from a publisher for my manuscript. I was ecstatic. No sooner had we celebrated our fortune at two pieces of good news than there was a third. The phone rang and it was for Tom. The *Journal Sentinel* editor was on the line, offering him the reporting job in Milwaukee. Could he start the first week of November?

Fortune was smiling on us that day, upending the morning's worries about moon phases and unlucky Friday the 13th. That night, the full moon would rise to mark the end of one chapter and the dawning of our next.

"FILE THE CASE IN FEDERAL COURT RIGHT NOW"

David Allen

Right on schedule, on the night of October 25, we presented our entire damage assessment to the Green Bay public. The Restoration and Compensation Determination Plan was built upon new restoration and damages work and incorporated all the formal pathway, injury, and damages determinations we had presented to the public over the previous two years. The plan itself had been six long years in the making (FWS 2000b). We were about to lay all our cards on the table to show the public, the scientific community, EPA, Wisconsin, and the paper companies that the damage assessment was no bluff. Decades of research had funneled into our formal administrative process, which pointed to how credible evidence and expert testimony could be presented to the federal district court in Milwaukee. We were signaling we had too much momentum to be stopped.

Bill Hartwig led the meeting, and I gave the main presentation, as we had done at our first big public meeting together back in May 1997. This meeting was even more important, and the audience was easily twice as big. Bill joked freely with the audience at the outset but soon turned serious about the enormity of the situation facing everyone now. Our agency had just completed one of the most comprehensive, detailed, and transparent Natural Resource Damage Assessments in history. It was time to act; there had been too many decades of company foot-dragging and governmental hand-wringing. Bill drove his point home with a quote:

> The matter of alleged Fox River and Green Bay pollution and its control is a subject of vital importance to all of us. To deal with it and reach its solution means we must deal with facts and properly analyze the facts to assign corrective measures.

Then the punch line: the quote was from the chairman of the Wisconsin Committee on Water Pollution at a public hearing held on December 17, 1948—*fifty-two years earlier*. Bill paused long enough for everybody to hear the murmurs run through the crowd, then summarized the recent PCB deliberations that had likewise dragged on for too long: the 1986 Green Bay Remedial Action Plan, the 1992 Fox River Coalition, and the 1997 Superfund listing proposal.

Bill now summoned all his charisma and intensity, drawing in his audience even more. "There's an obvious solution: EPA and DNR need to complete the RI/FS immediately and begin comprehensive cleanup of the Fox River," he said. "Only then can we make the public whole for the continuing losses beyond the reach of practical cleanup, from Little Lake Butte des Morts in Paper Valley to the Bays de Noc in the Upper Peninsula of Michigan."

It was my turn to explain how the community might finally be made whole after enduring decades of toxic pollution running through its backyard. But before launching into our new economics study, I painted a picture to remind the audience of all that the bay of Green Bay had to offer, and all it stood to lose, if the paper companies continued with business as usual. It was a picture of breathtaking beauty and economic power. I told of how Door County, once home to a string of sleepy backwater towns along the coast of the Door Peninsula, had won recognition in the early '60s as the "Cape Cod of the Midwest" and was now a world-class destination and playground for wealthy metropolitan Chicagoans (Lyttle 2008). I named some of the quaint small towns—Egg Harbor, Fish Creek, and Sister Bay—that nestled among dramatic limestone bluffs overlooking the bay, each tempting visitors with countless cafes, swanky boutiques, and pricey restaurants. I told of how bustling marinas, lush forests, and five state parks—the most state parks of any county in the United States—rounded out the Door County experience and helped swell the local population from 28,000 permanent residents to some 250,000 each summer.

It wasn't just tourists who were drawn to Door County. The bay of Green Bay was hugely attractive to fish and wildlife, and many species of both flocked to its diverse aquatic habitats, including riverine, near shore, and open water. The bay supported warm-water and cold-water fisheries. It had sandbars, estuaries, spawning and nursery habitats, rocky shorelines, and cold, deep waters. It had plankton, aquatic vegetation, insects, forage fish, and game fish. It had 250 species of birds, including vast annual influxes from the Mississippi Flyway. It had popular species like eagles, terns, herons, ducks, otter, and mink. It supported waterfowl hunting, sport fishing, commercial fishing, and subsistence fishing. Its watershed spanned warm- and cold-climate habitats with endless wetlands on the western shore, including emergent marsh, wet prairie, forested, and shrub-scrub. Its sprawling watershed included over 125,000 acres of agricultural wetlands, and over 14,000 acres of critical coastal wetlands. It was an invaluable treasure but under assault by decades of persistent, bio-accumulating PCBs.

I was passionate about the bay, and I knew the community was, too. It was my job to remind them of what many took for granted and others had forgotten after years of living with a compromised ecosystem. I wanted to remind them that Green Bay was one of the most polluted places in the country but, unlike most other polluted places, the bay remained a sparkling jewel of ecological vibrance and aesthetic beauty. It might be the most valuable place in the country that Superfund could still save. It was time to present the community with its options.

The "Total Value Equivalency" model devised by my team was the soul of the Restoration and Compensation Determination Plan for the Fox River and bay. The economics model knitted together the community's love for its waterways with how much it was willing to pay to reclaim the waters' full potential. It managed to do this by measuring the public's preferences when presented with a range of competing costs and values: higher or lower taxes; more or less sediment cleanup; more or less restoration to the river and bay; and a longer or shorter duration of PCB injuries to local waters, fish, and wildlife. Our experts had analyzed the choices made by the study's participants and used that data to build a groundbreaking economics model that showed how people in the community, on average, valued each restoration or cleanup program relative to the others, and how much they'd be willing to spend in additional tax dollars to achieve cleanup and restoration.

The Total Value Equivalency was our well-considered answer to an extremely difficult question: how should we compare realistic restoration opportunities around Green Bay with the losses caused by PCBs?

Finally, I could talk about the number, assuming a scenario where EPA actually made it across the finish line with its cleanup studies and actions. Our new economics model showed that the total *value* of eliminating PCB injuries to the Fox River and bay could be as high as about $600 million, but the *cost* of sufficient restoration to offset those same injuries was only as high as about $250 million. The lynchpin restoration and compensation study used the lower figure—the restoration costs—as the measure for ongoing PCB-related damages to everyone living in and around the bay of Green Bay. Fishing damages, defined as losses from fish consumption advisories for active Green Bay anglers, were calculated at around $100 million. To avoid double counting the future PCB-related damages (since anglers would be included in the forward-looking part of both studies), only past damages from the recreational fishing study were added to the total value study. That meant total damages could be between $176 million and $333 million, depending on how long cleanup actually took, how complete it was, and what mix of restoration options emerged as the most practical and cost effective.* Because 80 percent of the PCBs had already made their way out into the bay of Green Bay, and bay improvements provided the most bang for the buck, most of the proposed projects focused on restoration projects there. Among them: preserving and restoring wetlands and habitats, and reducing runoff pollution—particularly by

---

* $269 million to $508 million in 2020 dollars.

providing financial assistance for farmers to cut polluted runoff from their farmland.

The damage assessment number would be in addition to what would be an even higher price tag for cleaning up the PCB contamination in the river. The paper companies were responsible for paying all of it.

Rebecca Katers of Clean Water Action Council approached the microphone after the presentation. She was disappointed. The most vocal of Green Bay's environmental community had expected a dollar figure closer to the $1 billion settlement that Exxon Corp. had paid after the Exxon Valdez oil spill. "Our situation is worse," Katers said, noting the paper companies' PCBs had been allowed to linger in the river for decades despite the known health risks (Campbell 2000a). "They dragged their feet all this time intentionally. They should pay for their delay tactics."

A Madison resident was one of many in the audience to point out that Wisconsin DNR had not endorsed the Fish and Wildlife plan—despite a pledge in May that the two agencies would issue a joint plan. "That's a very conspicuous absence," he said.

Bill Hartwig and I weren't surprised by the criticism. The community was passionate about the river and bay, and the losses it had endured were hard to reconcile. But I also knew there was another milestone achieved in revealing the number. Bill and I had just served notice that Fish and Wildlife had credible results that could be used for negotiation—or litigation. The damage assessment was formalized leverage with the paper companies, and also the strongest inducement Fish and Wildlife could provide for EPA to move ahead with its authority to order a Superfund cleanup. It would also shine a bright light on a mountain of evidence so voluminous that Wisconsin could no longer look the other way.

Bob Cook, another audience member, seemed to read my mind. He stepped up to the mic and warned Bill not to wait. "File the case in federal court right now," Cook warned. "You'll regret it if you wait until after the election." Cook's suggestion carried weight. He had been deputy director of the entire U.S. Fish and Wildlife Service back in 1977–81 and was now retired in his home state of Wisconsin.

We had succeeded in publishing the Restoration and Compensation Determination Plan. The thick 692-page document bore Bill Hartwig's signature as lead authorized official on behalf of Fish and Wildlife, the Departments of Interior and Justice, the Oneida tribe, the Menominee tribe, the National Oceanic and Atmospheric Administration, the Little Traverse Bay bands of Odawa Indians in Michigan, and the Michigan Department of Justice.

The next step was a formal forty-five-day public comment period, and a series of public hearings in the region. It was time to take this show on the road.

CUTTING THE CORD

Susan Campbell

On November 11, I filed my last story at the paper. Fittingly, it was about the near completion of the Fort Howard dredging project at SMU 56–57. I liked that it had an air of finality to it, like lopping off another head of the many-headed Hydra. I made one last edit to the story, added my byline at the top, and turned off the computer. It was my last official day at the *Press-Gazette*, and perhaps my final day as a newspaper reporter. I'd already said good-byes to friends and colleagues. I would miss many of them, though some had already moved on. Saying good-bye to Carol Hunter had been the hardest. The executive editor had trusted me from the outset and given me the wings to fly, but always with a safety net below. She was the best editor I would ever know.

Hoping to avoid perception as a lame duck and miss out on a good news tip, I had waited as long as possible to say good-bye to David Allen and Jim Hahnenberg, my longtime sources at Fish and Wildlife and EPA. I'd bid farewell to my DNR sources as well: Bob Paulson, who had been my most transparent contact at the agency, and had been forbidden to speak with me for some months now; Bruce Baker, who had assumed Paulson's role as spokesman on the Fox River case; and George Meyer.

It was early evening when I finally finished writing, and most of my colleagues had already left to start celebrating the weekend. I wanted it that way. I looked around the newsroom with a mix of satisfaction and sadness, and left without saying anything. There was an unexpected knot in my throat.

I was back at the office the next week, unofficially, using up the last of my vacation time to clear out before the move to join Tom, who had already started his new job in Milwaukee. Today I was at my desk, downloading files and packing up banker boxes full of folders and notes, most of it about the Fox River. "Save your notes! This will be a book someday," several colleagues had urged me, as they had over the last couple years. I'd shrugged it off. It was hard to imagine wanting to revisit this story someday, any day, when I was trying so hard now to leave it behind.

Still, I wasn't quite ready to let it all go.

There was a sudden stir in the newsroom as several editors and my new replacement on the environment beat made their way toward the executive editor's office. The metro editor stopped and looked my way as if about to say something. He hesitated. "You don't want to know . . ." he half asked me. He ran his hand through his thick dark hair; it hadn't receded a bit. I looked at him and back at the mess of papers and folders piled around my desk. I did want to know. Desperately.

But we both knew that, technically, I wasn't even supposed to be there. More than that, we both knew it was time to cut the cord.

The news that day was indeed big. It was Wednesday, November 15, and George Meyer and Fort Howard had just met in Green Bay to publicly sign off on a new settlement. It was the first time the press and public heard of it, though Meyer had signaled it in the days after Fish and Wildlife unveiled its plan for damages totaling up to $333 million. Meyer had told the local *Green Bay News-Chronicle* that DNR hadn't seen enough data to support the federal plan and that the compensation formulas that fed it were weak. He'd forecast that his own compensation plan would be released later in November, and that it would supersede the federal assessment. "If we settle the state resources," Meyer was quoted saying, "then [Fish and Wildlife] couldn't claim them under their document" (Decker 2000).

The bottom line of the state's newest pact with Fort Howard: $7 million to achieve a claimed $55 million worth of restoration and improvements to the Fox River and bay, including restoring wetlands, improving fisheries, and building new picnic areas. Press accounts described a "complicated formula" in which the claimed $55 million value of the restoration package would cost Fort Howard less than 13 percent of that amount. The Sierra Club had another name for it: "creative financing" (Sandin 2000a, 2000b). "They should have come to the public before deciding," a spokeswoman said.

The settlement with Fort Howard was DNR's first complete NRDA settlement with any paper company of the Fox River Group. Meyer wouldn't speculate about whether it would serve as a template for deals with the other companies, but Katers and other environmentalists worried it might—and were doubly concerned because Fort Howard was one of the largest contributors of PCBs to the system.

Many were shell-shocked at what appeared to be a deal that came out of nowhere on the heels of Fish and Wildlife's comprehensive and publicly vetted damage assessment. "It seems a little surprising that a settlement occurred very quickly following the completion of the study," said a UW–Green Bay professor (Perry 2000). "The process matters a lot if you want legitimacy."

DAVID AND GOLIATH

David Allen

Soon after we published our restoration and compensation strategy, Bruce Baker let us know Wisconsin was moving forward with its Fort Howard settlement and that the Fort was planning a press conference criticizing Fish and Wildlife's findings. Wisconsin's project manager for Fox River cleanup—a man known for being so openly hostile that Greg Hill apologized to me for him being "rougher than a cob"—threatened to remove all Fish and Wildlife citations from the cleanup documents.

EPA overruled him. During this same period, Hill began accusing us of leaking information, no doubt trying to limit my continuing outreach to scientific groups, the press, and anybody else willing to listen. I ignored Hill and stopped worrying about his attempts to panic Fish and Wildlife managers. In November, Wisconsin and Fort Howard finally announced their new agreement to the public. For the next several days, I did little more than talk with reporters about the latest unilateral deal by Wisconsin, though I tried to preserve Charlie Wooley's sanity by not mentioning George Meyer by name.

My team dissected Fort Howard's documentation of its deal with Wisconsin and soon saw that the company had cleverly included a host of problems for DNR's own cleanup approach. Rather than argue with DNR about whose damage assessment was superior, my team concentrated on showing DNR and EPA experts how the Fort Howard deal introduced inconsistencies and problems for both the state and federal agencies' cleanup documents.

On November 29, I met for the first time with two reporters from the Madison-based *Wisconsin State Journal*. They were writing an in-depth article on the DNR deal and how it conflicted with the damage assessment. The pair would be conducting interviews and research for weeks and then publishing a major story on their findings. The reporters had my full attention until December 17, when the *Wisconsin State Journal* published "Fox River Sellout?" (Seely and Hall 2000) on the front page of its Sunday edition.

During the eighteen days leading up to the story, I'd maintained a laser focus on the reporters. I sent them factual materials, summaries, and the names of everybody touching the Fox River and Green Bay cleanup and damage assessment: Wisconsin staff, federal staff, tribal staff, Michigan staff, stakeholders, paper companies—everybody. The reporters called me regularly with follow-up questions after their interviews, especially with George Meyer, Bruce Baker, and Greg Hill. I tried to explain Wisconsin's positions fairly, and to gain the reporters' trust as a source of information that was rich and well documented. I even offered suggestions about how to portray complex information so that it was accessible and neutral. I wanted the newspaper's readers to draw their own conclusions about how raw information was relevant to conflicting positions.

Two days after the story ran, George Meyer sent an email to every DNR employee in the state accompanied by a copy of his letter to the editor attempting to justify Wisconsin's deal while complaining about the story and Fish and Wildlife. He quoted me by name—out of context (Meyer 2000). I guessed Charlie Wooley would be calling me again at home, and soon. I was right. Charlie was desperate to prevent me from writing my own letter to the editor in response to Meyer (Allen 2000c). I had already mobilized my experts to help me do exactly that. Charlie offered to write a letter instead, promising to use some of the content from mine. I agreed not to send my letter before Charlie and Frank Horvath could review it. It only took a few minutes for Frank to call. I relented. Charlie's letter to the editor was published soon after, with just enough of my text to mollify me (Wooley 2000).

Meyer's central arguments revolved around several themes. Chief among them were that our proposed Fox River settlement was much larger than those my agency had reached at two other U.S. sites, the Saginaw River in Michigan and Housatonic River in Massachusetts, and that my agency had a history of proposing inflated settlements but ultimately settling for less.

"The seven Wisconsin companies in this matter should pay a substantial amount of money for past damages to the Fox River from their former discharges," Meyer wrote. "However, should these Wisconsin employers pay twenty times what General Motors paid in Michigan or twenty times what General Electric paid in Massachusetts? That is the tough question that the *Wisconsin State Journal* did not ask."

As DNR had all along, Meyer also attacked our use of the economics model so criticized by the consultant the paper companies had hired for DNR.

In his published response, Charlie noted that Fish and Wildlife and its numerous federal partners and tribes had conducted a comprehensive evaluation subject to public scrutiny and technical peer review.

Responding to Meyer's statement that our agency had ultimately settled for lower amounts than originally proposed at other sites, Charlie was matter-of-fact: "It is true that government agencies often settle for less than their full estimate of damages. Indeed, this is the essence of a 'settlement.' However, negotiation strength increases with knowledge of the facts under discussion. The Service and its partners have conducted one of the most comprehensive, detailed assessments ever performed in the U.S." Charlie stressed that our agency still sought "a cooperative working relationship with Wisconsin."

"Rather than attempting to decide issues unilaterally with the companies and leaving the public to muddle through widely differing damage estimates, the Service's goal for the new year is to unify the public's NRDA claims," he concluded. "The Service is committed to redoubling our efforts to develop a unified position with Wisconsin."

I glanced out my living room window to see the Toyota Land Cruiser coming north on County Road M. That had to be my old friend Bill Conlon. Nobody else in the area drove a Land Cruiser.

Bill was going to love my stories this time.

Waiting with a fine crystal glass in hand, I greeted him in my gravel driveway as the Land Cruiser came to a stop and the driver's-side window powered down. Always the connoisseur, Bill held up the glass I handed to him and studied its translucent contents against the sky. Even before unbuckling, he breathed it in deeply. "Whisky," he pronounced. Then, after a pause, "Scotch." Next, he was out of the SUV with a quick handshake, a sip, and another deep breath. "Speyside single malt," he said, a gleam in his eye. Then, with a smirk, "I have some eighteen-year-old Macallan with me in the car, but we can swill down this twelve-year-old, for now." I bowed humbly at my old friend's latest demonstration of expertise. We laughed, unloaded the car, and went inside.

A few hours later, Bill broke out the older whisky and asked for the latest Fox River tales. I was ready. I handed Bill a copy of George Meyer's email to every DNR employee in Wisconsin, with Meyer's letter to the editor attached. Bill scanned it quickly. "Jesus, David, you really pissed him off this time." Then, with a smile, "Good job."

I filled Bill in on the latest news, including the Sheboygan and Fort Howard deals. He interrupted with questions as my stories serpentined through the main characters. But Bill kept returning to George Meyer. Finally, he asked, "What the hell is he thinking? I mean, all due respect, but you're just a peon. Why is he even bothering with you? Seriously, what's going on?"

"How the hell should I know?" I said. "I really am a peon. I don't travel in Meyer's rarefied circles. I don't know what all he has on his plate. I've no clue what it's like to live in Tommy Thompson's cauldron."

Bill pressed on. "Okay, you're right. You can't possibly know. But come on, man, you've gotta have some guesses. You've told me many times Meyer's no idiot, no sycophant. So what gives? Why does he keep carrying Thompson's water and going along with the paper companies? And why's he so mad at li'l ol' you?"

I had thought about this many times. Meyer wasn't likely a villain; indeed, he was well regarded by many in Wisconsin. In truth, I knew little of Meyer or his plight, and hadn't made it my business to find out. Better to focus on the facts, the law, and the public, and let people make up their own minds about the characters in this play. But Bill was right. I had a few guesses about the DNR secretary, and I could feel one of those familiar adrenaline surges focusing my mind and channeling my speech. I looked my friend in the eye. Meyer was a confounding crux of the story, a story that spanned nearly a decade and had suddenly come to a head—and had somehow become more personal. Bill took the hint. He wanted this insight, even if it revealed more about me than Meyer.

I launched into a soliloquy, my words streaming to release half-formed thoughts—the act of finally speaking them aloud crystallizing them for myself. I recalled a concern voiced by the environmental community at the time of Meyer's appointment: could a career bureaucrat like Meyer set aside his institutional loyalty if his bosses angled to sidestep the state's laws, people, and natural resources?

"I think Meyer cares about his institution as much as I care about facts," I said. "I think he actually cares about his position, his authority, and his institution. I don't give a shit about any institution when I'm chasing down information. I guess I don't really care about my title, either, as you can tell by my cheap Scotch."

Bill looked on encouragingly. I mused further. "I keep wondering if he's trying to prevent or snuff out recommendations and advice, even from his own experts and staff. I worry that he's trying to game the system to get the answers he knows he wants. I suspect he's too quick to reward institutional and personal loyalty, too slow to reward inconvenient facts." I smiled at Bill and added, "You know how hard it is for me to let that go." Bill grinned.

"On this Fox River thing, some truths just plain run into Tommy Thompson's politics. Meyer sees me trumpeting recommendations and trying to enforce the rules of the game, even when it leads to answers his boss doesn't want to hear. And there's no question he serves at the pleasure of that boss. Meyer sees me questioning his institution, his authority, and even the idea of institutional loyalty. I could see how that might really piss him off, particularly because I'm just a peon from Ohio—and a Fed."

I took another sip. Bill knew there was more on my mind. "Meyer might be in over his head," I ventured. "He's obviously smart, experienced, and dedicated. But he's probably not in the same league as Thompson and Thompson's political operatives. I know for sure he's not in the same league as our team in the Superfund arena. He's a professional lawyer, and maybe a professional politician. But he's up against a first-rate political machine on one side, and maybe the best Superfund team in the country on the other. He's caught in the middle. He probably doesn't realize how completely."

Bill, a devout atheist, summed it up with his typical ironical wit: "George can only see that you're a peon, David. He hasn't realized his own Philistine stature."

I laughed. "Well, if we're up against Goliath, I'm pretty sure he's employed by Fort Howard, not the State of Wisconsin. And nobody's gonna crown me king, even if we do somehow win this case."

In Madison, Gary George smelled a rat. The state senator from Milwaukee said the agreement between DNR and Fort Howard was the love child of a too-cozy relationship between a state regulator and the companies it is supposed to regulate.

Senator George called on state auditors to examine the deal the day after it was announced. "We need to find out if this settlement is adequate, and to find out why it was negotiated in secret and announced without public input," Senator George said in a November 16 statement appearing in the *Green Bay Press-Gazette* and the *Milwaukee Journal Sentinel* (Hildebrand 2000; Sandin 2000b). "We need to get to the bottom of it quickly."

A spokesman for Governor Thompson said legislators should commend, not criticize, the parties for reaching an agreement.

But George, who served as Senate co-chairman of the state's Legislative Audit Committee, was undeterred. DNR had stepped in with "a preemptive strike" to help Fort Howard after Fish and Wildlife's unveiling of much costlier damage assessment results, he said. "The people of the Fox Valley have been subjected to damage of many of their natural resources by this company, and now some people feel they are being ripped off by the DNR."

The *Wisconsin State Journal* story was big on its own, but Secretary Meyer had now guaranteed it would grow even bigger because of his editorial. I watched the fallout. Environmental groups and local stakeholders began publishing their own opinions and talking to reporters, needing no help from me. My team and I had already armed everybody we could reach with facts, expert opinions, and how to use them in a legal context. We had already opened ourselves up to years of past and future public scrutiny. We had already highlighted DNR's pattern of cutting unilateral deals with responsible parties after unusually cozy negotiations. I learned that the Madison reporters who broke the story were now using Wisconsin open records laws to delve deeper into the deal. Then, I heard directly from representatives of the Wisconsin Legislative

Audit Bureau that it was investigating DNR and the Fort Howard deal. I granted them an extensive interview.

As the controversy snowballed, DNR's Fox River staff became increasingly unhinged. In January 2001, I heard from the Sierra Club that George Meyer was calling Sierra Club staff members at home and lecturing them about the deal. Then, Jim Hahnenberg at EPA told me DNR was trying to withhold sediment volume calculations necessary for EPA's emergency cleanup of the SMU 56–57 hot spot. A few days later, the usually civil intergovernmental public relations conference call nearly disintegrated when DNR proposed quotes by Bruce Baker for the joint newsletter that were unacceptable to the federal agencies and the tribes. DNR relented only when I threatened to publish direct rebuttals to each of Baker's points in the same newsletter. Still in January, DNR told Jim Hahnenberg the state would not share drafts of the Remedial Investigation and Feasibility Study with Fish and Wildlife, despite EPA funding and legal obligations under federal regulations.

I continued to meet with stakeholders and the press, but I also tried to find opportunities to lessen DNR anger and anxiety. DNR was still the natural ally of Fish and Wildlife, and I remained convinced that DNR would eventually learn to operate in concert with the other governmental agencies. The paper companies did not share DNR's mandates and goals, and DNR would eventually remember its own vital public role. In late January, I worked with DNR's public relations team to focus on common goals, particularly related to cleanup, and on avoiding open conflict on damage assessment issues that would only add to the mounting scrutiny of DNR. The same day, DNR informed Rebecca Katers's Clean Water Action Council that DNR would not participate in a scheduled public meeting unless Fish and Wildlife was disinvited.

I was beginning to worry about the pace of rising conflict. Somebody was bound to get hurt. I didn't want anybody to lose their job over this, not even my harshest critics within DNR. But something would have to give, and soon.

Then, the tide suddenly changed. On February 2, Governor Tommy Thompson left Wisconsin to become the U.S. secretary of Health and Human Services, appointed by President George W. Bush. Four days after Thompson left, night became day in one surreal instant. I learned from the Wisconsin Department of Justice that the new governor would not reappoint George Meyer as DNR secretary. On February 12, I heard that the Legislative Audit Bureau and state senator George were taking aim at DNR and the deal with Fort Howard. Then, Fort Howard's plan unraveled. In March, Assistant U.S. Attorney Matt Richmond reported to me that the deal between DNR and Fort Howard had been cancelled.

I could almost hear the simultaneous celebrations break out in Fort Snelling, Boulder, Milwaukee, and DC. It was almost too good to be true. Somehow, my team and case had survived the Fort's best shot to date. Now, they were losing two key allies at the top of Wisconsin's government. The paper companies were probably soon going to face a truly unified intergovernmental partnership, for the first time.

Charlie Wooley instantly made plans to take full advantage of a new partnership with Wisconsin. Frank Horvath began charting a course to ride the wave of his region's damage assessment fame. Both of them made it clear they wanted me on their team in this new era.

The legal team was also happy. Justice began embracing its usual client, EPA. Interior welcomed a return to more traditional damage assessment territory, which followed the cleanup agencies' lead. Justice and Interior focused on proving to Wisconsin that the federal government would be a good partner.

I tried my best to join in the celebratory mood, but I wasn't quite sure everybody had thought this through. At least they hadn't thought through the role I might still realistically play in Green Bay. Nobody was going to forget their injuries after being subjected to my battering ram for all those years. Charlie Wooley was definitely going to keep me away from the press. Lawyers at Interior certainly were not going to tolerate any more steamrolling of their office to meet Fish and Wildlife's schedule and other demands. Main Interior also was not going to forget the budgetary knife fights or how often my team ignored the department's advice about how to spend the money. Before long, Justice was not going to need much help from Fish and Wildlife on cleanup issues as the attorneys closed ranks with their regular client, EPA. Most important, DNR, and especially Bruce Baker and Greg Hill, were not going to forget or hide their disdain whenever I showed up at a meeting. It wouldn't take long for Jim Hahnenberg to realize the advantages of keeping Fish and Wildlife out of the way as EPA began working more successfully with DNR.

I also was losing my most important and reliable conduit to the Green Bay public. Susan Campbell was leaving Green Bay, and maybe even journalism. It was true that we were never that close personally. In fact, I had always noticed she guarded her independence and professionalism as a journalist as fiercely as I protected mine as a civil servant. In our conversations it always felt like we were each on high alert. Still, she understood Paper Valley and Green Bay. She understood the government and the paper mills. She understood the technical issues. I thought she might even understand me, or at least the strange cauldron I'd been living in for the last nine years.

I could see my conducting gig was about to end. So, I resolved to spend whatever momentum I still enjoyed on the part of the case that was most authentic and personally meaningful for me: restoration of the waters and woods. They were still my church. And I would spend my remaining time in Green Bay—which I knew would be short—with the federal officials who would be most central to Fish and Wildlife's restoration successes beyond cleanup, after I left.

During my final winter on the Green Bay case, I led my last of many field tours. The destination was one of the most beautiful and important habitats in the entire region. My guests were Charlie Wooley, Frank Horvath, and the recently assigned lead attorneys on the case from Interior and Justice. We all drove together in a Fish and Wildlife minivan from Green Bay to Door County's Wagon Trail hotel and restaurant for two days of meetings and the field trip. The hotel was familiar territory to me. Here, nine years earlier, Ken Stromborg had taught me how to stand after donning insulated chest waders and a full-body monkey suit.

During the drive up the Door Peninsula, the conversation was sparse. Each of us was preparing for reforms to Fish and Wildlife's role in the Green Bay case, but it was anybody's guess whose influence would

The Wagon Trail resort, with Rowleys Bay (*right*), the Mink River Estuary (*upper left*), and the bay of Green Bay in the background. (Source Mark Dexter, with permission)

count most. The two DC attorneys tried to keep the mood light by bantering about the latest issue of *The New Yorker*. I joined in by arguing with DOJ's lawyer about whether Audi's new model, the TT, deserved its recent design accolades. And Charlie recounted tales of his recent musky fishing. Frank was even quieter than usual.

We were gathering for the last annual "summit" of the Green Bay Natural Resource Damage Assessment.* Everybody realized this would probably be the last one, and definitely the least well attended. I mostly ignored the meeting agenda and focused on the field trip: this last summit was going to be about the forest and the lake. I had picked the perfect spot to impress my colleagues with the sheer beauty of the site they were protecting and the critical importance the NRDA could still play, above and beyond the cleanup that would dominate their thinking in the coming years.

---

* The Green Bay NRDA team held seven approximately annual summits previous to this meeting on December 13–14, 2000. The previous summits were attended by most of the attorneys, managers, and experts working on the case at the time of each summit. This particular meeting was restricted to just a few people, and only Frank Horvath and I called it the eighth and final summit.

We left the van at the trailhead. It was cold—single digits—and there was a fresh dusting of new-fallen snow. We were at the Nature Conservancy's Mink River Estuary property. The pristine forest was glowing under a white winter sun. There was no breeze. The only sound was our soft footsteps in a light covering of snow. No banter now. The scene was breathtaking, the mood reverential. I led the party down the path in silence.

We were within an ideal example of the kind of place my team had designed the NRDA to protect. The Conservancy had protected this particular place for some of the same reasons. It was a rare and critical coastal wetland surrounded by nearly untouched cedar forest and related habitats. It was nestled between other protected properties, Wisconsin's Newport State Park and Mink River Estuary State Natural Area. The Conservancy lands surrounded the Mink River Estuary itself, which flowed to and from Lake Michigan not far from Spider Island, where Ken had been studying cormorants for more than a decade.

I had often visited this property on my own time. I had watched and listened to northern goshawks loudly complain about our intrusion into their nesting territory as Darlene and I traversed this same trail, hoping to find marsh marigolds and common green darners farther ahead. I had slept in my boat along a bank of this estuary on moonless, starlit summer nights. Now I was showing this quiet, secret place to the people who would carry the NRDA to its conclusion, people who could now visualize what might be restored or protected all around Green Bay and nearby Lake Michigan.

I broke the silence only after we arrived at the Mink River itself. Snow, ice, and water sparkled in the crystalline light. I reminded my guests that the PCB cleanup remained key, but restoration beyond cleanup was also critically important. No other action could make the public whole for losses that stretched well beyond the reach of any cleanup remedy. My team had already figured out how much was needed and where many of the best opportunities awaited. It was in places like this—places that, by their sheer splendor and ecological significance, made it all worthwhile.

AFTERWORD

As soon as DNR *actually* joined EPA and the co-trustees, starting in 2001, the intergovernmental partnership finally became functional. The federal government, two state governments, and several tribal governments became cylinders in a mostly well-oiled machine. DNR and EPA published the Remedial Investigation, Feasibility Study, and Proposed Remedial Action Plan in 2001–2 with co-trustee endorsement (Retec 2002a, 2002b; EPA 2001). Next came the Records of Decision in 2002 and 2003 (EPA 2002, 2003). Settlements between the governments and responsible parties started coming out every couple of years (DOJ 2001, 2002, 2003, 2006a, 2006b; EPA 2007; DOJ 2008, 2009a, 2009b, 2010, 2014a, 2014b, 2014c, 2017a, 2019). Leverage over the paper companies had increased exponentially, and real cleanup and restoration ramped up to a scale long imagined by Fish and Wildlife's team—but by few others (FWS 2003; Anchor Environmental 2008a, 2008b; EPA 2009; FWS 2013; EPA 2014).

The story about open warfare between agencies was replaced by the more predictable and mundane story of regulatory process between government and polluters. Still, even with unified governmental power, it would take another nineteen years to work out all of the settlements with the paper companies and complete the cleanup—and longer than that to finish the restoration projects.

Restoration projects began in 2002 using NRDA settlements. Dredging under the Superfund cleanup documents began in 2004. In five years, 372,000 cubic yards of contaminated sediment were dredged from the most upstream part of the Superfund site (GW Partners 2010).

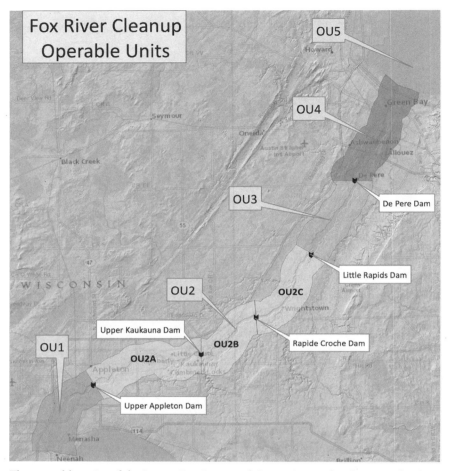

The operable units of the Lower Fox River and Green Bay under the Superfund cleanup. (Wisconsin DNR, dnr.wisconsin.gov)

This was in addition to the 90,000 cubic yards removed during 1998–2000 from the Deposit N and SMU 56–57 demonstration projects, and the emergency cleanup of the latter (EPA 2019).

Year after year, restorations continued all around the Fox River and Green Bay (FWS 2016). Total restoration settlements came to over $100 million, and were tacked onto the mounting cleanup costs. Fish and Wildlife and its co-trustees implemented seventy-eight natural resource restoration projects through 2016, using the first $43 million of settlements. These projects preserved 6,085 acres of wetlands and habitat, restored 3,961 acres of wetlands and habitat, improved 1,747 acres of habitat, enhanced eleven fisheries, and improved many public parks. The remaining settlements—more than half—were targeted for additional wetland and habitat preservation, as well as habitat improvements.

View from the shore of South River Bay on Garden Peninsula (also known as the natural resource trustees' Garden Bluffs Restoration Project and the Nature Conservancy's Haunted Forest Preserve), 2020. (P. David Allen II)

Limestone bluffs near South River Bay on Garden Peninsula, 2011. (P. David Allen II)

Meanwhile, EPA and DNR started dredging the rest of the Fox River in earnest. In 2009, they began dredging the main area of PCB contamination, especially below the De Pere Dam. For more than a decade, they removed an average of over 500,000 cubic yards of contaminated sediment *per year*—more each year than the total removed between 1998 and 2008 (Tetra Tech 2019).

On January 17, 2017, the federal DOJ announced the final phase of the cleanup (DOJ 2017b). Total cleanup costs were predicted to exceed $1 billion. On August 12, 2020, U.S. EPA administrator Andrew Wheeler came to Wisconsin to announce the completion of the cleanup, confirming that costs had in fact reached ten figures (Bollier 2020). Nearly a month later, on September 1, Wisconsin governor Tony Evers declared the cleanup a success during a public Zoom meeting* with other dignitaries, including Fish and Wildlife regional director Charlie Wooley (Schulte 2020). Enough PCB-contaminated sediments were dredged from nineteen miles of the river to fill Lambeau Stadium six times— over 6.5 million cubic yards, all placed in local landfills. Another 1,000 acres of river bottom were covered with specially engineered caps or clean sand.

Dignitaries at the September Zoom meeting, and various reporters afterward, estimated that the total cost to clean up and restore the Fox River and Green Bay under the Superfund law would reach $1 billion to $1.5 billion, the largest PCB cleanup in history and one of the largest sediment cleanups of any kind anywhere in the world. They said that PCBs had already been reduced by over 90 percent in river water and sediments, and that river walleye were close to reaching the "unlimited consumption" advisory level. They also said that DNR and EPA had successfully partnered as the lead technical and lead enforcement agency, respectively, and that the co-trustees—federal, state, and tribal—would continue to fund restorations throughout the bay using the money already received from settlements.

---

* Recording of the September 1, 2020 Zoom call: https://wiseye.org/2020/09/01/news -conference-gov-evers-dnr-federal-and-tribal-partners-announce-completion-of-fox-river -cleanup/.

The entire Fox River cleanup and restoration was funded by the paper companies at fault rather than by taxpayers who were already harmed by the pollution. The idea that polluters should pay to clean up their own messes—and make the public whole—prevailed. This principle succeeded in the face of Governor Thompson's early opposition, and it was implemented during the administrations of presidents Bill Clinton (D), George W. Bush (R), Barack Obama (D), and Donald Trump (R); Wisconsin governors Scott McCallum (R), Jim Doyle (D), Scott Walker (R), and Tony Evers (D); and Michigan governors John Engler (R), Jennifer Granholm (D), Rick Snyder (R), and Gretchen Whitmer (D). The principle prevailed despite fierce opposition from the paper companies and Tommy Thompson, and despite widespread skepticism from local supporters and opponents alike.

In short, the system worked. It prevailed without EPA ever finalizing the placement of the Fox River on Superfund's National Priorities List. It prevailed without the government ever taking the paper companies to a natural resource damages trial.

Fish and Wildlife's central damage assessment study for recreational fishing, calculating about $100 million in damages, matched the $100 million in NRDA settlements. Fish and Wildlife's preliminary estimate of damages for sediment restoration, about $700 million in 1996—or $1.2 billion in 2020 dollars—was also matched by the actual recovered cleanup costs. The Green Bay case influenced the private sector as well. In 2020, defense attorneys at some of the biggest Superfund sites in the country were noticing the Fox River and vowing to avoid Superfund litigation at their own sites (Carignan 2020).

The intergovernmental partnership won the central arguments. The evidence tells the story: the paper companies paid for the cleanup and restoration because the government proved that the mills created the mess.

EPILOGUE

David Allen and Susan Campbell

We left Green Bay—David in early 2001, and Susan in late 2000. Neither of us would participate in the fruits of our long labors. Our work was done. Susan had laid the foundation of reporting about Fox River PCBs and intergovernmental strife for most of a decade. David had set the table for the government to win two decades of orders and settlements that would drive the most comprehensive, systematic PCB cleanup and restoration in U.S. history. It was a bittersweet victory, as we each watched from afar the consequential events unfolding in Green Bay.

Since then, both of us have moved on again—David from environmental consulting for governmental agencies, and Susan from communications work for an environmental nonprofit. It's probably of little surprise that David, now retired, lives and plays the trombone in Marquette, Michigan. Susan left the communications field to promote and practice green real estate in Milwaukee. One thing that hasn't changed with time: we both still treasure walking the woodland trails and paths along the shores of the Great Lakes, gazing out over their arrestingly beautiful waters. It never grows old.

As for some of the others who played key roles in the Fox River story, they have moved on as well. Frank Horvath retired from federal service in 2010 and now splits his time between Rosemount, Minnesota and Venice, Florida. Ken Stromborg retired from federal service in 2007 and now lives near Denmark, Wisconsin. Joe Moniot retired from Fish and Wildlife's headquarters in 2012. He built or restored several wooden boats for David and lives in Kentucky. Josh Lipton retired from environmental consulting in 2018 and now lives in Boulder. Jim Hahnenberg retired from federal service in 2016 and now lives in Aurora, Illinois. Roger Grimes retired from federal service in 2004 and now lives on the north side of Chicago. Susan Schneider left Main Justice in 1999 and retired from federal service in Denver in 2013. Matt Richmond stayed with the case longest of all, from 1993 until nearly the end. Then he left for woods and waters unknown.

George Meyer has continued to serve Wisconsin's public and environment for decades since leaving DNR, including serving as the first executive director of the Wisconsin Wildlife Federation and being inducted into the Wisconsin Conservation Hall of Fame in 2017. Former governor Tommy Thompson completed his four-year stint as secretary of U.S. Health and Human Services in 2005. In July 2020 he was appointed to lead the University of Wisconsin system as interim president, stepping down from that post in spring 2022. After Thompson appointed Maryann Sumi to the Dane County Circuit Court in 1998, she was elected to the post in 1999, 2005, and 2011, and retired from the bench in 2014. Bruce Baker finally ascended to DNR's top post in the Water Division in January 2011, then promptly retired the following March.

In April 2016, Ken Stromborg and Jim Hahnenberg attended a governmental reunion for the Green Bay Natural Resource Damage Assessment. Both were disappointed that most other attendees did not remember the high-stakes drama of the 1990s, when EPA and Fish and Wildlife decided to force the paper companies to pay for cleanup and restoration. Ken thought somebody should find a way to record the inside story before it was completely forgotten.

By June of that year, Ken's musings and some prodding from others close to the story convinced us we should write this book. It had been decades since we had spoken to each other, as reporter to source or otherwise. Now, years later, we were about to learn each other's personal stories. We found out far more than we had ever revealed back in Green Bay, and we were usually happily surprised. Seeing our own experiences through each other's eyes was more than enlightening—it was thrilling. For the first time, we would tell our interwoven stories from a personal perspective.

The Green Bay story still matters to us because empirical facts and mechanistic principles are just as reliable in today's civic and political turmoil as they were during the arguments about Fox River PCBs in the 1990s. Facts and principles may seem elusive in the face of disinformation, blind allegiance to leaders and groups, rhetoric designed to gain tactical advantage without advancing truth, and angry discourse among divergent viewpoints.

Nevertheless, *every* citizen has access to credible information and to techniques for separating informational wheat from chaff. And every citizen can influence their own future, if they can occasionally pry themselves away from the addictive, numbing tonic of all our electronic distractions. We hope for a growing wave of people desperate to learn about the credibility and biases of information sources. We hope they will increasingly take time to seek reliable information and ignore obvious bias. We hope our fellow citizens will worry more about accuracy, precision, and depth than about finding temporary advantage for their favorite news channel, party, candidate, suspicion, or team.

Telling the Green Bay story matters to us, now, because our country's institutional power is still constrained by facts, principles, and the rule of law. Relatively few people can occupy positions of power at any given moment, but the rest of us can hold them accountable every day. Facts and principles are powerful levers within our legal system and within the institutions that bind us together in common cause as a nation. We hope that a growing chorus of citizens with diverse backgrounds, interests, and political leanings will demand honesty, transparency, and accountability from the people who represent them at every level of government. Power most certainly brings opportunities for abuse. Yet institutions of representative government that are rooted in law and based on facts and principle protect us all, even our leaders, from making the worst kinds of mistakes.

The Green Bay story still matters to us because open-mindedness and ethical fair play allow us, individually and collectively, to continue to be astonished by what turns out to be true and equitable, despite our expectations and prejudices. Life is richer and the future more boundless when we embrace the complexity of reality, when we give ourselves over to the pursuit of truth, despite our limitations in finding it. Our lives matter more when our causes are greater than ourselves but bounded by facts. Our ability to succeed together is magnified by concentrating on the facts and principles that are inalterable by opinions, and by agreeing to the compromises that are hard won through working the levers of our representative government. We do not have to agree about everything, but we can concur about many difficult issues through curious, open-eyed, principled, and disciplined attention to the details within our common grasp.

Let us begin by agreeing to care more deeply and consistently about what can be proven, and how and why. Let us rely on our own areas of expertise to test how various sources handle the topics we already know the most about. Most important, let's not believe purported facts only because they make us feel better, and let's apply healthy skepticism whenever we hear those with a vested interest tell us what is "fake" news. It's not all fake, nor is it always what we are hoping to hear—and that's as it should be in a democracy founded on the principle of open and spirited debate.

Apropos of that, we hope you will explore our story more deeply by looking at the details behind it—some of which still seem incredible to this day—and evaluate for yourself the story's authenticity.

This story is unusually well documented. First, we provide a little over twenty-two hundred pages of detailed handwritten notes taken daily during eleven years of internal and interagency meetings at EPA and Fish and Wildlife and extracted from the pages of the green notebooks referenced several times in the preceding pages (Allen 1991, 1992a, 1993, 1994a, 1995a, 1996, 1997, 1998b, 1999, 2000a, 2001, 2018a). You can search an electronic file of transcribed notes or try to read the handwriting from the original pages, captured in PDF files for each year. Second, there is a listing of 6,671 agency files from the Reading Room with categories, dates, and brief descriptions in another electronic file (Allen 2018c). Third, we downloaded many of the key agency documents from governmental websites. An electronic table lists three damage assessment indexes, five damage assessment planning documents, seven damage assessment determinations, fifteen settlement documents, fourteen cleanup and restoration documents, twenty-six papers, and seventeen scholarly presentations published in the scientific literature from the damage assessment work (Allen 2019a). Fourth, there is an electronic file listing 1,659 scientific papers that Fish and Wildlife accumulated for the damage assessment during the 1990s (Allen 2018b). Fifth, there is an electronic file with tables listing the key people who worked at Green Bay, both before the damage assessment and during it (Allen 2019b). Finally, we provide a short description of the most important outcomes of the damage assessment (Allen 2020).

REFERENCES

Abitz, Stephen. 1996. "Scare Tactics Used." *Green Bay Press-Gazette*, December 7, A-9.

Allen, P. D. 1991. Handwritten notes. www.papervalley.org.

———. 1992a. Handwritten notes. www.papervalley.org.

———. 1992b. Text from memorandum to F. Horvath, October 21. www.paper valley.org.

———. 1993. Handwritten notes. www.papervalley.org.

———. 1994a. Handwritten notes. www.papervalley.org.

———. 1994b. Text from memorandum to F. Horvath, April 14. www.papervalley .org.

———. 1995a. Handwritten notes. www.papervalley.org.

———. 1995b. Text from memorandum to F. Horvath and J. Smith, May 12. www .papervalley.org.

———. 1996. Handwritten notes. www.papervalley.org.

———. 1997. Handwritten notes. www.papervalley.org.

———. 1998a. "The Green Bay NRDA and Why CERCLA Liability Makes Sense for the Private Sector." Presented to the Appleton Rotary, Appleton, WI, October.

———. 1998b. Handwritten notes. www.papervalley.org.

———. 1999. Handwritten notes. www.papervalley.org.

———. 2000a. Handwritten notes. www.papervalley.org.

———. 2000b. Text from letter to G. Hill, July 20. www.papervalley.org.

———. 2000c. Unpublished letter to the editor, December. www.papervalley.org.

———. 2001. Handwritten notes. www.papervalley.org.

———. 2003. "The Green Bay Natural Resource Damage Assessment: Opening Significant Environmental Cases by the Government to Public and Scientific Scrutiny." Presented at the tenth annual meeting of the Wildlife Society, Burlington, VT, September 10. www.papervalley.org.

———. 2009. "Valuing Natural Resource Damages: How to Use Empirical Data and Estimation Techniques to Build Positions, Claims, and Leverage." In American Bar Association, *Proceedings of the 38th Annual Conference on*

Environmental Law, section of Environment, Energy, and Resources. www.
papervalley.org.

Allen, P. D. 2010. "Green Bay Natural Resource Damage Assessment: Why No
Habitat Equivalency Analysis?" Slides presented at the monthly meeting of the
National Oceanic and Atmospheric Administration, Assessment and Resto-
ration Division, Silver Spring, MD. www.papervalley.org.

———. 2018a. Daily notes, 1992–2001, relevant to the Green Bay Natural Resource
Damage Assessment, transcribed from notebooks. www.papervalley.org.

———. 2018b. List of scientific papers accumulated by the U.S. Fish and Wildlife
Service for the Green Bay Natural Resource Damage Assessment, 1992–1999.
www.papervalley.org.

———. 2018c. Table listing documents accumulated by the U.S. Fish and Wildlife
Service for the Green Bay Natural Resource Damage Assessment, 1992–1999.
www.papervalley.org.

———. 2019a. Table of publications for and from the Green Bay Natural Resource
Damage Assessment. www.papervalley.org.

———. 2019b. Tables 1–5: Key personnel working before and during the Green
Bay Natural Resource Damage Assessment. www.papervalley.org.

———. 2020. Skeleton key to the Green Bay Natural Resource Damage Assessment. www.papervalley.org.

Anchor Environmental. 2008a. "Lower Fox River Remedial Design, 60 Percent
Design Report for 2009 Remedial Actions," vol. 1. www.papervalley.org.

———. 2008b. "Lower Fox River Remedial Design, 60 Percent Design Report for
2009 Remedial Actions," vol. 2. www.papervalley.org.

Anderson, T. 1994. "Study May Hit Mills with PCB Damages." *Green Bay Press-
Gazette*, June 24, A-1.

Behnke, D. 2000. "Green Says Wording in Pending Bill Won't Affect Fox River
PCB Cleanup." *Appleton Post-Crescent*, June 27, B-1.

Berlin, W. H., R. J. Hesselberg, and M. J. Mac. 1981. "Growth and Mortality of Fry
of Lake Michigan Lake Trout during Chronic Exposure to PCB's and DDE."
Contribution 563 of the Great Lakes Fishery Laboratory, U.S. U.S. Fish and
Wildlife Service, Technical Paper 105, 11–22.

Bollier, J. 2020. "EPA Declares PCB Cleanup in Fox River, Lower Green Bay Complete, but More Work Remains." *Green Bay Press-Gazette*, August 12.

Bruss, S. 1998. "Dredging for PCBs Under Way on Fox River." *Green Bay Press-
Gazette*, November 24.

Campbell, S. 1996a. "Cooperation or Confrontation." *Green Bay Press-Gazette*,
December 20, B-1.

———. 1996b. "Feds' Role in Fox Cleanup Stirs Trouble." *Green Bay Press-Gazette*,
November 24, 1996, A-1

———. 1996c. "Frustrated Activist: It's Time to Leave." *Green Bay Press-Gazette*,
September 17, A-1.

———. 1996d. "Little Said on Fox Cleanup Negotiations." *Green Bay Press-Gazette*, December 21, B-1.

———. 1996e. "Open Doors on Water Meetings." *Green Bay Press-Gazette*, December 30.

———. 1997a. "The Politics of Pollution." *Green Bay Press-Gazette*, May 14, A-1.

———. 1997b. "Public Gets Update on Fox River Cleanup." *Green Bay Press-Gazette*, May 22.

———. 1997c. "Seven Mills Target Fox Pollution." *Green Bay Press-Gazette*, January 31, A-1.

———. 1998a. "Assessment of PCB Danger Key to Fox River Cleanup." *Green Bay Press-Gazette*, August 2, A-1.

———. 1998b. "Bill Would Give Governors Veto of Superfund Designation." *Green Bay Press-Gazette*, June 18, B-4.

———. 1998c. "Cancellations Leave Just One Speaker on PCBs." *Green Bay Press-Gazette*, April 25, B-2.

———. 1998d. "The Debate over PCBs: Q & A with Theo Colborn and John Giesy." *Green Bay Press-Gazette*, August 2, A-13.

———. 1998e. "EPA Leader Takes Hard Line on PCBs, Health." *Green Bay Press-Gazette*, July 19, A-2.

———. 1998f. "Fish-Eating Warnings Posted along Fox River." *Green Bay Press-Gazette*, June 23, B-1.

———. 1998g. "Fox Proposed for Superfund: EPA to Accept Public Comment for 60 Days." *Green Bay Press-Gazette*, July 29.

———. 1998h. "Fox Proposed for Superfund: Potential Remains for Voluntary Cleanup." *Green Bay Press-Gazette*, July 10, A-1.

———. 1998i. "Fox Restoration a Challenge." *Green Bay Press-Gazette*, October 11, A-1.

———. 1998j. "Fox River Dredging Plan Makes Some Residents Nervous." *Green Bay Press-Gazette*, August 27, A-1.

———. 1998k. "Fox's PCB Count Mounts." *Green Bay Press-Gazette*, June 19, A-1.

———. 1998l. "Opinions on Fox Flood EPA." *Green Bay Press-Gazette*, September 20, A-1.

———. 1998m. "PCBs' Effects on Humans Argued." *Green Bay Press-Gazette*, July 28, A-1.

———. 1998n. "PCBs' Total Impact Unknown." *Green Bay Press-Gazette*, April 28.

———. 1998o. "Scientists Feel Left out of Fox Debate." *Green Bay-Press Gazette*, August 26, B-1.

———. 1998p. "Superfund Stakes High All Around." *Green Bay Press-Gazette*, July 19, A-1.

———. 1998q. "Superfund Status Weighs Heavily on Fox." *Green Bay Press-Gazette*, April 19, A-1.

Campbell, S. 1998r. "Thompson: Superfund Bad Idea." *Green Bay Press-Gazette*, May 15, B-2.

———. 1999a. "Bay Added to Fox River PCB Cleanup Studies." *Green Bay Press-Gazette*, October 29, B-1.

———. 1999b. "DNR Touts Early Data on Fox PCBs." *Green Bay Press-Gazette*, February 9, A-1.

———. 1999c. "Dredging Project Faces Downsizing." *Green Bay Press-Gazette*, January 22, A-1.

———. 1999d. "Dredging Project Might Meet Only Half of Its Goal." *Green Bay Press-Gazette*, November 4, A-1.

———. 1999e. "EPA Hears Mostly from Superfund Site Advocates." *Green Bay Press-Gazette*, February 8, A-1.

———. 1999f. "Federal Report Says PCBs Drift into the Bay." *Green Bay Press-Gazette*, August 31, B-1.

———. 1999g. "Fish Advisories May Cost Mills Millions." *Green Bay Press-Gazette*, November 8, A-1.

———. 1999h. "National Group to Observe Work on PCBs." *Green Bay Press-Gazette*, July 16, A-1.

———. 1999i. "Panel Wraps Up PCB Hearing." *Green Bay Press-Gazette*, September 29, B-1.

———. 1999j. "Residents Can't Dispose of Mussels." *Green Bay Press-Gazette*, June 4, A-1.

———. 1999k. "Survey on Fox River Finds Health Concerns." *Green Bay Press-Gazette*, October 21, A-1.

———. 2000a. "Compensation Amount Hinges on Cleanup Plan." *Green Bay Press-Gazette*, October 26, A-1.

———. 2000b. "Environmentalist Group Wants EPA to Clean Up Fox." *Green Bay Press-Gazette*, March 8, B-8.

———. 2000c. "Environmentalists Take Fox Cleanup Fight to U.S. Senate." *Green Bay Press-Gazette*, June 28, B-2.

———. 2000d. "EPA Boosts Estimate of Dioxin Risk." *Green Bay Press-Gazette*, July 5.

———. 2000e. "Fort James to Resume Fox River Dredging." *Green Bay Press-Gazette*, May 26, A-1.

———. 2000f. "Mills Urged to Finish Dredging." *Green Bay Press-Gazette*, March 16, B-1.

———. 2000g. "Paper Mills' TV Ad Campaign Will Address Fox Cleanup." *Green Bay Press-Gazette*, March 19.

———. 2000h. "State Pact on PCB Site Worries Feds: DNR Offers Settlement for Sheboygan River Pollution." *Green Bay Press-Gazette*, July 22, B-1.

Carignan, S. 2020. "Lawyers Predict Fewer Long Court Battles with EPA over Superfund." *Bloomberg Law*, August 14.

Cioni, T. 1998. "County Panel Doesn't Oppose Superfund." *Green Bay Press-Gazette*, July 7, B-1.

Colborn, T., D. Dumanoski, and J. P. Myers. 1996. *Our Stolen Future.* New York: Dutton.

Cole, F. 1998. "Residents Don't Fear Fox Cleanup: Open House Explains Dredging." *Green Bay Press-Gazette,* December 6, A-1.

Connolly, J. F., T. F. Parkerton, J. D. Quadrini, S. T. Taylor, and A. J. Thumann. 1992. *Development and Application of a Model of PCBs in the Green Bay, Lake Michigan Walleye and Brown Trout and Their Food Webs.* Prepared for U.S. EPA, October 2. http://udspace.udel.edu/handle/19716/1437.

Content, T. 1998. "PCB Damage Called Heavy: Report Backs State Fish Advisories." *Green Bay Press-Gazette,* December 11, B-1.

Culhane, E. 1998. "Public Forum Outlines the Health Dangers of PCBs." *Appleton Post-Crescent,* April 28, A1.

Custer, T. W., and C. Bunck 1992. "Feeding Flights of Breeding Double-Crested Cormorants at Two Wisconsin Colonies." *Journal of Field Ornithology* 63 (2): 203–11.

Decker, Jeff. 2000. "State, Feds Feud over Fox Proposals." *Green Bay News-Chronicle,* October 31.

DePinto, J. V., R. Raghunathan, P. Sierzenga, X. Zhang, V. J. Bierman, P. W. Rodgers, and T. C. Young. 1994. *Recalibration of GBTOX: An Integrated Exposure Model for Toxic Chemicals in Green Bay, Lake Michigan.* https://semspub.epa.gov/work/05/417179.pdf.

DeVoogt, P., and U. Brinkman. 1989. "Production, Properties, and Usage of Polychlorinated Biphenyls." In *Topics in Environmental Health,* vol. 4 of *Halogenated Biphenyls, Terphenyls, Naphthalenes, Dibenzodioxins and Related Products,* edited by R. Kimbrough and A. Jensen, 3–46. Amsterdam: Elsevier.

Dobkin, L. 2010. "The Sawdust Trail." *Milwaukee Magazine,* February 22. https://www.milwaukeemag.com/TheSawdustTrail/.

DOJ (U.S. Department of Justice). 2001. Consent Decree with Appleton Papers Inc. and NCR Corporation. www.papervalley.org.

———. 2002. Consent Decree with Fort James Operating Company (Fort Howard). www.papervalley.org.

———. 2003. Consent Decree with P. H. Glatfelter Company and WTM 1 (Wisconsin Tissue Mills). www.papervalley.org.

———. 2006a. Consent Decree with Appleton Papers Inc. and NCR Corporation. www.papervalley.org.

———. 2006b. Consent Decree with NCR Corporation and Sonoco-U.S. Mills Corp (U.S. Paper). www.papervalley.org.

———. 2008. Consent Decree with P. H. Glatfelter Company and WTM I Company (Wisconsin Tissue Mills). www.papervalley.org.

———. 2009a. Consent Decree with City of De Pere and George Whiting Company. www.papervalley.org.

———. 2009b. Consent Decree with 12 De Minimis Parties. www.papervalley.org.

———. 2010. Consent Decree with Brown County and the City of Green Bay. www.papervalley.org.

DOJ (U.S. Department of Justice). 2014a. Consent Decree with Kimberly Clark Corporation. www.papervalley.org.

———. 2014b. Consent Decree with NewPage Wisconsin System Inc. (Consolidated Papers). www.papervalley.org.

———. 2014c. Consent Decree with State of Wisconsin and Other Cashout Settling Defendants. www.papervalley.org.

———. 2017a. Consent Decree with NCR and Appvion, Inc. (Appleton Papers, Inc.). www.papervalley.org.

———. 2017b. "NCR Corporation Agrees to End Litigation and Complete Massive Superfund Cleanup at Wisconsin's Fox River." Press release. www.papervalley.org.

———. 2019. Consent Decree with P. H. Glatfelter Company and Georgia-Pacific Consumer Products L.P. (Fort Howard). www.papervalley.org.

Durkin, P. 2018. "George Meyer Still Standing His Ground." *Wisconsin State Journal*, April 7.

Eadie, B.J., G.L. Bell, and N. Hawley. 1991. *Sediment Trap Study in the Green Bay Mass Balance Program: Mass and Organic Carbon Fluxes, Resuspension, and Particle Settling Velocities.* National Oceanic and Atmospheric Administration. https://repository.library.noaa.gov/view/noaa/11277.

EPA (U.S. Environmental Protection Agency). 2000. Enforcement Action Memorandum: Determination of Need to Conduct a Time-Critical Removal Action at Sediment Management Units 56 and 57, Part of the Lower Fox River NRDA/PCB Releases Site, Winnebago, Outagamie, Brown, Oconto, Marinette, Kewaunee, and Door Counties, Wisconsin and Menominee and Delta Counties, Michigan, Site ID# A565. www.papervalley.org.

———. 2001. Proposed Remedial Action Plan, Lower Fox River and Green Bay. www.papervalley.org.

———. 2002. Record of Decision, Operable Unit 1 and Operable Unit 2, Lower Fox River and Green Bay Site Wisconsin. www.papervalley.org.

———. 2003. Record of Decision, Operable Units 3, 4, and 5, Lower Fox River and Green Bay site, Wisconsin. www.papervalley.org.

———. 2007. Unilateral Administrative Order to Eight Companies for Lower Fox River and Green Bay Superfund Site, Operable Units 2–5. www.papervalley.org.

———. 2009. Five-Year Review Report for Fox River Natural Resource Damage Assessment/PCB Releases Superfund Site. www.papervalley.org.

———. 2014. Second Five-Year Review Report for Fox River Natural Resource Damage Assessment/PCB Releases Superfund Site. www.papervalley.org.

———. 2019. Third Five-Year Review Report for Fox River NRDA/PCB Releases Superfund Site. www.papervalley.org.

Eschmeyer, P. H. 1957. "The Near Extinction of Lake Trout in Lake Michigan." *Transactions of the American Fisheries Society* 85 (1): 102–19.

Fitzsimons, J. D. 1995. "The Effect of B-Vitamins on a Swim-up Syndrome in Lake Ontario Lake Trout." *Journal of Great Lakes Research* 21 (supplement 1): 286–89.

FWS (U.S. Fish and Wildlife Service). 1994. Preassessment Screen and Determination, Lower Fox River and Green Bay, Wisconsin. www.papervalley.org.

———. 1996. Assessment Plan: Lower Fox River/Green Bay NRDA. www.paper valley.org.

———. 1997. Assessment Plan Addendum: Lower Fox River/Green Bay NRDA. www.papervalley.org.

———. 1998a. Fish Consumption Advisories in the Lower Fox River/Green Bay Assessment Area. www.papervalley.org.

———. 1998b. Lower Fox River/Green Bay Nrda Initial Restoration and Compensation Determination Plan. www.papervalley.org.

———. 1999a. Injuries to Avian Resources, Lower Fox River/Green Bay Natural Resource Damage Assessment. www.papervalley.org.

———. 1999b. Injuries to Fishery Resources, Lower Fox River/Green Bay Natural Resource Damage Assessment. www.papervalley.org.

———. 1999c. Injuries to Surface Water Resources, Lower Fox River/Green Bay Natural Resource Damage Assessment. www.papervalley.org.

———. 1999d. PCB Pathway Determination for the Lower Fox River/Green Bay Natural Resource Damage Assessment. www.papervalley.org.

———. 1999e. Recreational Fishing Damages from Fish Consumption Advisories in the Waters of Green Bay. www.papervalley.org.

———. 2000a. Lower Fox River/Green Bay NRDA, Third Assessment Plan Addendum. www.papervalley.org.

———. 2000b. Restoration and Compensation Determination Plan, Lower Fox River/Green Bay Natural Resource Damage Assessment. www.papervalley.org.

———. 2003. Joint Restoration Plan and Environmental Assessment for the Lower Fox River and Green Bay Area. www.papervalley.org.

———. 2008a. Green Bay Natural Resource Damage Assessment Reading Room Index of Documents. www.papervalley.org.

———. 2008b. Green Bay Natural Resource Damage Assessment Reading Room Index of Documents. www.papervalley.org.

———. 2008c. Green Bay Natural Resource Damage Assessment Reading Room Index of Documents. www.papervalley.org.

———. 2013. Restoration Progress Report for the Lower Fox River and Green Bay Natural Resource Damage Assessment. www.papervalley.org.

———. 2016. Lower Fox River and Green Bay Natural Resource Damage Assessment and Restoration, Update to the Restoration Plan and Environmental Assessment. www.papervalley.org.

Gailani, J., C. K. Ziegler, and W. Lick. 1991. "Transport of Suspended Solids in the Lower Fox River." *Journal of Great Lakes Research* 17:479–94.

Gamble, D., and P. Heyda. 2016. *Rebuilding the American City: Design and Strategy for the 21st Century Urban Core.* New York: Routledge, 73–78.

Great Lakes Water Quality Board. 1987. "Report on Great Lakes Water Quality: Appendix A, Progress in Developing Remedial Action Plans for Areas of

Concern in the Great Lakes Basin, Report to the International Joint Commission" Presented at Toledo, OH, November.

Green Bay Press-Gazette. 1996. "Continue Cooperation on River." November 30, A-9.

———. 1998. "Local Fox Cleanup Still Best." July 12, A-14.

———. 1999a. "Don't Scale Back Fox River Project." January 31, A-14.

———. 1999b. "The River as We See It." Appleton Papers advertisement, February 7, A-5.

GW Partners. 2010. "Remedial Action Certification of Completion, Lower Fox River Operable Unit 1." www.papervalley.org.

Hildebrand, S. 2000. "Fort James Deal May Spur Audit." *Green Bay Press-Gazette,* November 17, B-1.

Hildebrand, S. and Campbell, S. 1997a. "EPA: Add Fox to Superfund List." *Green Bay Press-Gazette,* June 19, A-1.

———. 1997b. "Fox, Bay Fish-Eating Tips Offered." *Green Bay Press-Gazette,* February 20, A-1

Holey, M. E., R. W. Rybicki, G. W. Eck, E. H. J. Brown, J. E. Marsden, D. S. Lavis, M. L. Toneys, T. N. Trudeau, and R. M. Horrall. 1995. "Progress toward Lake Trout Restoration in Lake Michigan." *Journal of Great Lakes Research* 21 (supplement 1): 128–51.

Hunter, C. 1998. "We Look Forward to a 1999 Full of Change." *Green Bay Press-Gazette,* December 27.

International Joint Commission. 1990. *Fifth Biennial Report under the Great Lakes Water Quality Agreement of 1978 to the Government of the United States and Canada and the State and Provincial Governments of the Great Lakes Basin.* Part 2. Washington, DC: International Joint Commission.

Jones, M. L., G. W. Eck, D. O. Evans, M. C. Fabrizio, M. H. Hoff, P. L. Hudson, J. Janssen, D. Jude, R. O'Gorman, and J. F. Savino. 1995. "Limitations to Lake Trout (Salvelinus namaycush) Rehabilitation in the Great Lakes Imposed by Biotic Interactions Occurring at Early Life Stages." *Journal of Great Lakes Research* 21 (supplement 1): 505–17.

Jones, R. P. 1995. "Thompson's Actions Called 'Childish.'" *Milwaukee Journal Sentinel,* June 10.

Keith, J. A. 1966. "Reproduction in a Population of Herring Gulls (Larus argentatus) Contaminated by DDT." *Journal of Applied Ecology* 3 (supplement): 57–70.

Klas, P. and P. DeKeyser. 2000. "Tecumseh Disappointed with EPA's Plan." Tecumseh Products, letter to the editor, *Sheboygan Press,* July 2, A-7.

Knuth, B. A., S. Lerner, N. A. Connelly, and L. Gigliotti. 1995. "Fishery and Environmental Managers' Attitudes about and Support for Lake Trout Rehabilitation in the Great Lakes." *Journal of Great Lakes Research* 21 (supplement 1): 185–97.

Kubiak, T. J., H. J. Harris, L. M. Smith, T. R. Schwartz, D. L. Stalling, J. A. Trick, L. Sileo, D. E. Docherty, and T. C. Erdman. 1989. "Microcontaminants and

Reproductive Impairment of the Forster's Tern on Green Bay, Lake Michigan, 1983." *Archives of Environmental Contamination and Toxicology* 18: 706–27.

Lyttle, B. 2008. "The Cape Cod of the Midwest." *New York Times*, September 11.

Mac, M. J. 1981. "Vulnerability of Young Lake Trout to Predation After Chronic Exposure to PCB's and DDE." Technical Papers of the U.S. Fish and Wildlife Service 105. https://www.usgs.gov/publications/vulnerability-young-lake-trout -predation-after-chronic-exposure-pcbs-and-dde.

Manchester-Neesvig, J. B., A. W. Andren, and D. N. Edgington. 1996. "Patterns of Mass Sedimentation and of Deposition of Sediment Contaminated by PCBs in Green Bay." *Journal of Great Lakes Research* 22 (2): 444–62.

Manthe, Laura. 1997. "Trying to Frighten Workers." *Green Bay Press-Gazette*, January 3, A-7.

Meyer, G. 2000. Letter to the editor. *Wisconsin State Journal*, December 19. Forwarded to David Allen by Wisconsin DNR staff. www.papervalley.org.

Meyer, J. 1994. "Five Mills Blamed for PCBs in the River." *Appleton Post-Crescent*, June 25, A-1.

Millard, Pete. 1998a. "Garvey Says Governor's Restructuring Clears Path for Special Interest Groups." *Milwaukee Business Journal*, February 1. https://www .bizjournals.com/milwaukee/stories/1998/02/02/story6.html.

———. 1998b. "A Year Later, Business Leaders Praise Governor's Restructuring of State Government." *Milwaukee Business Journal*, February 1. https://www .bizjournals.com/milwaukee/stories/1998/02/02/story1.html.

Murphy, T. 1997. "Feds Ripped on Fox Cleanup." *Green Bay Press-Gazette*, June 7, A-5.

Pearson, R. F., K. C. Hornbuckle, S. J. Eisenreich, and D. L. Swackhamer. 1996. "PCBs in Lake Michigan Water Revisited." *Environmental Science and Technology* 30:1429–36.

Perry, T. 2000. "Fort James, DNR Deal Leaves Some Questions." *Green Bay Press-Gazette*, November 19, B-1.

Retec. 2002a. Final Feasibility Study, Lower Fox River and Green Bay, Wisconsin. www.papervalley.org.

———. 2002b. Remedial Investigation Report, Lower Fox River and Green Bay, Wisconsin. www.papervalley.org.

Sandin, J. 2000a. "Fort James Corp., State Agree on Pollution Settlement." *Milwaukee Journal Sentinel*, November 15.

———. 2000b. "George Seeks Audit of Pollution Deal." *Milwaukee Journal Sentinel*, November 16.

Schulte, L. 2020. "'Still a Lot More to Do' as Evers, Environmental Leaders Announce End of Fox River Dredging Project." *Milwaukee Journal Sentinel*, September 1.

Schultze, S. 1995. "DNR Chief Says Governor Pressed Him." *Milwaukee Journal Sentinel*, June 8.

Seely, R., and A. Hall. 2000. "Fox River Sellout?" *Wisconsin State Journal*, December 17, A-1.

Seppa, N. 1993. "Meyer Facing Unhappy Campers." *Wisconsin State Journal*, January 17, 1.

Swackhamer, D. L., and D. E. Armstrong. 1987. "Distribution and Characterization of PCBs in Lake Michigan Water." *Journal of Great Lakes Research* 13: 24–36.

Sweet, C. W., T. J. Murphy, J. H. Bannasch, C. A. Kelsey, and J. Hong. 1993. "Atmospheric Deposition of PCBs into Green Bay." *Journal of Great Lakes Research* 19 (1): 109–28.

Tetra Tech. 2019. Remedial Action Summary Report, Lower Fox River Operable Units 2–5. www.papervalley.org.

Tillitt, D. E. et al. 2005. "Thiamine and Thiaminase Status in Forage Fish of Salmonines from Lake Michigan." *Journal of Aquatic Animal Health* 17 (1): 13–25.

Velleux, M., and D. Endicott. 1994, "Development of a Mass Balance Model for Estimating PCB Export from the Lower Fox River to Green Bay." *Journal of Great Lakes Research* 20 (2): 416–34.

Velleux, M., D. Endicott, J. Steuer, S. Jaeger, and D. Patterson. 1995. "Long-Term Simulation of PCB Export from the Fox River to Green Bay." *Journal of Great Lakes Research* 21 (3): 359–72.

Versar. 1976. *PCBs in the United States: Industrial Use and Environmental Distribution. Task 1.* Final Report, February 25. Washington, DC: USEPA Office of Toxic Substances.

Williams, L. L., and J. P. Giesy. 1992. "Relationships among Concentrations of Individual Polychlorinated Biphenyl (Pcb) Congeners, 2,3,7,8-Tetrachlorodibenzo-P-Dioxin Equivalents (Tcdd-Eq), and Rearing Mortality of Chinook Salmon (Oncorhynchus tshawytscha) Eggs from Lake Michigan." *Journal of Great Lakes Research* 18 (1): 108–24.

Wilson, Dan. 2000. "Fort James Steps Up on PCB Dredging." *Post Crescent*, May 26, A-1.

Wooley, C. 2000. "Fish & Wildlife Estimate Based on Solid Research." Letter to the editor. *Wisconsin State Journal*, December 24, B-2.

ABOUT THE AUTHORS

 P. David Allen II is a retired wildlife biologist and environmental consultant, who has worked for federal, state, tribal, and local governments in twenty-five states. He is a contributor to *Economics and Ecological Risk Assessment and Applications to Watershed Management*. His publications have appeared in numerous journals and programs including *Proceedings of the 38th Annual Conference on Environmental Law, Fisheries, Southwest Hydrology, Environmental Toxicology and Chemistry* and *Archives of Environmental Contamination and Toxicology*. He currently resides in Marquette, Michigan.

 Susan Campbell is a former environmental reporter for the *Green Bay Press-Gazette* and has covered politics, government, and civil and criminal courts for local newspapers in suburban Philadelphia and Boston. She is also the coauthor of *Beyond Earth Day: Fulfilling the Promise*, with the late Earth Day founder, Sen. Gaylord Nelson. Her articles have appeared in the *Milwaukee Journal Sentinel, Psychology Today,* and the *Journal of Soil and Water Conservation*. She is a former communications manager at the Chicago-based Allliance for the Great Lakes and adjunct journalism instructor with the University of Wisconsin–Green Bay. She currently practices sustainable real estate in Wisconsin.